AMERICAN
PANIC

AMERICAN PANIC

PANIC

A

HISTORY

of

WHO SCARES US

and

WHY

MARK STEIN

palgrave
macmillan

First published in 2014 by PALGRAVE MACMILLAN® in the United
States—a division of St. Martin's Press LLC, 175 Fifth Avenue, New York, NY
10010.

Where this book is distributed in the UK, Europe and the rest of the world,
this is by Palgrave Macmillan, a division of Macmillan Publishers Limited,
registered in England, company number 785998, of Houndmills, Basingstoke,
Hampshire RG21 6XS.

Palgrave Macmillan is the global academic imprint of the above companies and
has companies and representatives throughout the world.

Palgrave® and Macmillan® are registered trademarks in the United States, the
United Kingdom, Europe and other countries.

ISBN 978-1-62953-325-4

Design by Letra Libre, Inc.

Printed in the United States of America.

A Book Club Edition

To Harry and David

Contents

Acknowledgments

This book began on a hunch that the political panics that have erupted in American history emanate from common sources. With little more than that hunch, my friends Mark Olshaker, Janet Bickel, David Dugoff, Ben Tannen, along with my sister, Roberta Redfern, and nephews Daniel L. Goldberg and Matthew Kahn, raised questions or mentioned works that enabled me to develop this idea into a manuscript. During this process, I was fortunate to receive insights from scholars such as Arthur Goldschmidt, Jr., Omar Khraishah, Marianne Noble, David Pike, and Richard Zweigenhaft. I also wish to thank Arlene Balkansky of the Serial and Government Publications Division of the Library of Congress, for her assistance with my research. I thank her especially for reading each chapter on her own time, and for marrying me over thirty years ago. I have also been blessed to have been represented by Kenneth Wright and Alec Shane at Writers House, under whose guidance this book was given birth and brought to Karen Wolny at Palgrave Macmillan. Here again I was blessed, for Karen's skills and insights, backed by copyeditor Bill Warhop's keen eyes and laser logic, kept this panic-prone writer feeling safe in their blue-pencil-wielding hands.

Introduction

"It is better TO LIGHT A CANDLE
than curse the darkness."

—Chinese proverb

Political panic, the irrational fear that one's government is in danger, is by no means unique to any country. In America, it dates back to the 1692 Salem witch hunt, though conceivably earlier panics may have occurred among Native American tribes. The panic that began in Salem commenced after seizures suddenly afflicted three girls, ages nine through twelve. When the colony's physicians could not explain it, fear arose that sorcery was taking place in Salem and endangering its Puritan rule. After the first suspect was arrested and charged with witchcraft, a capital crime, more accusations quickly followed, many of them leveled by individuals who stood to gain from the conviction of the people they accused. In little over a year, nineteen colonists were executed, eight others awaited execution, fifty awaited sentencing, and 150 still awaited trial when the colony's governor ended the proceedings by fiat.

What happened in Salem over 300 years ago continues to reverberate in the United States. "Witch hunt" remains a phrase in the American vernacular, ensconced in our dictionaries as an investigation of disloyalty based on unverified assertions and public fear. In other ways, too, the Salem witch hunt entailed elements of political panic that have continued to contribute to a pattern in American political panic. That there is a pattern in political panic can be seen when William Gribbin, concisely describing today's Tea Party movement, wrote, "Growing out of neighborhood protest rallies, burgeoning in a climate of hostility toward established politicians . . .[it] soon became an organized political force. It fostered a raw democracy, attacked every hint of special privilege, and so drove even its foes to emulation."[1] The pattern emerges from the fact that Gribbin was not writing about the Tea Party. He was writing about the Anti-Masonic Party, an early nineteenth-century movement barely remembered today.

An element regarding the present-day Tea Party that echoes an element from the Salem witch hunt surfaced when *Washington Post* commentator Susan Jacoby wrote in the paper's October 20, 2010, online edition, "All of the Tea Party/Republican candidates this year are ignorant." The statement did that which statements by Tea Party adherents frequently do: stereotype a group of people. In so doing, the statement entered the realm of panic by *doing that which it fears.* Similarly, during the Salem witch hunt, one of the townspeople urged a slave in the community to prepare a "witch's cake," a confection made with urine from a person whom the devil has possessed. The cake is then fed to a dog. The dog's ingesting of the cake was believed to cause the devil to spit out, from the possessed person's mouth, the identity of his agent. Here, too, panic resided in doing that which one feared; in this instance, fearing that sorcery was endangering the community, the townsperson engaged, via the slave-made "witch's cake," in sorcery.

This book seeks to illuminate such elements that form this recurring pattern in American political panic. It seeks to light a candle rather than curse those who curse the darkness since, as the pattern to be unearthed will show, none of us is immune from political panic. Most of us, upon becoming aware of other groups, have entered the portals that can lead to panic. "On one level or another, we're all drawn to conspiracy theories," the legendary FBI profiler John Douglas observed with Mark Olshaker in *The Anatomy of Motive* (1999). "They make the world seem comprehensible." The danger one feels when sensing conspiracy is the same sense of danger that is present in the panics explored in this book. Among these panics have been fears of conspiracies by witches, Catholics, communists, capitalists, Muslims, and the Japanese after Pearl Harbor. Others sensed danger to the republic emanating less from conspiracy than what they perceived to be the nature of Native Americans, Africans and their African American descendants, Jews, Chinese, Latinos, homosexuals, and women. As with fears of conspiracy, fears based on stereotypes help make the world comprehensible. What makes none of us immune is that *the perception of a pattern,* which makes the world comprehensible to those who fear conspiracies, is what enables all of us to understand concepts and events.[2]

Along with the fact that none of us is immune from political panic is the fact that *not all political alarm is panic.* Panic is a type of alarm, the elements of which will be unearthed and assembled in the pages that follow. As the elements that compose this pattern assemble, they will in turn illuminate why some people panic and others don't. Here, too, events at Salem set the stage. Some accusers, as previously suggested, may have participated in the panic for personal gain. Others, quite likely, simply went along to get along. Of those who did not succumb to panic, many probably, even if privately, did not believe in sorcery. One highly influential Massachusetts colonist who did believe in sorcery but remained skeptical of the panic in Salem was Cotton Mather. Mather, a prominent Boston minister and physician, was the author of a 1689 book, *Memorable Providences Relating to Witchcrafts and Possessions.* Still, he criticized the Salem trials. Three elements that recurred in subsequent panics surface via Cotton Mather. The first is a *misbegotten assertion*—in this case, that witches exist—misbegotten because it was based on a second recurring element in political panic, an *unverified claim.* Such a claim in Mather's book is exemplified in his statement, "The blessed God hath made some to come from the Damned, for the Conviction—may it also be for the Conversion—of us that are yet alive." Though Mather undoubtedly believed this statement, no basis existed to verify his claim other than faith. Ironically, Mather's criticism of the trials in Salem resulted from the court's acceptance of unverified claims. He vigorously objected to the admission of "spectral evidence," testimony that a defendant appeared to a witness in a vision. That Mather fell victim to an unverified claim and yet criticized the use of the same element reveals a third element that recurs in political panic: *alarmists cannot be stereotyped.*

Confessions, which can serve as verified claims, are another element that we will see recur in many political panics, including the panic over witchcraft. During the trials, the slave who prepared the "witch's cake," Tituba, confessed to seeing particular accused women "ride upon sticks" and "hurt the children."[3] In an account written shortly after the episode by Robert Calef, he records Tituba later claiming "that her master [Samuel Parris, the father of one of the accused girls] did beat her [Tituba] and otherways abuse her to make her confess."[4] At the time of the trial, Tituba's confession saved her life, but also bestowed credence on the claims of the accusers—much as confessions continued to do in panics to come.

The panic over witchcraft reached the point where two dogs were put to death after coming to be suspected of possession by the devil.[5] While the execution of dogs for witchcraft may appear to be the high-water mark of the panic, these acts occurred when widespread panic was receding. As will be seen in many of the episodes examined in this book, panic intensifies in some individuals as they perceive it to be diminishing among others.

One important difference between the panic at Salem and those that commenced later is that the Salem witch hunt predated the Constitution. For that reason, the witch hunt helps illuminate the extent to which the Constitution of the United States has affected political panic. One immediately recognizable difference is how suddenly the panic at Salem ended. "I have also put a stop to the printing of any discourse one way or the other," Governor William Phips wrote to the king, " . . . because I saw a likelyhood of kindling an inextinguishable flame if I should admit any publique and open Contests. . . . They are now stopt till their Majesties pleasure be known."[6] Lacking a constitutionally mandated freedom of speech, right to assemble, and system of checks and balances among the colony's executive, judicial, and legislative functions, the king's appointed governor had the authority to end trials, vacate verdicts, and prohibit speech or gatherings. After the American Revolution and the adoption of the Constitution, political panic in America would not be so easy to halt.

Though the colonists in Salem did not have the Constitution, they did have something Americans associate with the Constitution: founding fathers. Political panics in the United States—both those emanating from the political right and left—have been and remain replete with references to the nation's founders. For American Puritans in 1692, their foremost founding father was John Winthrop, who articulated the vision for this new community while en route with his fellow Puritans in 1630. Winthrop declared, "Wee must be knitt together in this worke as one man . . . [and] abridge ourselves of our superfluities." He then invoked the biblical image of a New Jerusalem when he added, "Wee shall be as a Citty upon a Hill."[7] Seven decades later, Cotton Mather lamented how far they had strayed from the vision of their founders. "They will not find New England a New Jerusalem," he wrote, adding that "many of the rising generation . . . grow weary of their Church-State."[8]

Few people today think of John Winthrop as one of America's founding fathers, but the quest he expressed has remained deeply rooted in the nation's political landscape. In *Puritan Origins of the American Self* (1975), historian Sacvan Bercovitch detailed how Americans altered the Puritan quest to create a New Jerusalem in the New World by turning it into a secular mission in which the United States would change the world as a beacon of freedom and democracy. President John F. Kennedy echoed John Winthrop when he declared in his 1961 inaugural address, "The eyes of all people are truly upon us, and our governments, in every branch . . . must be as a city upon a hill—constructed and inhabited by men aware of their great trust and their great responsibilities." President Ronald Reagan, in his 1989 farewell address, reprised, "I've spoken of the shining city all my political life . . . a tall proud city built on rocks stronger than oceans. . . . And if there had to be city walls, the walls had doors and the doors were open to anyone with the will and the heart to get here."

In exploring the political panics that have erupted in America, this book will progress as chronologically as possible, given the varying lengths and overlaps of the panics. It will also progress from identifying recurring elements to analyzing them. This exploration will not present full histories of the resistance of those groups over whom there was panic, or of those Americans who spoke out against panic, except when such responses significantly impacted on the panic. Ultimately, this book will seek to determine whether such episodes can be avoided, or at least minimized. Can this nation's political landscape be drained of the muck of hysteria? To find out, we must put on political rubber gloves and dig into three centuries of battered and often blood-soaked earth.

One

"Hyenas in human form—no good
INDIANS except those that are dead."

—Chicago Tribune headline, January 3, 1891

Of all the political panics in American history, none has been more
deadly than that which fueled the ethnic cleansing of the people who
populated what is now the United States prior to the arrival of Europeans.
Far more unarmed Native American women, children, and elderly were
killed in the United States than all the people killed in the nation's other
political panics combined. The treatment of Native Americans provides insight into a fundamental question regarding political panic: When is violence against a group of people an act of panic as opposed to an act of war?

From the colonial era through the nineteenth century, whites often
viewed Native Americans as a threat to the expansion of settlements believed
necessary for economic and political security. One of the first such conflicts
was the Pequot War (1637–38). In that war, panic clearly surfaced when
the colonists surrounded a fortified Pequot encampment and, recognizing
the danger of charging into it, opted to burn it and kill anyone who tried to
escape the flames—including women, children, and the elderly. *Any* Pequot
was thus regarded as a threat. Commanding officer John Mason justified
this killing of women and children when he wrote in his report, "But God

was above them who laughed his enemies and the enemies of his people to scorn, making them as a fiery oven. . . . Thus did the Lord judge among the heathen, filling the place with dead bodies!"[1] It is conceivable that God favored the colonists over the Pequots, but it is not verifiable. As in the actions taken against accused witches, people were killed on the basis of an unverified claim.

Actions based on unverified claims are not, in and of themselves, acts of panic since we often act on the basis of assumptions. What is beginning to surface from the witchcraft panic and the massacre of the Pequots, however, is that an individual is susceptible to panic to the extent that he or she acts on the basis of unverified claims.

Panic in the Newly Born United States

In both the American Revolution and the War of 1812, Native Americans fought on both sides, based on what each tribe perceived to be its political best interest. In August 1813, Creek Indians from the Red Sticks tribe attacked American forces at Fort Mims in Alabama, where many noncombatants had sought safety. In this instance, it was the Native Americans who set fire to the premises, resulting in the deaths of scores of unarmed elderly, women, and children—and demonstrating that Native Americans, too, are susceptible to panic.[2]

The massacre of whites at Fort Mims also illustrates other elements that recur in political panic. The first of these is, not surprisingly, *panic breeds panic.* This element can be seen in the *Universal Gazette* of Washington, D.C.; its October 29, 1813, report on the massacre described the Red Sticks as "savages" who lack "feelings of common humanity." This stereotype is, in turn, predicated on two elements that recur in political panics right up to the present day. One of these elements is the use of an *absolute*—in this instance, the assertion that *all* Red Sticks lack empathetic feelings. The assertion is akin to the absolute implicit in John Mason's claim regarding God's condemnation of all the Pequots. Surfacing as well in the *Gazette* statement is the use of a *filtered fact.* The absolute the newspaper applied to the Red

Sticks filtered out white people who had also indiscriminately killed men, women, and children.

Indeed, in a subsequent engagement with the Red Sticks during the War of 1812, General Andrew Jackson made no secret of such genocidal intentions when he wrote of the Battle of Horseshoe Bend. "Determining to exterminate them, I detached General Coffee . . . to surround the bend in such a manner as that none of them should escape," he wrote. After killing more than 550 who were now trapped on a peninsula, Jackson reported that his men "continued to destroy many of them who had concealed themselves under the banks of the river until we were prevented by night." The murders resumed at sunrise.[3]

During Jackson's presidency, panic regarding Native Americans helped fuel the federal government's premier act of legislated ethnic cleansing, the 1830 Indian Removal Act. The legislation mandated the relocation of Native Americans from much of the southeastern United States. "Doubtless it will be painful to leave the graves of their fathers," Jackson declared in that year's State of the Union message. But, he went on to say, "is it supposed that the wandering savage has a stronger attachment to his home than the settled, civilized Christian? Is it more afflicting to him to leave the graves of his fathers than it is to our brothers and children?"[4] Jackson's remarks contained an unverified claim and a filtered fact. His comparison of the "wandering savage" to the "civilized Christian" asserted an unverified claim that the culture of Native Americans is inferior to that of Christians. His assertion that Native Americans leaving their ancestral land was no more painful than Europeans leaving their ancestral land to come to America filtered out millions of Europeans who chose *not* to leave their ancestral land—a choice this legislation denied to Native Americans.

Some tribes, recognizing the inevitable, voluntarily complied. Others did not. Of them, one soldier who participated in the removal wrote, "Women were dragged from their homes by soldiers whose language they could not understand. Children were often separated from their parents and driven into the stockade with the sky for a blanket and the earth for a pillow. And often the old and infirm were prodded with bayonets to hasten them to the stockades."[5] Among the 16,000 Cherokee forced to relocate, some 4,000 died on the trek to the reservation set out for them in what is now Oklahoma. In the months that followed their arrival in this new environment, another 4,000 are estimated to have died. The Cherokee speak of it still as *Nunna dual Tsuny,* rendered in English as the "Trail of Tears."

The Social Soil Beneath the Trail of Tears

The panic over Native Americans was the first to erupt from a social soil in which racial prejudice was deeply rooted. Joining the biblical justification offered for the wholesale slaughter of the Pequot, racial justifications rooted in Nature were increasingly offered as the nation entered the nineteenth century while simultaneously expanding westward. With the death toll along the Trail of Tears mounting, beliefs about racial determination of character had become so deeply rooted that George Turner wrote, in *Traits of Indian Character* (1836), "His reason . . . is less corrupted and perverted while he roams in his native forests than in an unrestricted intercourse with civilized man." Fearing, on behalf of the Indians, that contact with whites corrupts and perverts their reasoning, Turner did that which he claimed to fear by justifying the exile of Native Americans based on reasoning corrupted and perverted by an unverified claim regarding their reasoning (unverified because Turner was not fluent in any of their languages), and possibly further perverted and corrupted by the fact that Turner was a prominent land speculator.

As the United States expanded to the Pacific Ocean and its population began to fill those lands, increasing numbers of Americans contemplated the extinction, and among some the active extermination, of all Native Americans. On August 14, 1851, the *National Intelligencer* in Washington, D.C., commented on epidemics of smallpox among Native Americans: "There are few persons, we suppose, who do not anticipate the entire extinction of all the present tribes of North America." While lack of vaccination for smallpox (medically known since 1796) among Native Americans was one element in these epidemics, so too were acts of political panic. Connecticut's *Norwich*

Courier reported on April 18, 1855, of an army captain who, "in view of the anticipated troubles with the Indians in Nebraska, suggests that blankets taken from small pox hospitals be freely distributed among the different tribes."

As early as the French and Indian War, General Jeffrey Amherst (for whom towns in Massachusetts, New Hampshire, New York, Ohio, Wisconsin, and a county in Virginia are named) inquired during a battle for present-day Pittsburgh, "Could it not be contrived to send the small pox among the disaffected tribe of Indians?" Justifying his view with Nature, Amherst stated that Indians were "the vilest race of beings that ever infested the earth, and whose riddance from it must be esteemed a meritorious act for the good of mankind."[6] William Trent, one of the officers under Amherst, subsequently recorded in his diary, "We gave them two blankets and an handkerchief out of the small pox hospital. I hope it will have the desired effect."[7] Amherst's directive did that which it feared, which was an emerging hallmark of political panic: Fearing Native Americans were "the vilest race of beings" on earth, Amherst urged and oversaw one of the vilest acts conceivable.

The degree to which smallpox-infected blankets were used to exterminate Native Americans cannot be stated with certainty. What can be stated with certainty is that other forms of indiscriminate massacres—actions embedded in an absolute, that *all are a danger*—increasingly occurred as the nation expanded. The degree to which this absolute became rooted in the nation's political landscape can be seen in a brief news item in the May 17, 1871, *Savannah Advertiser* on an encounter at Camp Grant, Arizona, in which nearly 150 Apaches were killed, many of whom were women and children seeking food rations at the outpost: "The people of Arizona have determined to protect themselves against the Indians, and after the massacre at Camp Grant they started in pursuit. Soon after they came upon them encamped and killed eighty-five of the party."

In March 1863, U.S. troops under the command of Colonel Patrick Conner slaughtered 224 members of the Shoni tribe along the present-day Idaho-Utah border in reprisal for the murder of several miners by three Shoni. The murder of those miners was indeed a capital crime. But to sentence an entire tribe to death without trial by jury or congressional declaration of war is to do that which one fears: Fearing *all* Shoni were a danger to the United States because some of its members violated U.S. laws, Conner and his troops endangered the United States by dispensing with the due processes of law that are the country's pillars.

Following the Civil War, General Philip Sheridan led troops in an attack on the Montana-based Piegans, killing 173 of their men, women, and children. Georgia's *Macon Telegraph* declared in its March 8, 1870, report of the incident, "The Indians are a filthy, degraded race," revealing another element that frequently recurs in political panics: a *blank to be filled in.* In this instance it resides in the word *degraded;* this use of the word leaves it to the reader to determine what constitutes the gradations of race based on his or her own knowledge, needs, and fears.

The mass murder of Native Americans reached its climax on December 29, 1890, when the Seventh Cavalry charged upon a band of Sioux at Wounded Knee Creek on the tribe's Pine Ridge Reservation in South Dakota. Between two and three hundred men, women, and children were killed. Absolutes abounded in newspaper accounts, such as that in the *St. Paul Pioneer Press,* which declared, "The teeth of these treacherous wild beasts *must* be drawn as a *guarantee* of safety in the future," or when the *Omaha World Herald* concluded, "There is *no alternative.*"[8] (Italics added in both quotations.)

That those who justified the violence at Wounded Knee did so on the basis of unverified claims became apparent within weeks of the event. A report to the commissioner of Indian Affairs from one of the agency's representatives at the Pine Ridge Reservation stated, "The party [of Sioux] was not a war party . . . but a party intending to visit the agency. . . . I do not credit the statement which has been made by some that women carried arms and participated in the fight."[9] The military leaders at Wounded Knee would well have recognized that the approaching Sioux were not a war party based on observations previously made by the army's preeminent Indian fighter, General George Armstrong Custer. In his widely read book, *My Life on the Plains* (1874), Custer stated, "Indians contemplating a battle, either offensive or defensive, are always anxious to have their women and children removed from all danger." That General Custer wrote these words is all the more revealing since the rage demonstrated by the Seventh Cavalry at Wounded Knee was partially fueled by revenge for the 1876 massacre by the Sioux at the Battle of Little Big Horn, an episode remembered today as "Custer's Last Stand." In that episode, five companies in the Seventh Cavalry were wiped out, along with General Custer.

These twin massacres illuminate the difference between political panic and war. Many of the 268 U.S. troops killed at Little Big Horn were wantonly murdered by Sioux. Those murders were acts of panic committed during warfare. The distinction surfaced immediately after the massacre, when the victorious Sioux made no effort to pursue their advantage by attacking Billings, Montana, sixty miles distant, where white women and children resided. Quite likely battle panic was also present at Wounded Knee. In that episode, however, the indiscriminate killing of *any* Native American revealed widespread political panic, underscored by the fact that the Sioux were clearly not approaching with the intention to attack.

Diminishment of the Panic

Even before the massacre at Wounded Knee brought to a close two centuries of warfare between whites and Native Americans, widespread panic over Native Americans had begun to abate. One of the earlier indications surfaced in an 1879 legal challenge by Chief Standing Bear of the Ponca tribe. When the federal government discovered it had inadvertently granted to the Sioux a region in present-day Nebraska that the government had previously granted to the Ponca, Standing Bear and his tribe were forcibly removed and marched to a reservation in present-day Oklahoma. Unhappy in this new environment, Standing Bear walked back to his ancestral land (a distance of some 400 miles) where, upon arriving, he was promptly taken into custody by the U.S. army. In this instance, however, a local attorney went to court on Standing Bear's behalf, seeking a writ of habeas corpus. Enshrined in Article I of the Constitution, a writ of habeas corpus requires the government to declare what law a person has been charged with violating or to release the person. Indian Inspector Edward C. Kemble, who had overseen the relocation of the Poncas, defended the incarceration of Standing Bear on the basis that Native Americans were genetically inferior. "In dealing with Indians," he asserted, "we must sometimes do as we do in dealing with children . . . and may have to decide for them what is best." Federal judge Elmer S. Dundy was not so certain, ruling that "an Indian is a 'person' within the meaning of the laws of the United States."[10]

Citizenship for selected Native Americans also commenced prior to Wounded Knee. In 1885, a Department of Interior report stated, "The Indian problem could be easily solved by simply withdrawing all government supervision over these people and conferring upon them the rights of American citizenship." In defending this view, the report cited a key element in what turned out to be its widespread acceptance by the public when it noted, "After incorporating into our body politic four million blacks in a state of slavery and investing them with citizenship and suffrage, we need not strain at the gnat of 260,000 Indians."[11] That the threat white Americans felt from Native Americans was now equivalent to that of a gnat became evident with the passage of the General Allotment Act of 1887. It provided a means for Native Americans to become citizens by altering the ownership of tribal land in a way that enabled tribe members to sell their individual parcels. The law reflected the fact that white Americans were now far more land thirsty than bloodthirsty.

As citizens, Native Americans turned out to be as law-abiding as non–Native American citizens. Representative of their loyalty to the nation is the fact that some 12,000 Native Americans served in World War I, with soldiers of Choctaw descent earning particular distinction as "code talkers" who translated sensitive military messages into their native language—so linguistically different from European languages it was beyond the abilities of enemy code breakers to decipher it. Similarly during World War II, Navajo soldiers served as code talkers. In that war, more than 44,000 American Indians served in the armed forces (several being awarded the Medal of Honor, the highest military award in the United States), and another 40,000 left their reservations to work in ordnance depots, factories, and other war industries.[12]

To this day, assumptions about the inferiority of the character and culture of Native Americans remain, though widespread panic is long past. In its aftermath, however, winds of guilt continue to blow through ravines in the soul of the nation now living on the land it conquered. Those winds, however, have blown right by equally deep-rooted prejudicial views regarding the other major group present since the nation's founding: African Americans.

Two

"There are plenty of people in this country of ours who would far rather see ... the entire white race here rotted by heroic injections into their veins of all the SAVAGERY AND CRIMINALITY IN THE NEGRO than have any number of the latter ... in any way inconvenienced."

—R. W. Shufeldt, M.D., The Negro: A Menace to American Civilization (1907)

Fear that African Americans endanger the United States is the most enduring panic in the history of the United States. It predates the American Revolution and continues to sprout in the nation's social landscape. In 2010, some demonstrators opposed to President Barack Obama's proposed health care law shouted "nigger" at Congressman John Lewis, a hero to many for his leadership and the beatings he withstood during the Civil Rights Movement. Others displayed placards depicting President Obama as an

African witch doctor. The intensity of this panic can be seen in the fact that roughly 4,000 African Americans have been lynched in the United States, yet not until the latter half of the twentieth century was anyone known to have been convicted for the crime.[1]

How did it come about that government officials and so many influential members of the community abided these atrocities? The answer is that the roots of this particular panic are deeper than those of any other, and they emanate from biblical times. Twelve hundred years before Europeans began to settle in the New World, Saint Augustine wrote, "The condition of slavery is the result of sin. This is why we do not find the word 'slave' in any part of Scripture until righteous Noah branded the sin of his son with this name."[2] Augustine was referring to Genesis 9:24–26 in which it says, "Ham the father of Canaan, saw his father's nakedness and told his two brothers. . . . When Noah . . . learned what his youngest son had done to him, he said, 'Cursed be Canaan. The lowest of slaves shall he be to his brothers.'"

This justification for enslaving black people resulted from the unverified claim that sub-Saharan Africans descended from Middle Eastern Canaanites. Such, for example, was the claim of British slave trader Richard Jobson when he attached the absolute "undoubtedly" to his 1623 assertion about Africans: "Undoubtedly these people originally sprung from the race of Canaan, the sonne of Ham."[3] By 1852, then-popular American author Josiah Priest expanded on the three lines in Genesis to explain all racial differences and behavioral characteristics. God, he asserted, "superintended the formation . . . of the sons of Noah in the womb of their mother . . . giving to these children each such forms of bodies, constitutions of nature, and complexions of skin, as suited his will. . . . He caused Ham to be born black . . . in the particular of animal generation as relates to the human race."[4]

After the Civil War, the biblical justification shifted from slavery to white supremacy. "How can any person who believes in the Bible admit for a moment that God intended to teach it that all men are born free and equal?" John Ambrose Price wrote in *The Negro: Past, Present, and Future* (1907). Price asserted that "the blackness of the prognathous race, known in the world's history as Canaanites, Cushites, Ethiopians, black men or negroes, is

not confined to the skin, but pervades in a greater or less degree the whole in-
ward man." In 1914, Mississippi senator James K. Vardaman declared, "God
Almighty never intended that the Negro should share with the white man
in the government of this country, and you cannot improve upon the plans
of God Almighty or defeat His purposes either by legislative enactments." In
1966, Georgia governor Lester Maddox echoed Vardaman's view in stating,
"God set up the boundaries of the habitations of people, by continent, and I
think that our trouble today has been brought about by integration."[5]

Josiah Priest's 1852 biblically based assertion that connected dark skin
and animals other than humans emanated from both his interpretation of the
Bible and from a second deeply rooted source: genetics. As far back as 1638,
Thomas Herbert wrote of Africans, "Their language is apishly founded, with
whom tis thought they mixe unnaturally."[6] In *History of Jamaica* (1774), Edward Long asserted, "When we reflect on the nature of these men, and their
dissimilarity to the rest of mankind, must we not conclude that they are a
different species of the same genus?" Connecting this justification to the
panic over the early women's rights movement, anthropologist James Hunt
declared in 1864, "It cannot be doubted that the brain of the Negro bears
a great resemblance to the European woman or child's brain, and thus approaches the ape far more than the European, while the Negress approaches
still nearer to the ape."[7] Here too the element of panic results from—as in
Cotton Mather's treatise on witchcraft—a misbegotten assertion, as none of
these "scientific" conclusions can stand up to empirical scrutiny.

Among the scientific claims of black inferiority, one source of misbegotten assertions surfaced in the nineteenth century. In *Race Traits and Tendencies
of the American Negro* (1896), statistician Frederick Hoffman correlated race
with data regarding disease, income, and crime. "It became more and more
apparent," he concluded, "that there lie at the root of all social difficulties or
problems, racial traits and tendencies." In so concluding, Hoffman engaged in
a fallacy in statistical interpretation: *Correlation does not imply causation.* (An
often cited example of this lapse in logic is condemnation of milk, based on
the fact that over 99 percent of all murderers drank milk, as children.) From
his misbegotten assertion, Hoffman concluded, "It is not the conditions of life,

but in race and heredity that we find the explanation of the fact to be observed in all parts of the globe, in all times and among all peoples, namely, the superiority of one race over the other, and of the Aryan race over all."

A form of filtered facts also surfaced in racial research by virtue of measures not used. Like Frederick Hoffman, physician R. W. Shufeldt published his studies of racial traits in his 1907 book, *The Negro: A Menace to American Civilization*. "I have met with a good many very worthy negro men in life," Shufeldt wrote in introducing his work, going on to assert (as had Hoffman), "I have no special prejudice against them, and . . . I have in no case or instance been actuated by any other motive than telling the truth." There is reason to believe Hoffman and Shufeldt thought they were not prejudiced or panicked. Nevertheless, Shufeldt's book ended up concluding, "Our ancestors permitted large numbers of these savage and cannibalistic blacks to be landed on the shores. . . . Owing to the ever-present desire to ravish the white women . . . the negro demonstrates to us . . . that, in spite of fire [and] hanging . . . he intends to gratify this heinous lust." One fact that Shufeldt's research filtered out was comparison with the percentage of white men who desire to ravish white, or black, women. The absence of this comparison is underscored by the fact that Shufeldt himself observed, "During the days of slavery, untold thousands of hybrids were produced, due to a crossing of the black and the white races." But here Shufeldt filtered out a key variable: Nowhere does he address the percentage of these "hybrids" resulting from white men impregnating black women compared to black men impregnating white women. (My own guess would be that the vast majority were the offspring of white fathers.) By filtering out that variable, Shufeldt further filtered out the possibility that some (my own guess would be most) of such instances were nonconsensual—rape, or, to use Dr. Shufeldt's terminology, white men ravishing black women.

In the United States, the fissure over the inherent equality or inequality of Africans and their American descendants deepened and branched at the point where it intersected with a previously mentioned element in American political panic: reverence for the Founding Fathers. Most notably, Thomas

Jefferson, who penned the words, "all men are created equal," also penned "Blacks, whether originally a distinct race or made distinct by time and circumstances, are inferior to the whites in the endowments of body and mind."[8] In this and other ways, Jefferson and other Founding Fathers begat a dysfunctional family. Among those offspring was Abraham Lincoln, highly revered for his Emancipation Proclamation, who nevertheless had also proclaimed, "There is a physical difference between the white and black races which I believe will ever forbid the two races living together on terms of social and political equality. . . . I as much as any other man am in favor of having the superior position assigned to the white race."[9]

So deep and so branched are these fissures that they continue to divide Americans of all educational levels right up to the present. In 1969, professor Arthur Jensen at the University of California, Berkeley, correlated IQ scores with race and concluded that it is "not an unreasonable hypothesis that genetic factors are strongly implicated in the average Negro-white intelligence difference."[10] In 1994, similar claims were asserted by Harvard professor Richard Herrnstein and behavioral scientist Charles Murray in their widely read book, *The Bell Curve*. Scores of colleagues challenged the validity of this research, based on a form of filtered facts—in this instance, variables not included in the collection of data. Along with previous works that claimed credibility on the basis of being scientific, such filtered data can generate another key element that frequently fuels political panic: While correlation does not imply causation, *it can cause assumption*.

Based on assumptions about race, the longest lasting laws through which government participated in the nation's panic over African Americans were state prohibitions of interracial marriage. Such so-called antimiscegenation laws were enacted in forty-one of the fifty states (the exceptions being New Hampshire, Vermont, New York, Connecticut, New Jersey, Wisconsin, Minnesota, Alaska, and Hawaii). Not until 1967, when the Supreme Court ruled in *Loving v. Virginia* that such laws were unconstitutional, did they come to an end in the sixteen states where they had not yet been repealed.

First Acts of Panic

As early as 1712, a New York journalist reported an insurrection by "Negroes to the number of twenty-five or thirty . . . having conspired to murder all the Christians here, and by that means thinking to obtain their Freedom."[11] After suppressing the rebellion, in which nine whites died, New York executed twenty-one slaves. Some were hanged, some were burned alive, and one was crushed by wheel. A white man convicted of providing weapons to the slaves was also executed. This panic was fed by the fact that it was not the first such slave rebellion. Nor, despite the extreme reprisals, would it be the last.

"Disagreeable rumors having reached this City of an insurrection of the slaves in Southampton County," the *Richmond Whig* told readers on August 23, 1831, in the first report of what would come to be known as Nat Turner's Rebellion. Over the course of two days in Southampton County, Virginia, Turner and his followers killed fifty-six whites in their effort to liberate themselves from slavery. Among their victims were unarmed women and children, a sign of panic yet again recurring among some in the midst of battle—and a sign that African Americans are no more immune to panic than Native Americans or whites. In suppressing the rebellion, whites killed over 120 slaves, also including women and children, as panic similarly played a role. In the case of these whites, however, racial prejudice revealed what it can add to panic. Sadistic acts of torture and maiming of blacks in Southampton County were so widespread in the days that followed, and so exceeded the brutalities inflicted upon the whites, that the commander of Virginia's militia, after arriving on the scene, threatened to impose martial law to halt what he called these "revolting . . . acts of atrocity."[12]

Intersecting of Panics

In 1837, women's rights advocate Sarah M. Grimké wrote, "We are in much the situation of the slave."[13] Grimké, born on a South Carolina plantation, was not alone in her view; Lucretia Mott, Lydia Ann Moulton Jenkins, and publisher Henry Brown Blackwell voiced the same sentiments at the 1854

Woman's Rights Convention in Cleveland. Just as the fissure over racial equality/inequality has continued to modern times, so too has this analogy with women. In 1969, *Psychology Today* published an article entitled, "Woman as Nigger," and in 1972 John Lennon and Yoko Ono recorded their song, "Woman Is the Nigger of the World."

What we see in these examples we will continue to see in other panics. Often, leading voices will seek to increase the octane in their efforts to fuel concern by tapping other ongoing panics. In some instances, so many issues become so interconnected they take on a life of their own. The modern-day Tea Party movement is one such instance, being an amalgamation of Americans who are concerned—variously but by no means unanimously—about the federal deficit, the growing extent of federal authority, the rights of gun owners, immigration, and the preservation of once-prevailing attitudes regarding marriage and sexuality. While the Tea Party has not, as of this writing, amalgamated to the point of being an independent political party, previous amalgamations did become third-party political organizations—most notably as the Anti-Masonic Party, in the early nineteenth century, and some decades later the Know Nothing Party. Being amalgamations, their names are not entirely accurate descriptions of their members. Many in the Anti-Masonic Party, for instance, did fear the secrecy of the freemasons but, as the previously mentioned historian William Gribbin observed, the movement also included many who joined the movement due to "hostility toward established politicians . . . [and] every hint of special privilege."[14] The name Know Nothing Party referred not to any presumed ignorance of its adherents, but rather to those in its original nucleus saying they "knew nothing" of plans being secretly formulated to prevent Catholics from entering the United States. Though the core adherents of the present-day Tea Party movement oppose higher taxes, the movement's name is similarly inaccurate since the event from which it derives, the 1773 Boston Tea Party, was not a protest against higher taxes; it was a protest against taxation without representation.

In the case of attitudes regarding African Americans, its connection with the women's rights movement influenced both the panic over African Americans and the panic over women. One example of this influence is the many women who both opposed slavery and sought to increase their political role in the United States by participating in Abolitionist organizations (a fact that, as we shall later see, not all abolitionist men were happy about). On the other side of this racial fissure, an example from after the Civil War reveals how women increased their political participation through public expressions of panic over African Americans. "When courts fail to convict . . . [these] lust-filled fiends in human shape, then husbands and fathers will rise . . . and rebuke the crime with a short shrift and a strong rope," Rebecca Latimer Felton, who went on to become the first woman to serve in the United States Senate, wrote in a December 19, 1898 letter to the editor of the *Atlanta Constitution*. "If it takes lynching to protect woman's dearest possession," she went on to add, ". . . I say lynch a thousand a week if it becomes necessary."

As seen in Rebecca Felton's statements, the emancipation of the slaves increased the intensity of the soon-to-spread panic over African Americans. Two years after the Civil War, author Hinton Helper proposed that African Americans (and, linking to the panic over Chinese, other nonwhites) "be colonized in a State or Territory by themselves . . . and there, under suitable regulations, required to remain strictly within the limits assigned them."[15] As in Nazi Germany, concentration camps were not Helper's final solution. He went on to say, "We should so far yield to the evident designs and purposes of Providence as to be both willing and anxious to see the negroes, like the Indians and all other effete and dingy-hued races, gradually exterminated from the face of the whole earth."

That same year, a brief item in the *Milwaukee Sentinel* noted, "A mischievous secret society, called Klan, has been organized in Giles County [Tennessee], composed chiefly of young men of rebel proclivities."[16] Within a year, the newly formed Ku Klux Klan murdered five African American men in Tennessee. In his 1877 book, *KKK Sketches, Humorous and Didactic,* James Melville Beard prefaced his collection of racial anecdotes: "The intelligent reader will see no politic, nor evidence of political bias in the pages of this volume." Assuming he truly believed this statement, Klan-member Beard did not view himself as panicked, just as Frederick Hoffman and

R. W. Shufeldt avowed themselves unbiased in writing books we have seen to be replete with panic.

At the time *KKK Sketches, Humorous and Didactic* was published, African American migration northward and westward was accompanied by panic over their presence. School segregation laws had already been passed in Ohio, Pennsylvania, and numerous municipalities in New York. Prohibitions on African Americans owning real estate, entering into contracts, bringing lawsuits, or testifying against a white person had been enacted in Ohio, Iowa, California, and Oregon. Indiana's 1851 constitution had stated, "No Negro or Mulatto shall come into, or settle in, the State." A similar exclusion was sought in Illinois, which we call today "the land of Lincoln." In that state, nineteen African Americans were lynched between 1882 and 1962. Sixteen were lynched in Ohio during those years, fourteen in Indiana, six in Pennsylvania, and four in Minnesota. In New York City, at least twelve African Americans were murdered in 1863 during four days of draft riots, with an unknown number of others possibly washed away by the Hudson and East rivers.[17]

The South, however, remained the region in which panic was most intense. In addition to scores of lynchings and double lynchings that took place between 1890 and 1915 (a year whose significance will soon be seen), newspapers frequently reported the lynching of as many as ten African Americans in a single incident in states throughout the south.[18] Exceeding even these incidents was the number of African Americans killed in Wilmington, North Carolina, on Election Day in 1898. At least twenty were murdered when the town's African Americans tried to exercise their right to vote—the precise number being unknown due to inadequate record keeping and the number of blacks who fled the backlash, never to return.

The degree to which filtered facts can morph into grotesque misinformation fuelling panic of deadly intensity surfaced in Alabama's *Birmingham Age Herald* when it headlined its coverage of Wilmington's Election Day deaths, "North Carolina Will Be Redeemed From Negro Domination." Filtered from the news report was the fact that, at the time, African Americans, who constituted one-third of North Carolina's population, occupied only three of the 120 seats in the state's House of Representatives and two of the fifty seats in its Senate.

1915: The Curse of a Nation

In the era of African American migration to the North, animosity on the part of white northerners provided common ground on which they and their Southern counterparts could begin to heal the national wound that remained from the Civil War. In this regard, two significant events took place in 1915. The first was the nationwide projection of the new unity between North and South in the acclaim that greeted D. W. Griffith's block-buster film, *The Birth of a Nation*. A review in the November 9, 1915, *Philadelphia Inquirer* stands out less for what it said than what it didn't say. It made no mention that this "remarkable picture, wonderfully well done" showed whites being forced from voting by the freed slaves and African Americans dominating the legislature with unshod feet propped up on the desks as they booze it up while enacting a law allowing interracial marriage. At no point did the review mention the film showing a white woman leaping to her death to avoid an amorous black man, or the lynching of that man by the Ku Klux Klan. That such plot points are unmentioned suggests such events were widely viewed as common knowledge, and that execution without trial of African Americans was widely viewed as acceptable. Even in Boston, where the heart of Abolitionism once beat, the view that the film was historically accurate was expressed when the April 13, 1915, *Boston Morning Journal* commended its "remarkably realistic illustrations of the historical times revolving around the Civil War" and praised the "superbly staged" battle scenes involving the "adventures of the celebrated Ku Klux Klan."

Considerably greater historical validation was bestowed on the film by no less a figure than President Woodrow Wilson, who arranged for it to be shown at the White House—an event that had never before happened. Wilson's influence extended beyond the fact that he was the president; he was also highly regarded as an intellectual, having been a professor at, and president of, Princeton University. He had already bestowed official validation on racism when, shortly after entering the White House, he issued directives segregating public facilities in the District of Columbia and all offices of the federal government. His use of the federal government to participate in the panic was flanked by similar actions by countless other high-ranking and highly respected officials. Particularly notable were university presidents and regents—among the most respected minds in society—who imposed segregation at their institutions. In this social landscape, *The Birth of a Nation* was (in the opposite sense of the term) the biggest bomb in Hollywood history, landing not with a thud but with augmented explosiveness.

The second significant event in 1915 regarding panic over African Americans occurred when *The Birth of a Nation* opened in Atlanta. Alongside an ad for the film was an ad for the "greatest, Secret, Patriotic, Fraternal, Beneficiary Order"—a newly minted Ku Klux Klan, being revitalized by William J. Simmons. Soon to become the preeminent leader of the Ku Klux Klan, Simmons succeeded in attracting some 500,000 new members over the next five years. "Klaverns" were created nationwide, including in such places as the University of Wisconsin, where it was one of the school's fraternities. Ten years later, a mass gathering of the Klan in Washington, D.C., was highlighted by an unprecedented parade down Pennsylvania Avenue. "The area was fairly blanketed with the white hoods and robes of the order," the *Washington Post* reported on August 9, 1925. The article revealed the widespread respect for the Klan when it noted that, for the first time ever, the police escort that leads the way in the city's public parades rode behind "the three horseman who formed the color guard." No longer an escort, the police department of the nation's capital was now a participant.

Still, a key question remains. Why then? Why did this fear over African Americans gather such force between 1915 and 1925, rather than the decade before or after? The answer, to a large extent, is that D. W. Griffith was indeed a groundbreaking filmmaker. But a keyword in that statement is "film." Motion pictures were a new development in communications that, near the end of the nineteenth century, began to be exhibited in nickelodeons throughout the United States. Because nickelodeons were inexpensive, this new form of entertainment was popular across the economic spectrum.

Because the films were silent, the nation's huge immigrant population could follow the plotlines even if unable to read the simply worded inter titles. By 1915, motion pictures were the most effective technological messenger yet devised. And this film's message was the most potent yet produced. It not only further united northerners with southerners, it provided immigrants a path for acceptance: Adopt the view that African Americans are a danger to the nation. An Irish American family, it is worth noting, was at the center of Hollywood's next blockbuster that adulated the Ku Klux Klan: *Gone with the Wind.*

As an alarmist, D. W. Griffith, like so many others, eludes categorization. His passion in life was motion pictures, not race or politics. Nor, as an artist, was Griffith driven to explore his private world on a public screen. In *The Birth of a Nation,* African Americans are vengeful and irresponsible, whereas the most irresponsible person in Griffith's life was his father. Jake Griffith abandoned his Kentucky farm for drinking and gambling sprees that ultimately cost the family its land. The least vengeful people in D. W. Griffith's life were the family's former slaves, who were at his father's bedside when he died.[19] The future filmmaker, also present, was seven years old. No doubt there is a pattern that connects the life of D. W. Griffith with the films he made, but it is as intricate as a cobweb, and located in the dark recesses of his mind.

While film made Griffith a highly effective messenger, he received the message from another highly effective messenger: Thomas Dixon, author of *The Clansman,* a best-selling novel that became a hit play that became a motion picture called *The Birth of a Nation.* Dixon, who grew up on a North Carolina farm, received a scholarship to study political science at Johns Hopkins University. But he gave it up to pursue acting; then he gave up acting for law school. Rather than practice law, he ran for the North Carolina legislature. He was elected, but left politics after one term and became a minister. Dixon advanced from a pulpit in North Carolina to Boston's Dudley Street Church to New York's Twenty-Third Street Baptist Church, where, at age twenty-five, he led one of the largest congregations in the city. But he remained unsatisfied. Leaving the ministry, Dixon tried his hand as a novelist and was, yet again, immediately successful. When *The Clansman* sold over 100,000 copies in its first few months, he adapted it for the stage, and when the play was a hit in New York and in touring companies, he turned to the movies, approaching a former actor he knew named David W. Griffith. When *The Birth of a Nation* triggered efforts to ban it, Dixon turned to another friend, this one from his days at Johns Hopkins—Thomas Woodrow Wilson. Beneath this network Dixon acquired in his peripatetic career is a common denominator. Thomas Dixon wanted to be a great messenger. And finally he had found his message: the danger of African Americans.

The reunification of northerners and southerners provided by their shared panic over African Americans, joined with the unification this panic provided for immigrants with native-born whites, propelled the panic to the point that organized acts of ethnic cleansing commenced. In 1921, a mob attacked and burned to the ground the Greenwood section of Tulsa, Oklahoma, where the town's African Americans lived. Twenty-six blacks were known to have died in the carnage—though many more are believed to have been killed and dumped elsewhere. A precise death toll could not be assessed since many African Americans fled and did not return, even after those who remained rebuilt their community. Two years later, a mob attacked and burned down the predominantly African American community of Rosewood, Florida. Six African American deaths were officially listed, though unofficial estimates range as high as twenty-seven. All that remains of Rosewood today is a roadside marker. No charges were filed against the participants in either of these episodes. The same was true, as we shall come to see, with similar acts of ethnic cleansing inflicted by mobs on Irish Catholics, Chinese, and Hispanics.

Even in courthouses, deadly filtering of facts now sprouted on a scale of government sanctioned mass-execution of African Americans. In 1931, two white women accused nine young black men, ranging in age from twelve to nineteen, of raping them on a freight train they were all riding. At the trial that followed in Scottsboro, Alabama, the examining physician testified that all the sperm he found in the women were dead, indicating that they last had engaged in sexual relations prior to riding the train. Nevertheless, the

Scottsboro Boys, as they came to be known, were convicted and sentenced to death (with the exception of the twelve-year-old, who was sentenced to life in prison). By filtering the medical facts, the verdict and sentences were clearly acts of panic. That the judge did not exercise his prerogative to void the verdict gave official sanction to the panic.

The Beginning of the End of Widespread Panic

The Scottsboro case went on to have larger significance in the history of the panic over African Americans. The executions were ultimately prevented due to nationwide outrage that resulted after the Communist Party seized upon this injustice as an example of capitalist rulers seeking to divide the working class along racial lines. While the preponderance of African Americans were wary of the Communist Party, many became mindful of the effectiveness not only of the mass rallies organized by the Communists during the Scottsboro trials but also of collective action by the more politically accepted labor movement (despite so many unions at the time denying membership to blacks). After World War II, African Americans adopted collective action, thereby launching the modern Civil Rights Movement.

In other ways, too, the racial equation changed during the years of the Great Depression and World War II. Though athletic abilities in African Americans could be racially dismissed, as could the achievements of African American entertainers, intellectual achievements were more difficult to brush off. Between the onset of the Great Depression and the end of World War II, African American authors had published highly acclaimed fiction, such as *The Ways of White Folks* (1934) by Langston Hughes (already a widely respected poet), Zora Neale Hurston's *Their Eyes Were Watching God* (1937), and Richard Wright's *Native Son* (1940). Nor could white Americans dismiss the importance of African American physician Charles Drew's newly developed process for preserving blood plasma, which enabled the United States to provide vitally needed transfusions to the wounded in World War II. At the same time, the Tuskegee Airmen, the military's first African American aviators, destroyed 262 German aircraft, along with some

950 railcars and trucks, and sent a German naval destroyer to the bottom of the sea.

But the service of African Americans in World War II and the wars that preceded it did not reduce panic as much as such service did in other political panics (as we shall see in the chapters about Catholics and Jews) because African Americans fought in segregated units. Consequently, their valor went largely unwitnessed by white soldiers. On the home front, persecution of African Americans erupted into riots in cities such as New York, Philadelphia, Baltimore, Detroit, and elsewhere.

Following the war, momentum shifted significantly when the Supreme Court ruled in 1954 that racial segregation in public schools is unconstitutional. As seen in the Salem witch hunts, when the waning of widespread panic intensified the vehemence of some to the point of executing dogs, likewise vehemence intensified as widespread panic over African Americans began to wane. In response to the Supreme Court ruling, one reader of the June 15, 1954, *Baltimore Sun* wrote, "Secession is the only alternative now left." Panic resides less in the suggestion of secession than in the use of the absolute, "only." Other absolutes governed the letter writer's subsequent reference to "Nine Old Men and the agitators who would bring disorder and *complete ruination* down on us." (Italics added.)

The following year, momentum further shifted. This time the shift occurred not in one of the nation's highest venues but on a city bus. African American seamstress Rosa Parks refused to yield her seat to a white person and was arrested, commencing an episode in which African Americans employed the tactic of collective action that they had witnessed during the Scottsboro case: They boycotted the buses in Montgomery, Alabama. While some Southern whites recognized that times had changed, many did not. "City commissioners posted a $500 reward today for information leading to convictions for the bombing of the home of a Negro leading a race boycott of city buses," Alabama's *Anniston Star* reported on January 31, 1956. The targeted leader was a twenty-seven-year-old minister named Martin Luther King, Jr. Though local officials sought to quell such violence, they also sought to maintain the old equation by arresting the boycotters at their gatherings, including Martin Luther King, who spent two weeks in jail.

But the equation was changing in another way, too. Once again a new technology in communication was spreading throughout the United States: television. When the bus boycott commenced at a packed mass meeting, television cameras broadcast the scene. Television showed the damage to Martin Luther King's house after it was bombed. When King was arrested, television showed that too. And in December 1956, television viewers watched King board a bus in Montgomery, after the city had yielded to national pressure and ended segregated seating.

For many in panic, however, an additional result of their logic having been trampled by their fears and needs was their inability to adjust to the impact of television. Despite the presence of network cameras, southerners continued to respond to the nonviolent protesters with violence. More than thirty African Americans were murdered for their participation in the Civil Rights Movement, including four girls, ages eleven to fourteen, who perished when a bomb destroyed the Birmingham, Alabama, church in which they were attending Sunday school, and a thirteen-year-old boy shot later that day by teenagers coming from a rally celebrating the bombing. Not included in this count were those murdered for traditional reasons, such as the 1955 lynching of fourteen-year-old Emmett Till, accused of whistling at a white woman. The final murder specifically connected to the Civil Rights Movement took place in 1968. Its victim was Martin Luther King, Jr. Even in this death toll the altered equation surfaced. As in the previous episodes of such violence, a lesser number of whites died as well—eight in this instance—except now the whites died because of their *support* for African Americans.

In 1964, Congress passed the Civil Rights Act, followed the next year by the Voting Rights Act. These laws reflected the fact that, by the mid-1960s, anti-black attitudes had been sufficiently marginalized to end the centuries-long national panic. Still, regional panic continued in much of the South and in the North. In 1966, a white crowd in Cicero, Illinois, hurled bottles and bricks at civil rights marchers who were protesting that no African Americans lived in the Chicago suburb despite the fact that many worked there. In the 1970s, Boston was the scene of repeated racial violence over mandated bussing of students to achieve school integration.

Though these and others episodes subsided by the end of the twentieth century, their embers have remained volatile. On February 6, 2012, a self-appointed neighborhood watchman in Florida shot and killed an unarmed seventeen-year-old African American in a confrontation that commenced over watchman George Zimmerman's suspicion of Trayvon Martin, based on Martin's head being covered by his sweatshirt's hood. Zimmerman maintained he felt his life was in imminent danger from this unarmed, 158-pound teenager, despite the fact that twenty-eight-year-old Zimmerman, who outweighed Martin by nearly thirty pounds, was armed with a 9 mm semiautomatic pistol. Zimmerman's justification for shooting Martin was backed by a 2005 Florida law allowing people to shoot to kill in self-defense in any place where "he or she has a right to be."[20] Known as the Stand Your Ground law, its significance lay in the fact that it eliminated any obligation to retreat or escape if reasonably possible. "People want to know we stand on the side of victims of crime instead of the side criminals," Florida legislator Dennis Baxley explained.[21] Baxley's explanation was governed by a panic-inducing blank to be filled in. It left it to others to decide what constitutes being on the side of criminals. When signing the legislation into law, Governor Jeb Bush combined a panic-inducing absolute with an unverified claim when he stated that the law eliminated the dangerous requirement to "have to retreat." The governor's claim that one *had* to retreat (an absolute) was verifiable—but verifiably false. In the state of Florida there had been many recent instances in which charges were not filed against individuals who killed in self-defense, outside their home, fearing they had no reasonable ability to retreat or escape.[22] Nevertheless, following Florida's enactment of its Stand Your Ground law, more than thirty other states passed similar legislation.

The killing of Trayvon Martin raises a question. Did panic over African Americans and panic over the Second Amendment intersect? The organization most involved in advocating Stand Your Ground laws has been the National Rifle Association (NRA). "Our Founding Fathers knew that without Second Amendment freedom, all of our freedoms could be in jeopardy," NRA leader Wayne LaPierre declared at a 2013 meeting of the American Conservative Union.[23] His assertion was replete with elements frequently seen in political panic. Along with his reference to the Founding Fathers was an unverified claim regarding what they knew—a claim that is also a form of absolute, since it asserts they *all* knew it. The statement then employed another absolute when it referred to *all* of our freedoms. Though far into the portal to panic, LaPierre's statement stopped short of entering the realm of panic when he said *could* be in jeopardy as opposed to *would* be in jeopardy.

These views are a relatively recent position on the part of the NRA. In 1934, the organization supported the National Firearms Act, which mandated the registration of certain newly manufactured firearms. The NRA later lent its support to the Gun Control Act of 1968, which required a license to engage in interstate sales of firearms. In the mid-1970s, however, the NRA began to oppose such laws. It was also in the era between the mid-1960s and the mid-1970s that widespread panic over African Americans began to wane. During those same years, membership in the NRA surged. While the NRA's 2013 claim of 5 million members has been questioned, its growth is uncontested.[24] Though the NRA does not release figures on the demographics of its membership, every indication suggests that only a very small percentage is African American. Even as approximate figures, these two estimates suggest that many who remained fearful of blacks (often based on their correlation of race and crime) may have joined the NRA to cloak that fear, now socially less acceptable, in the Second Amendment right to bear arms.

Nevertheless, the underlying momentum away from panic over African Americans has continued to prevail. Following the killing of Trayvon Martin, for which George Zimmerman was acquitted, a commission appointed by Florida's governor concluded that the state's Stand Your Ground law was an "unnecessary and dangerous departure from the traditional law of self-defense."[25] As of this writing, efforts are being made in the Florida legislature to retract the law.

"It's a racial stalemate we've been stuck in for years," Democratic presidential nominee Barack Obama stated in the 2008 election, aptly describing the currently prevailing momentum. "But I have . . . a firm conviction . . . that working together we can move beyond some of our old racial wounds . . . . For the African American community, that path means embracing the burdens of our past without becoming victims of our past. . . . In the white community . . . [it] means acknowledging that what ails the African American community does not just exist in the minds of black people. . . . This union may never be perfect, but generation after generation has shown that it can always be perfected."

That year, Americans elected Barack Obama as their forty-fourth president, and the first African American president of the United States.

Three

"[T]o prepare for the overthrow of the government, no measure could be more effectual than the toleration of THE INSTITUTION OF FREE-MASONRY, which inculcates principles of arbitrary power and slavish obedience, the most abhorrent to freedom."

—James Odiorne, OPINIONS ON SPECULATIVE MASONRY (1830)

It is hard to imagine the middle-class guy who occasionally parades around wearing a red fez with sequins and a tassel belongs to a group once feared as a danger to the nation. Harder still is it to grasp that James Odiorne, quoted above, believed an organization whose members had included George Washington was secretly plotting *slavish obedience most abhorrent to freedom.* Yet Odiorne was not alone in sounding this alarm. During the first three decades of the nineteenth century, fear that freemasons were a threat to the nation became so widespread that a political party came into existence, the Anti-Masonic Party. Though today the Anti-Masonic Party is largely forgotten, its imprint remains by virtue of its having been the first political party to nominate its presidential candidates openly at a national convention.

The panic over freemasons was primarily fueled by an element that played a central role in the Salem witchcraft panic: secrecy. While the notion of clandestine conclaves was part of both panics, in this instance the claim was not unverified. Freemasons were, in fact, sworn to secrecy regarding their oaths and rituals. In addition, Founding Father anxiety, so frequently an element in American political panics, surfaced for the first time in this panic in regard to the men who led the Revolution. Being a panic among the generation that followed those men, its references to the founders displays most vividly the anxieties attached to turning the nation's founders into legends. Also revealing itself particularly clearly in this panic are the ways ambitious individuals can use panic for personal purposes. Indeed, such individuals *created* this panic.

Among the nation's founders, George Washington, Benjamin Franklin, John Hancock, and James Monroe had all been members of the freemasons. In their era, the organization consisted of well-established individuals in the New World and in Europe who shared an interest in the advancement of science and philosophy. Freemasonry's secret oaths of mutual support attracted such men because their advanced philosophies—such as the notion that all men are created equal—ran counter to the interests of monarchs. In keeping with their philosophy of equality, these freemasons began to include a wider variety of members, resulting in a large influx of new members. In the United States, this influx was augmented as increasing numbers of Americans migrated westward toward the Northwest Territory and newly acquired Louisiana Purchase. Freemasonry provided them with new social bonds and business connections to replace those that had been severed by leaving their hometowns in the East.[1]

The wider variety of men who now joined for a wider variety of reasons eventually broke with the intellectual brand of freemasonry practiced by their more patrician forbearers, returning the emphasis to the ancient organization's medieval bonds made sacred by rituals known only among its members. Founding Father anxiety can be seen by comparing the funerals of freemasons Benjamin Franklin and George Washington. Some 20,000 people gathered to watch Franklin's funeral procession in Philadelphia, which featured the American Philosophical Society, the brotherhood of Revolutionary War officers known as the Society of the Cincinnati, political officials, and clergy—but not a single representation from his fellow freemasons. Comparable numbers assembled at the funeral of George Washington, where the procession featured his Masonic lodge accompanying the casket.

Anxiety over those Founding Fathers who were freemasons resulted not only from a change in membership but also from a change in Europe. As seen in that which was salvaged following the panic over witchcraft, the new United States was erected as a beacon of democracy—a beacon that soon cast its light on France, contributing to its 1789 revolution. Because it was far more dangerous to plan the *overthrow* of a king, as opposed to *independence* from a king, the secret oaths and pacts of freemasonry attracted revolutionaries. When, however, the French Revolution turned into a decades-long bloodbath of rage and revenge, many Americans became conflicted in their views of revolution—and freemasons. In 1820, a resolution was introduced before the Presbyterian Synod of Pittsburgh to exclude freemasons from church membership. Regarding the Founding Fathers, one memoirist of the era recorded, "Time or other causes have, I am sorry to say, weakened the popular memory of the events which gave birth to the Republic. The Fourth of July celebrations are by no means as universal. Nor is the sense of gratitude to the fathers and founders of our government." That memoirist was Thurlow Weed, the man who, more than any other individual, ignited widespread panic over freemasons.[2]

The anti-Masonic panic began in the wake of a local panic—not over freemasons but among freemasons. In 1826, the Batavia, New York, lodge of freemasons denied membership to a newcomer in town named William Morgan, despite the fact that Morgan had been a member of a lodge in Rochester, New York. Morgan relocated to Batavia after a fire destroyed his place of business, inflaming his alcoholism and, taken together, rendering him bankrupt. In Batavia, his frequent inebriation resulted in being denied membership in the town's newly forming Masonic lodge, at which point his anger and need for funds drove him to write and arrange for the publication of a book revealing freemasonry's secret oaths and rituals.

Morgan's manuscript triggered a panic within the Batavia lodge. Seeking to prevent publication of the revelations, members of the lodge abducted Morgan. That this act was one of panic resides in the kidnappers doing that which they feared. Fearing Morgan's book would subject their activities to public view, they abducted him, thereby inevitably drawing attention to their activities. Worse, for these panicked freemasons, whatever became of William Morgan has remained a mystery—and mystery, as seen in the Salem witch hunt, is a blank to be filled in that enables others' fears and needs to participate in their assessment. In September 1826, newspapers nationwide picked up an item from the *Batavia Advocate* that had filled in the blank with a tantalizing surmise regarding Morgan's fate: "There is some reason for the horrible apprehension that his life has been secretly sacrificed."[3]

Whatever the fate of William Morgan, who was indeed never seen again, why did his manuscript arouse such panic? Over twenty works revealing the rituals of the Masons had been published during George Washington's lifetime.[4] None of their authors had been kidnapped, let alone murdered. How had freemasonry—at least, in Batavia, New York—come to this? The answer is, yet again, the nation's newly emerging Founding Father anxiety. When the founders established the new nation on the basis of a secular document, they left unanswered who would oversee the nation's sacred rituals. Back in 1793, the laying of the cornerstone of the United States Capitol was ritualized by the Grand Lodge of Maryland freemasons and Virginia's Alexandria Lodge, who anointed the cornerstone with corn, wine, and oil, followed by a Masonic chant. Similar ceremonies marked the openings of other public projects in the early years of the republic. Many Americans who were not freemasons were uncomfortable with this emerging secular clergy.[5]

In western New York, where Batavia is located, many were also uncomfortable with what was then the nation's preeminent public works project: the Erie Canal, whose construction through the region would connect commerce on the Great Lakes with the Hudson River. Those with access to the canal stood to gain considerably, but those without access would be cut off when the routes of commerce would dramatically shift. The fact that the canal's most ardent proponent, New York governor De-Witt Clinton, was a freemason raised additional fears of secret pacts. Both these unstable elements—one commercial, the other spiritual—were on display at the grand opening of the canal in 1825. The ceremony was led by a procession of some 300 freemasons who offered a prayer to the Grand Architect of the Universe and blessed the canal's capstone by sprinkling it with corn and wine. When, less than a year later, William Morgan planned to publish his book, it was not fear of embarrassment that panicked the men who abducted him; it was, in their minds, heresy—a threat to the nation's nascent secular priesthood.

Two months after William Morgan's abduction, four members of the Batavia lodge were arrested and soon convicted of conspiracy to kidnap. The available evidence would not support a charge of kidnapping, per se, let alone murder, since Morgan's fate remained uncertain. That uncertainty made for a news story that captured the nation's imagination for reasons best expressed by the judge who sentenced the defendants. Whatever they had done to Morgan, he declared, resulted from "the dictates of the secret councils and conclaves" of freemasonry.[6]

That there was growing fear of freemasons is evidenced by New York City's *Spectator,* which devoted half of its March 9, 1827, front page to re-porting on a gathering of citizens calling itself the "Lewiston Convention," which had declared its intention to demand answers to Morgan's disappear-ance. "It was represented," the article noted, "that Mr. Weed, Editor of the *Rochester Telegraph,* who was appointed one of the delegates to the Lewiston Convention, did not go in consequence of having been threatened by the Masons." Filtered from the article was who selected Thurlow Weed to be a delegate. As one of the organizers of the event, Weed quite likely appointed himself. His assertion that he had opted not to go because he had been threatened by the freemasons was a panic-inducing unverified claim. While an unverified claim is not necessarily false, what is verifiably true is that Weed's absence at the gathering drew attention to him by creating a panic-inducing blank to be filled: Who and how many were secretly targeting him?

The publicity generated by the Lewiston Convention contributed to a grand jury charging six others with involvement in Morgan's abduction. Panic, however, was not yet sufficiently widespread to trample the judicial system. Unlike Salem's theocratic judiciary during the witchcraft panic, the Bill of Rights contributed to New York's judiciary maintaining its threshold for verification of claims via the rules of evidence. The defendants were acquitted. Those constitutional safeguards, however, also inadvertently served to further inflame panic.

"Fellow Citizens," began an advertisement in the September 25, 1827, *National Intelligencer* that asserted the recent acquittals resulted from secret pacts among freemasons who were now among our judges and jurors. "If one private society can established and execute laws," the ad declared, ". . . the mantle of darkness will, in the first place, envelope the conspirators and defend them from your grasp." But far worse, it warned, "Your Government shall be overthrown . . . by effecting the destruction of your liberties." The ad was signed by one Solomon Southwick. He too would achieve fame as he joined with Thurlow Weed in sounding alarms over freemasonry. Neither, however, succeeded in igniting nationwide fear until October 7, 1827, when a body washed ashore on Lake Ontario.

Widespread Panic Detonates

"Thurlow Weed, being sworn," stated the Oak Orchard, New York, coroner's report, "says that he came here in company with others . . . to examine the body and that he assisted in disinterring it."[7] The reason the corpse needed to be disinterred was that the coroner, after originally examining it, had ruled the remains unidentifiable and ordered it buried. Weed, learning of this, immediately gathered a group composed of Morgan's wife and close associates. The group demanded that the body be disinterred and, after viewing the remains, agreed the corpse was William Morgan.[8]

Weed's news scoop put an exclamation point on a book just published by Solomon Southwick: *A Solemn Warning Against Free-Masonry* (1828). In and of itself, Southwick's book was regarded by many with credibility by virtue of Southwick having been a freemason. As with Tituba in the witchcraft panic, confessions (even recanted, as was Tituba's) often function as verified claims. Much as Weed had lamented his generation's disconnection from the nation's July 4th founding, Southwick too sought to reconnect his readers with the recently departed Founding Fathers. In so doing, however, he displayed his anxiety over the nation's preeminent freemason founder, George Washington, by filtering facts. Regarding Washington's lifelong membership in the freemasons, Southwick argued, "Could the Patriarch, as well as the Hero of his country, who had drank deep at the Fountain of Light which emanated from the Divine Mission of the Redeemer of Mankind . . . slake his thirst for improvement in the scientific and moral deserts which comprise the domains of Free Masonry?" Presenting certitude instead of evidence, Southwick entered the portal to panic by continuing, "I boldly answer, NO. He could not; he did not." Southwick capped this claim by citing Washington's Farewell Address. "It warns us, in that clear and emphatical language which characterizes all that Washington ever said or wrote, to 'BEWARE OF SECRET ASSOCIATIONS.'" Here Southwick proceeded further into the portal to panic by filtering out the fact that George Washington never made that statement. What Washington had warned was that political "combinations and associations, under whatever plausible character . . . are likely, in the course of time and things, to become potent engines, by which cunning, ambitious, and unprincipled men will be enabled to subvert the power of the people."[9] He did not say, "Beware of secret associations," because he was referring to the newly (and not at all secretly) forming political parties, a phenomenon George Washington hoped would not take root in the new United States. Southwick would soon enter the realm of panic by doing that which, in citing Washington's warning, he claimed to fear. He soon joined with others to form the Anti-Masonic Party.

Southwick's book also contained an element seen in the panic over African Americans and that we will see again in the panic over gay

Americans: sexuality. For those fomenting panic, sex has not only its obvious allure but also arouses uncertainties and fears for many, if not all, of us. Southwick confided to his readers that, in freemasonry's initiation ritual, the newcomer "submits to being stripped naked . . . under the indecent and ridiculous pretense of ascertaining his sex" and is led blindfolded around the room on a leash. Ruefully he confessed, "How often I retired in disgust from those nocturnal orgies." Baring his soul (and visions of young naked boys), he lamented, "I shudder at the idea of . . . youth going like a lamb to slaughter, to poison the virgin purity of his mind . . . in a dark and secret conclave . . . of men who pass in the world for gentlemen and Christians." Five months later, Solomon Southwick was nominated for governor of New York.

Southwick's book was soon joined by a spate of anti-Masonic books, including *Revelations in Masonry* (1827) by "A Late Member of the Craft"; *Free Masonry: Its Pretensions Exposed, Its Dangerous Tendency Exhibited* (1828) by "A Master Mason"; and *Free Masonry: Deadly Foe to Equal Liberty* (1830) by "A Citizen of Massachusetts." In remaining anonymous, these authors created blanks to be filled in that, in the context of the Morgan affair, many Americans filled with the fear that the freemasons would seek vengeance if they knew who the author was, just as they had against William Morgan. Those in panic filtered out the fact that other anti-Masonic authors in these same years did put their names on their books, and none was subsequently killed, kidnapped, or assaulted.

Thurlow Weed also published a book, though he did so in the same way that he got Morgan identified as the corpse: through a group he could control. His 1827 book, *A Narrative of the Facts and Circumstances Relating to the Kidnapping and Presumed Murder of William Morgan,* was the "official" report of the Lewiston Convention, at which Weed had gained prominence through his absence. Unlike Southwick, however, Weed did not seek public office. In what would become a long and powerful political career, he always operated behind the scenes.

That Weed and Southwick both published their books in 1827, the year Morgan's alleged corpse washed ashore, suggests they wrote quickly—which

they did because 1828 was an election year. The citizens group that had originally formed to investigate Morgan's abduction now reconvened as a state-
wide anti-Masonic gathering. Among the members of its steering committee
was Thurlow Weed. After the delegates nominated Solomon Southwick for
governor, the April 1, 1828, *United States Telegraph* wryly noted, "Thurlow
Weed, of the anti-humbug paper at Rochester, will not support Solomon
Southwick for governor. Now, if this antimasonic fever was genuine, why
not support Solomon?" The question yields the first evidence that Weed was
fanning fears more than he was fearful. He did not support Southwick because he was not about to back a candidate who had no chance of winning.
Southwick did indeed lose New York's gubernatorial race to Martin Van Buren in a three-way race in which Southwick garnered only 12 percent of the
vote. Still, the election marked the debut of the Anti-Masonic Party, which
succeeded in capturing fifteen seats in the New York State Assembly—a fact
that did not escape Thurlow Weed.

The month after New York's anti-Masonic convention, a bill was proposed in the state legislature to prohibit freemasons from holding public
office, along with anyone who had taken a nonjudicial oath—a remedy previously suggested in Solomon Southwick's book. The bill failed to pass, however, due to concerns over the Constitution's guarantee of free speech and the
right to assemble. During this same period, nineteen Baptist churches in
western New York held a convention of their own for the purpose of urging
churches to excommunicate any freemason congregant who did not publicly
renounce the organization. On March 7, 1828, the *New Bedford Mercury*
in Massachusetts reported, "We learn Mr. Thurlow Weed, formerly editor
of the *Rochester Telegraph,* is about to publish there a new newspaper under
the title of the *Anti-Masonic Enquirer.*" Notably, the article's New York correspondent added, "Nor is this excitement confined to our state . . . but
is spreading fast, as we are informed, into the western part of Pennsylvania." On November 24, 1829, the *Delaware Gazette* told readers, "The anti-
Masonic excitement . . . has been extended to the state of Vermont."

The incident that caused panic to erupt in Vermont involved yet another
element that would recur in panics to come: guilt by association. Joseph

Burnham, a convicted sex offender reported to have died in prison, was suddenly said to have been seen in New York City. Burnham was already notorious; his trial, for the rape of a young girl who was lured and held down by two women, had captured considerable attention. On the basis of the rumors that he had been seen—which remained, in effect, "spectral evidence"—a local attorney named Richard Ransom, soon to be a candidate for Congress, claimed Burnham's escape resulted from a conspiracy involving the prison's superintendent, warden, and physician, all of whom were freemasons. Filtered from his claim was the fact that Burnham was not a freemason. But his son was. Joseph Burnham was thus "Masonized," much as, in a later panic, individuals would be "communized."[10]

The legislatures of Pennsylvania and Rhode Island now joined those of Vermont and New York in launching official investigations into freemasonry. Witnesses summoned before committees faced interrogations very similar to those in Salem's witch hunt, with the significant difference that they now had the protection of the Constitution. When, for example, one witness brought before Pennsylvania's investigating committee was asked to reveal the initiation ceremonies and secret oaths of freemasonry, he refused to answer, asserting instead his "solemn protest against a committee . . . possessing any authority under the Constitution to cause a citizen to appear and give evidence . . . touching such a question"—a response that would be echoed in twentieth-century congressional investigations of communists. Pennsylvania's anti-Masonic investigating committee reacted with a resolution "to take into custody all the above named persons . . . to answer for contempt committed against this House"—also echoed by the twentieth-century House Un-American Activities Committee when it charged the "Hollywood Ten" with contempt of Congress, resulting in prison sentences for those who continued to refuse to answer the committee's questions about their associations.[11]

In 1830, delegations from Vermont, Massachusetts, Rhode Island, Connecticut, Pennsylvania, New Jersey, Ohio, Alabama, and New York assembled in Philadelphia in the first national Anti-Masonic Party convention.

The delegates created a committee "to report what measures can constitutionally . . . be used to effectuate the extinction of freemasonry" and announced
their intention to nominate a presidential candidate when they reconvened
prior to the 1832 presidential election. At that next convention, and for the
first time in American history, a political party openly voted in nominating
its presidential candidate. The man that the Anti-Masonic Party chose was
William Wirt, thereby raising a question: Who was William Wirt?

When the delegates arrived in Baltimore for the 1832 convention, many
had other nominees in mind. Thurlow Weed, too, had been hard at work
seeking a candidate to challenge the reelection of Andrew Jackson, a member
of the Masons. But there was a critical difference between Weed's outlook
and that of the other delegates. They wanted an anti-Mason candidate; Weed
wanted a winnable candidate. Privately, he had approached Henry Clay, the
presumptive candidate of the National Republican Party (not to be confused
with today's Republican Party). Like Andrew Jackson, Henry Clay was also
a Mason. Unlike Jackson, a Democrat, Henry Clay's political party was in
its in final stages of decay. Weed urged Clay to abandon his party, renounce
freemasonry, and tap into the popularity of the anti-Masonic movement by
running as its candidate. Clay demurred.[12]

Eventually Weed ended up approaching William Wirt, a respected
former U.S. attorney general. Lacking the stature of a Henry Clay, Weed
conceived of a different strategy to make Wirt electable. Wirt too was a
freemason, but rather than urge him to renounce it, Weed urged him to
redefine it. At the Anti-Masonic convention, Wirt proclaimed that the party
had "no other object in view then, in effect, to assert the supremacy of the
laws of the land." It did not seek to prohibit anyone from "the enjoyment of
those social rights which are secured to them by their Constitution." As for
amending the Constitution or making nonjudicial oaths illegal, those efforts
were now refashioned by the party's presidential candidate into using the
"elective franchise [by] deeming every man unfit for office who . . . considers his Masonic oaths and obligations as superior to his obligations to the
Constitution."[13]

The Final Phase of the Panic

Wirt's address reflected the kind of compromise that can widen a movement's appeal but weaken the commitment of its core supporters. Moreover, it can destroy the movement by turning those core supporters into enemies. As seen in the execution of dogs during the Salem witch hunt, and in every political panic that followed, as widespread panic diminishes, panic among those who remain so alarmed often intensifies. In this instance, a petition circulated during the presidential campaign declared, "Those who went into anti-Masonry from honest principles are opening their eyes to the shameless sporting with integrity by Thurlow Weed . . . [and] the abandonment of original principles by the leaders in the coalition."[14] In the election that followed, William Wirt received less than 8 percent of the vote.

The 1832 election was a defeat for the Anti-Masonic Party, but not for Thurlow Weed. Through the party, he had advanced from New York to the national arena. For him, Wirt's poor showing gave Weed more of what he needed: information. He now knew it was time to bail. Thurlow Weed soon left the party he helped form to join the emerging Whig Party.

At the third Anti-Masonic Party convention, those who remained opted not to nominate their own candidate. Instead they nominated William Henry Harrison, a Whig. Even with their support, Harrison lost to Jackson's handpicked successor, Martin Van Buren. Following this defeat, the Anti-Masonic Party quietly faded away.

In terms of political panic, the Anti-Masonic movement is significant for two reasons. It sheds light on the way the Constitution can protect individuals during a panic—though in so doing can also further fuel a panic. Also seen particularly clearly in this episode were ways ambitious individuals can avail themselves of the fears that fuel panic and even create widespread panic. Thurlow Weed exploited the panic from behind the scenes and went on to become one of his era's preeminent power brokers. He managed the career of William Seward, putting deals in place that enabled Seward to win election to New York's governorship and the United States Senate. Seward was considered a shoo-in for the 1860 presidential nomination, but Weed inaccurately assessed a one-term Illinois congressman making a long-shot bid. Seward had to settle for becoming Abraham Lincoln's secretary of state.

Solomon Southwick exploited the panic in a way that sought the spotlight by authoring a book and running for governor. When that effort sputtered out, he went on to seek the spotlight on other stages. He next became involved in the newly emerging temperance movement, offering a resolution at the 1833 gathering of the New York Temperance Society to "call loudly upon all professing Christians to clear themselves of even the slightest imputation of a sin so foul" as alcohol.[15] He then turned to the newly forming abolitionist movement. In 1838, three antislavery poems Southwick wrote were set to music and sung at an abolition rally in his hometown of Albany.

The end of widespread panic over freemasons did not end the alarms. Works espousing fear of freemasons have periodically continued to appear.[16] None has triggered panic, as the nation's social landscape has changed. Those changes, however, provided the groundwork for the political panics that followed.

Four

"The despots of Europe are attempting, by THE SPREAD OF POPERY IN THIS COUNTRY to subvert its free institutions."

—Samuel F. B. Morse, FOREIGN CONSPIRACY AGAINST
THE LIBERTIES OF THE UNITED STATES (1835)

The 1776 North Carolina constitution stated, "No person, who shall deny the being of God or the truth of the Protestant religion . . . shall be capable of holding any office or place of trust or profit in the civil department within this State." Likewise the original constitutions of South Carolina, Georgia, New Jersey, and New Hampshire all prohibited non-Protestants from holding political office. The reasoning behind this distrust of Catholics holding public office in the United States was stated in works published in the United States in its early years—such as *The Master Key to Popery* (1812) or *The Mysteries of Popery Unveiled* (1820)—which argued that Catholics, by virtue of their religion being ruled by the pope, were a danger to democracy. When, in the closing decades of the 1700s, Catholic immigrants fled to the United States to escape political upheavals in France and Ireland, American fears that they were bringing cultures of tyranny from their homelands caught fire beyond the five states that prohibited Catholics from holding office.

This first nationwide anti-Catholic panic manifested itself in the 1798 Alien and Sedition Acts, which made it a federal crime to engage in any form of "false, scandalous, and malicious writing" about the federal government and authorized the deportation of any immigrant the president deemed dangerous.[1] These new laws became a campaign issue in the 1800 election, pitting incumbent President John Adams, who had signed the legislation, against Thomas Jefferson, who had opposed it. Jefferson won the election. Ironically, though unintentionally, Jefferson then set the stage for a new wave of anti-Catholic fears.

The Louisiana Purchase: New Ground for Fear

President Jefferson's 1803 Louisiana Purchase added a vast region to the United States, into which the fears underlying the anti-Catholic panic expanded and branched. An April 23, 1803, letter to the editor of the *Port-Folio* revealed that reader's fear of Catholics as a danger to the nation in the concern it expressed about this new region, predominantly populated at the time by French Catholics. It declared (in that era's often plural use of the nation's name), "[T]he United States never wish to see the province of Louisiana republicanized, but by the gradual emigration of their own citizens."

Panic, however, did not spark among the pioneers. Facing a host of more imminent dangers, they had to rely on each other. This era of anti-Catholic panic flared in the Northeast. "In the great valley of the Mississippi, a cloud arises," a speaker at an 1844 New York campaign rally declared. "Every day it gathers strength. That cloud is Catholicity."[2] Samuel F. B. Morse, the widely admired developer of the telegraph, expressed in his 1835 book, *Foreign Conspiracy Against the Liberties of the United States,* the reason Catholics triggered political fears. Catholics, he told readers, "are but obedient instruments in the hands of their more knowing leaders to accomplish the designs of their foreign masters."[3] Such fear would echo over a century later in the panic over communist subversion when FBI director J. Edgar Hoover declared, "The Communist Party USA is . . . [a] foreign-directed, international conspiracy . . . completely subservient to Moscow."[4]

Among numerous others for whom the acquisition of this new land triggered fear that Catholics were a danger to the nation, one is notable for the way her prominence in the anti-Catholic panic paved the way for her later role in the women's rights movement and the panic it triggered. Anna Ella Carroll wrote in her 1856 book, *The Star of the West,* "In the vast margin of the West yet to be filled, it becomes a question of the first moment to the nation that it be occupied by Protestants, whose education tends to strengthen our liberties, while that of Romanism is designed to subvert them." Whether Carroll genuinely feared that Catholics endangered the nation or availed herself of others' fear for personal political gain is open to question. Though raised as a Protestant, among her many Catholic relatives had been Charles Carroll, a signer of the Declaration of Independence. How does it happen, then, that in another book Anna Ella Carroll published that same year, *The Great American Battle* (1856), she declared, "It becomes our duty . . . to prohibit a Papist to hold office or cast a ballot in our box, until he shall have proved himself the friend of liberty . . . by expressly foreswearing, without mental reservation, all allegiance to the Pope."[5]

Anna Ella Carroll's parents, though of mixed Protestant and Catholic lineage, were married in a Catholic ceremony but raised their children as Protestants.[6] A likely source for daughter Anna's political distrust of Catholics surfaced in the years that followed her opening remarks in *The Great American Battle:* "As a woman, I have no affiliations with any principles which place her in a sphere at variance with that refined delicacy to which she is assigned by Nature. I have no aspirations to extend her influence or position." With the outbreak of the Civil War, despite her claim of having "no aspirations to extend her influence," Carroll published a legal defense of President Lincoln's suspension of *habeas corpus* that so rivaled that of any attorney it brought her to Lincoln's attention. She subsequently prepared a report for him analyzing Confederate defenses in the region of the Tennessee River's watershed and suggested changes in the route of invasion.[7] Now a widely respected political figure, Carroll went on to serve on the board of the National American Woman Suffrage Association. For Anna Ella Carroll, the anti-Catholic panic provided a career opportunity. She may genuinely have been alarmed by the massive influx of Catholic immigrants. But she did not hesitate to betray her claim of having no aspirations to extend her influence or position—just as Thurlow Weed had not hesitated to betray the Anti-Masonic Party when it suited his agenda. Their two careers illuminate a fundamental aspect of political panic. Social conflicts unleash emotions that can empower any alarmist with the ability to harness those emotions— including alarmists from groups that are politically underempowered.

During this era, another new ground was opening up that also augmented the fear of Catholics. This new ground was the widespread expansion of schools. One book from this period warned parents that Catholic educators will "disarm you and lull suspicion to sleep, then . . . stealthily lead the confiding mind of your child out of the reach of parental control."[8] Another warned, "Only give them the education of one generation of our citizens and, as everyone knows, they can do with the next whatsoever they please."[9] Just as Samuel Morse's warning over Catholics was so closely echoed in J. Edgar Hoover's warning over communists, we will also hear these warnings echo in the second half of the twentieth century (and into the twenty-first) in fears regarding homosexuals.

Likewise, echoes from the witchcraft panic were now sounding in the panic over Catholics. Maria Monk's 1836 book *Awful Disclosures* called the sacramental wine used in the Catholic Eucharist "the wine of fornication," and echoed the Salem witchcraft panic when it continued, "Nothing but the powers of darkness could work up the young girl to receive it, unless by subtlety of the devil, and the vile artifices of the Nuns." *Awful Disclosures,* one of a series of escaped-nun confessionals, depicted convents as alluring refuges that, once women crossed their thresholds, became dens of iniquity. Satan leading a coven of witches permeates the book's subtext in describing the punishment meted out to one young nun. Tied to a bed, a second mattress was placed over her and a priest "sprung like a fury upon it, and stamped on it with all his force. He was speedily followed by the nuns." Soon, "all was motionless and silent beneath it." The book led its readers into underground spaces in which evil lurked, as when it recounted Monk's being sent to the cellar for coal: "I passed three small doors . . . fastened with large iron bolts . . . each having a small opening above, covered with a fine grating secured by a smaller lock." The dungeon-like bowels of the convent then became more macabre as she told of coming upon a space where "the earth appeared as if mixed with some whitish substance . . . [and] a hole dug so deep into the earth that I could perceive no bottom. . . . I knew that lime is often used by Roman Catholics in burying-places." The book thus artfully merged an imaginative notion of this bottomless pit as a passageway to hell with what Monk suspected to be its actual use as an open gravesite.

Whether or not its revelations were true, what is true is that the actual author of *Awful Disclosures* was a man named Theodore Dwight. Dwight thus entered the realm of panic by doing that which he feared. Fearing Catholics engaged in secrecy, much of it involving women, he sought to combat it by doing likewise. To his credit, however, he did it effectively and artfully, crafting the book's revelations in the popular (and still popular) gothic tropes of horror fiction. Like Thomas Dixon's *The Clansman,* Dwight's ghost-authored *Awful Disclosures* was an enormous success. Also as with Dixon, *Awful Disclosures* enabled Dwight to achieve a long-sought prominence. After failing to achieve fame as a poet, Dwight turned to travel books, though their success paled in comparison with earlier travel books by his uncle, Timothy Dwight, president of Yale University. In addition he tried his hand as the author of guides to parenting and classroom teaching before hitting the jackpot with *Awful Disclosures;* he soon revealed his authorship and published, under his own name, *Open Convents.* The purported author, Maria Monk, did indeed exist and did relate to Dwight her experiences living in a convent. As with William Morgan, who sought to improve his situation by joining the freemasons and, when that did not succeed, to improve his situation by publishing an exposé of the freemasons, Maria Monk sought to improve her situation by becoming a nun and, when that did not succeed, to do so by publishing *Awful Disclosures,* though she later raised questions as to the liberties Dwight took, both with her story and her royalties from sales of the book. Little more than ten years after the appearance of the still wide-selling *Awful Disclosures,* Maria Monk was sent to prison for theft. She died the following year at the age of thirty-three.[10]

The secular version of the witchcraft panic's Puritan mission was invoked when the nationally known orator Lyman Beecher warned in 1834 of the danger of Catholics by declaring, "If this nation is, in the providence of God, destined to lead the way in the moral and political emancipation of the world, it is time she understood her high calling and were harnessed for the work." The work involved defeating the "Catholic system," which Beecher declared to be "adverse to liberty."[11] His fiery words were soon followed by actual fire when a mob burned the city's Ursuline Convent to the ground. The following day, Irish Catholic men from nearby towns converged on Boston. "Much credit is due to Bishop [Benedict] Fenwick," the *National Intelligencer* reported on August 18, 1834, "for the exertions he made to dissuade the Catholics from all acts of retaliatory violence." But Lyman Beecher interpreted the bishop's intervention differently. "Has it come to this" he asked, "that the capital of New England has been thrown into consternation by the threats of a Catholic mob, and that her temples and mansions stand only through the forbearance of a Catholic bishop?"[12] One could conclude Lyman Beecher was simply a bigot, but Beecher stands as an example that alarmists cannot be stereotyped. His lifelong ministry included even greater efforts to abolish slavery and extend a hand to African Americans.

The panic over Catholics that spread through the nation as its population spread into the Louisiana Purchase was further fueled when that new land became economically joined to the east via the Erie Canal and the railroads that followed. These enabled the rapid industrialization that created massive numbers of new jobs. Those jobs, in turn, attracted immigrants, many of whom were Irish Catholics escaping famine when their country's potato crop fell victim to disease in the 1840s. These shifts in America's social and literal landscape unsettled the sense of security of so many native-born citizens that a movement commenced that culminated in the creation of the Know Nothing Party. Its aim was to keep America American.

While the Know Nothing Party was not solely anti-Irish or anti-Catholic, it centered Irish Catholics in its crosshairs. "Most of the Irish who come to this country are as ignorant as children seven years old," Nathaniel Hopper, a Know Nothing candidate, declared in 1843.[13] Fearing that Catholics, in obedience to the pope, would vote as a bloc, Hopper continued, "Who is it that commit most of the robberies, and thefts, and murders in this city and country? . . . And then don't these same fellows, as soon as they come among us, walk right up to the ballot boxes and become our rulers?" The following year, a Know Nothing speaker raised the specter of ethnic cleansing when he declared, "These Irish bog-trotters must be sent back to their native obscurity."[14] Invoking two increasingly familiar elements of political panic, he continued, "We must rally round the Bible which Washington wove [sic] in the holy cause of our country." Another declared that the upcoming election "is no less than a declaration of independence. . . . Are Americans prepared to admit Catholicity," he asked, "the means of robbing us of our rights? . . . Never let it be said that the descendants of Washington and Jefferson tamely bowed down to a papal power and give papists up the ballot box."

Also as seen before, vehemence was soon followed by violence. "Dreadful Riot at Philadelphia," headlined a May 8, 1844, account in the Washington, D.C., *National Intelligencer* of a mob's attempt to burn down a convent. In Cincinnati, a riot ensued in 1853 when a mob attempted to lynch the papal nuncio, visiting on a goodwill tour. Ethnic cleansing took place that same year when a mob descended on an Irish neighborhood in Salmon Falls, New Hampshire; as the *Bangor Daily Whig* reported on June 6, "the Irish families therein having moved out in accordance with previous notice sent them by the mob, the buildings were demolished." The news report noted that "the authorities showed no disposition to interfere."

The following year, Catholic churches were destroyed by arson in New Hampshire and Maine. A bomb leveled a Catholic church in Massachusetts, and an Irishman was murdered during the sacking of a Catholic church in New Jersey. The *Boston Atlas* reported on October 19, 1854, "The Rev. Mr. Bapst, a Roman Catholic priest from Bangor, was tarred and feathered and rode on a rail at Ellsworth, Maine, on Saturday evening." Also in 1854, violence between Catholics and Protestants erupted in St. Louis. "For forty-eight hours this city has been the scene of one of the most appalling riots that has ever taken place in the country," one correspondent reported. "Men have been butchered like cattle, property destroyed, and anarchy reigns supreme."[15] Louisville was the scene of an 1855 attack on Irish Catholics that erupted into a riot costing twenty lives.

Legislation was proposed that year in Massachusetts and Michigan authorizing inspection of convents. The measure failed to pass in Michigan but was enacted in Massachusetts and, in the years ahead, in Georgia and Florida. None uncovered evidence of any of the accusations. In Congress, anti-Catholic legislation was proposed by New York representative Thomas Whitney, a founder of the Know Nothing Party. Whitney sought to amend the naturalization law by requiring the oath taken by applicants for citizenship specifically include "that he doth absolutely and entirely renounce and abjure all allegiance and fidelity to every foreign . . . state or sovereignty whatever, both civil and ecclesiastical."[16] By now, however, citizenship and voting rights were more explosively connected to slavery than to fear of Catholic loyalty, since the 1854 Kansas-Nebraska Act allowed voters to decide about slavery in their state or territory. That contest (ultimately won in both states by antislavery advocates) caused Whitney's bill to fail, as most immigrants did not support slavery.

The Civil War years were a time-out for anti-Catholic rage. New York City's previously discussed military draft riot by a largely Irish mob was neither an Irish reaction to anti-Catholic rage, as shamefully evidenced by the mob murdering African Americans, nor a display of disloyalty by Irish-American citizens, as the rioters were primarily recent arrivals. Irish-Americans served on both sides in the war, loyal in the same way as Protestants. But suspicions of Catholic disloyalty resurfaced after the war. An editorial in the February 2, 1870, *Boston Investigator* warned that "papists are fully, perfectly, and entirely under the control and government of the . . . Bishops, Priests, and Clergy." The editorial then added another recurring fear, seen in the panic over witches and freemasons, when it said, "The system of Popery is of such a character that all affairs can be transacted in the most secret, hidden, disguised manner."

In addition to yet a new generation of anti-Catholics books, the emerging art of political cartoons joined the fray. A Thomas Nast image in the May 8, 1875, issue of *Harper's Weekly* depicted what appeared to be crocodiles arriving on our shore—the crocodiles, on second glance, being the mitered heads of Catholic bishops. Nast's widely popular images also appeared in the magazine *Puck,* where they were joined by similar depictions drawn by another of the nation's premiere cartoonists, Joseph Keppler.

The Decline of the Panic

While the pause for the Civil War appears to not have diminished anti-Catholic passions, the war did produce the seed that, as it sprouted, would diminish the panic. An 1872 *Methodist Quarterly* review of George Hughey's *Political Romanism* told readers, "He makes it as sure as a mathematical demonstration that a good papist cannot consistently be an American patriot."[17] The seed, tiny though it be, is the word "consistently." Catholics, after all, had just fought and died with the same loyalty (to their respective regions) as Protestants. Not until the blood of Catholic and Protestant Americans mixed on the battlefields of several more wars, however, would "consistently" fully flower.

In 1875, the clause in New Hampshire's constitution barring Catholics from elective office was proposed for inclusion in the Colorado constitution. Colorado, however, opted not to include it, and one year later New Hampshire deleted it as well. In 1886, former priest Charles Chiniquy published memoirs in which an entire chapter detailed his claim that the Catholic hierarchy secretly arranged the assassination of Abraham Lincoln.[18] Much like the Puritan execution of "bewitched" dogs in 1692, this astonishing claim turned out not to represent a new high-water mark in the anti-Catholic panic, but rather a desperate effort to reenergize a panic that was beginning to wane. No clamor resulted following the book's publication. There was response to John Brandt's 1895 *America or Rome: Christ or the Pope?* It was typified in *The Congregationalist,* a Protestant publication that told its readers "much of which it states is exaggerated, and the impressions which the book makes need to be corrected by statements of other sides of the truth."[19]

A new anti-Catholic political association similarly sought to revitalize the crusade of the now-defunct Know Nothing Party. The American Protective Association formed in 1887 "to oppose the election or appointment of any Catholic citizen to political position of whatever degree or nature, including positions of any kind in connection with our public schools."[20] But the APA failed to achieve the impact of its predecessor. An article in the October 27, 1894, issue of the formerly anti-Catholic *Harper's Weekly* said, "Ignoring the splendid patriotism of many distinguished Roman Catholics . . . the A.P.A. sees in all Roman Catholicism a constant menace to the rights, liberties, and perpetuity of the American republic." By the end of the decade, the APA faded from the pages of the American press.

Still, the embers of anti-Catholic fear flared anew in 1928 when the Democratic Party nominated New York governor Al Smith for president. When Smith, a Catholic, was first proposed in 1924, a mail campaign was inaugurated "to guard against Jesuit schemes for the mastery of America."[21] In the run-up to the 1928 campaign, Alabama senator J. Thomas Heflin declared, "Protestants of America are determined to keep Popery out of the White House."[22] Smith's Catholicism (and his opposition to Prohibition) resulted in Herbert Hoover winning nearly 60 percent of the vote.

One of the last widely read anti-Catholic alarmists, Paul Blanshard, also sought to attain prominence at this time—but not as an anti-Catholic. Blanshard sought recognition as an advocate of socialism. "The labor movement is made up of good Catholics, good Jews, indifferent Protestants, Bolsheviks, Southern Presbyterians, and infidels," he wrote in an article for the August 1923, issue of *Forum*. Twenty-six years later, he declared, "American Catholic bishops who praise democracy always utter their praises with an important mental reservation, that the real source of the authority of the American government, and of all governments, is God and not the people . . . [by which] they mean the particular Catholic Deity who established Roman primacy through St. Peter, whose Vicar on earth is the Pope."[23]

What happened to all that togetherness? In 1948, the still relatively un-known Blanshard published an article in the *Nation* criticizing the Vatican for declaring it a sin for Catholics to marry non-Catholics or send their children to a public school when a Catholic school was available. For the first time in his career, Blanshard made national news when that issue of the *Nation* was removed from school libraries in New York at the behest of the Catholic Church. He at once set to work on a book, *American Freedom and Catholic Power*, which appeared the following year. It became a best seller. (Blanshard went on to expand his book in a 1958 edition; it was reissued in 1960 and 1984.) Following in the footsteps of prior alarmists, who also raised the octane fueling their warnings by connecting them to other panics, Blanshard published *Communism, Democracy, and Catholic Power* in 1951, tapping into that era's widespread fear of communist subversion.

By now, however, "consistently" was blossoming for American Catholics. In the Spanish-American War, World War I, World War II, and at that moment in Korea, Catholics fought and died alongside other Americans. Moreover, American Catholics were among the most prominent of the anti-communist alarmists—most notably senators Joseph McCarthy and Pat McCarran. Also during this era, Catholics joined other (white) Americans in a massive migration out of ethnic urban neighborhoods, resettling together in suburbs.

In 1960, the Democratic Party again nominated a Catholic for president. Having foreseen the possibility that John Fitzgerald Kennedy would be nominated, Blanshard published *God and Man in Washington* earlier that year. Others, too, continued to fear a president who was Catholic. "We cannot turn our Government over to a Catholic President who could be influenced by the Pope and by the power of the Catholic hierarchy," the former president of the Arkansas Baptist Convention declared.[24] Fear remained sufficiently widespread that Kennedy devoted an entire speech to his religion and his loyalty.

"I believe in an America where the separation of church and state is absolute," he told a gathering of Protestant ministers, "where no Catholic prelate would tell the President, should he be Catholic, how to act . . . and where no man is denied public office merely because [of] his religion." Directly addressing the Catholic American loyalty written in blood on battlefields, Kennedy said, "This is the kind of America I believe in, and this is the kind I fought for in the South Pacific, and the kind my brother died for in Europe. No one suggested then that we may have a 'divided loyalty,' that we 'did not believe in liberty,' or that we belonged to a disloyal group that threatened the 'freedoms for which our forefathers died.'" Kennedy then invoked the nation's founders when he added, "And in fact, this is the kind of America for which our forefathers died."[25] His assertion, though stirring, filtered out the fact that the founders in five of the nation's first thirteen states prohibited Catholics from holding public office. But those states no longer did, nor did most Americans still fear that Catholics endangered democracy. In November 1960, John F. Kennedy was elected president of the United States.

Five

"The menace to the Western world lies in the ... MILLIONS OF YELLOW MEN.... There is a certain integrity ... a sympathy and comradeship and warm human feel which is ours ... and which we cannot teach to the Oriental."

—Jack London, "The Yellow Peril" (1910)

Upon a signal at 9:30 am on November 3, 1885, "many hundred citizens congregated" in Tacoma, Washington, the *San Francisco Bulletin* reported, "marching quietly along the streets to the Chinese houses, requesting the occupants to pack their goods and leave." Three weeks earlier, a circular had informed the town's Chinese residents that if they remained in Tacoma after November 3, they would be killed.[1] The *Bulletin* correspondent, omitting that detail, went on to report, "No trouble occurred, order prevailed and everything was quietly consummated. . . . Six weeks ago, there were 700 Chinamen at Tacoma." No law or ordinance led to this expulsion. Nevertheless, sheriff's deputies observed the proceedings but did not intervene. The expulsion resulted from a rally at which the speakers denounced the Chinese as a menace to their community and a danger to the United States. The rally's keynote speaker was the mayor, Jacob Weisbach, an immigrant from Germany.

Tacoma's ethnic cleansing of its Chinese residents, like similar acts seen involving Native American settlements and African American communities, was the product of those elements that create political panic. But the nation's anti-Chinese panic marked a new milestone. Three years before Tacoma's Chinese residents were rounded up and escorted out of town, the federal government participated in the panic by enacting the Chinese Exclusion Act. The law prohibited any further Chinese immigration for the next ten years. Ten years later, Congress renewed the prohibition for another ten years, and did so again when that period expired. As for those Chinese already in the United States, the law stated that "hereafter, no State court or court of the United States shall admit Chinese to citizenship."[2] Never before had a panic resulted in federal legislation prohibiting a particular race from entering the United States. Race had, of course, long been a primary fissure in the nation's social groundwork, both in regard to African Americans and Native Americans. With the emancipation of the slaves, the nation's racial groundwork shifted, fissures intersected, and social earthquakes erupted. In the case of the Chinese, historian Najia Aarim-Heriot has observed that "the best way to reconstruct the dynamics of the Chinese exclusion movement . . . is to relate it to the dynamics of black-white relations."[3]

Commencement of the Panic

In 1849, news that vast gold deposits were being discovered in the Sierra Nevada range in California triggered a gold rush by the now proverbial "Forty-Niners." Among those pouring into this region were immigrants from China who, along with other immigrants and native-born Americans, hoped to get rich quick. In that first heady year, a correspondent for New York's *Albany Evening Journal,* fascinated by these oddly dressed men with long hair worn in pigtails, wrote how "the quietness and order, cheerfulness and temperance which is observable in their habits is noticed by every-one . . . and their cleanliness exceeds that of any other people."[4] Their readiness to adopt American customs was described in San Francisco's May 1, 1851, *Weekly Pacific News* when it reported that the growing number of Chinese in the city "have already become so much anglicized as to distinctly pronounce, 'How d'ye do.'"

But competition in the gold-bearing regions was causing conflict. Within months of the "How d'ye do" article, a spark of ethnic cleansing was reported. A confrontation between American and Chinese miners near Marysville, California, turned violent. The Chinese miners "were vanquished and driven off," Virginia's *Richmond Enquirer* reported on June 15, 1852. Other such sparks followed. On November 16, 1852, San Francisco's *Alta California* reported on miners in Jacksonville, California, "expelling the Chinese." In Oroville, California, a white mob set fire to the town's Chinese section, destroying its shops and approximately 100 homes.[5]

Anti-Chinese resolutions were cheered into effect at rallies in Calaveras County (1857), Shasta County (1859), and Siskiyou County (1860).[6] The Calaveras County resolution invoked the Founding Fathers when it proclaimed "that the requirements of patriotism to preserve the 'inalienable rights' of American freemen . . . demand of us decisive and energetic action on the momentous question of Asiatic aggression in the mines." This assertion was saturated with elements of political panic. Aside from the widespread pre–Civil War filtering of the phrase "inalienable rights," which in the Declaration of Independence follows from "all men are created equal" (not "all American freemen"), the resolution asserted an unverified claim regarding Chinese aggression in the mines. This unverified claim itself filtered out the fact that the only verified instances of aggression in the gold mines had been attacks upon the Chinese. The Calaveras resolution went on to declare that the Chinese must leave the area within six months, after which its signers bound themselves, at "the risk of our lives, to carry out the spirit and intention of these resolutions to the very letter." The Chinese miners complied. So too, in response to similar resolutions, did Chinese miners in nearby Mariposa, Diamond Springs, Horsetown, French Gulf, and Rock

Creek. In all, some 200 such incidents of ethnic cleansing of the Chinese took place in the states west of the Rocky Mountains.[7]

This panic that now flared in the West attracted the attention of the rest of the nation. In Massachusetts, the *Barre Gazette* told readers on October 31, 1851, "The Chinese are destined to exert an important influence in this country. For the last six months they have supplied a larger number of immigrants than any other country." But its report was not panicked, even as it predicted tectonic social changes soon to come, possibly because those changes were (at the time) 3,000 miles away. "Events of great moment in the history of the world are destined to grow out of the rapid colonization of this Pacific shore," it stated. "A turning and overturning is at hand. The Chinese emigration to California is one link in the chain." An item in a Sacramento newspaper was far terser. "Six hundred and fifteen Chinese arrived on Monday," it reported, adding, "it is said that there are ten thousand awaiting passage to this country."[8] San Francisco's *Alta California* estimated the Chinese population in California to have grown from fifty, at the outset of 1849, to nearly 12,000 in June 1852. Still, it told readers that "there is no necessity for the hue and cry which has been raised relative to this particular class of foreigners."[9]

While there may have been no necessity for the "hue and cry," California governor John Bigler had a necessity for votes if he was to win reelection. He had previously been elected by a 370-vote margin, 1 percent of the total. Though he had never advocated anti-Chinese legislation, Bigler now declared that "measures must be adopted to check this tide of Asiatic immigration."[10] Being the governor, his warning significantly spread the fear by enhancing its credibility.

The spread of panic over Chinese immigrants was further fueled by its intersection with yet another fissure in America's industrial landscape, this one between labor and management. Many business owners and corporations welcomed this influx into the labor supply. Some actively sought it, contracting to pay voyage costs in return for labor at prearranged rates. Such Chinese workers were called *coolies,* a derivation of the Chinese word for *slave.* The derivation of the term did not go unnoticed by Governor Bigler in his quest for votes from the growing working class. In urging that the gates be closed to Chinese immigrants, he declared, "I allude particularly to a class of Asiatics known as 'Coolies,' who are sent here . . . in a state of voluntary or involuntary servitude."[11] In one stroke, vote-hungry Bigler tapped into three of the era's panics: fear that the nation faced danger from the Chinese; fear of a virtual expansion of the slave-holding South; and fear of capitalist corporations. One week after delivering this message to the legislature, a bill was introduced "to prevent coolie labor in the mines and to prevent involuntary servitude."[12] On Election Day, Bigler became the first California governor to win reelection.

But a question remains. By seeking the votes of angry white miners, didn't Bigler worry about alienating the multitude of Chinese miners? At this point in time, Chinese immigrants were not yet prohibited from becoming citizens. Bigler himself raised the question in the same message to the legislature when he noted, "A question around which there has been thrown some doubt is whether Asiatics could, with safety, be admitted to the enjoyments of all the rights of citizens."[13] He then went on to speculate that, since federal law (at the time) enabled any "free white person" to become a citizen, the case could be made that the Chinese were not white, and therefore could be banned not only from citizenship, but from serving as jurors or giving testimony against a white person.

The following year, Bigler's legal musings became legal precedent. George Hall, a white miner in California, robbed and murdered Ling Sing, a Chinese miner. Three other Chinese miners witnessed the deadly assault. Hall was found guilty and sentenced to death. But the California Supreme Court overturned the conviction, ruling that a section of California law—"No black or mulatto person, or Indian, shall be allowed to give evidence in favor of, or against, a white man"—was intended to exclude all non-Caucasians. George Hall went free.

The court ruling didn't stop there. The opinion handed down by the court justified this exclusion of Chinese testimony on the basis of the Chinese being a race "whose mendacity is proverbial; a race of people whom nature has marked as inferior, and who are incapable of progress or intellectual development beyond a certain point."[14] Following the court ruling, a man identified in the press only by his last name, Alden, drew his pistol when passing a small group of Chinese men and murdered one without provocation.[15] Alden was arrested later that night but released the next day, since the only witnesses were the dead man's Chinese friends. Two weeks later, a group of white men robbed a Chinese mining camp near Auburn, California, and lynched three of its miners. Those who survived knew who the assailants were, but the inadmissibility of Chinese testimony against white people prevented prosecution.[16] When, in 1868, the Fourteenth Amendment bestowed citizenship and guaranteed equal protection and due process of law not only to the recently freed slaves but to all persons born in the United States, California was not among the states that voted to ratify it (although it did so symbolically in 1959).

Backed by the credibility of California's governor and state supreme court, alarm over Chinese immigrants had sufficient fuel to spread widely. But it did not yet do so. While one reason was the massive influx of Chinese being confined to the West Coast, another was that widespread panic over capitalist corporations was just beginning to harness steam. Not only did industrialists look with favor on this added supply of cheap labor, but most of the nation's newspapers were either owned by, or financially dependent on, the advertising of wealthy industrialists or their corporations. The effectiveness of this blockade around the anti-Chinese panic in California, and the intensification of rage resulting from that blockade, can be seen in an August 1, 1853, letter to the editor of the *Alta California*. "I notice with sorrow that the newspapers throughout the State avoid the discussion," it calmly began in regard to Chinese immigration. Anger toward industrialists then began seeping out as it continued, "Truly there is an object to be gained by this course—a great, a detestable, a damnable object—and that object is the degradation and reduction of the price of labor." Full-throated rage against the Chinese followed. "The only force to oppose this inundation of half humans is the outraged and insulted American laborer," the letter writer declared, brandishing unnamed consequences if "he may see himself surrounded by long-tailed blue skins . . . contact with whom his very soul revolts, and himself put on a level with them."

The Civil War sidetracked the anti-Chinese panic, just as it did the panic over Catholics. Shortly before the onset of the war, however, a portent appeared of what would later dominate the nation's fear of a "Yellow Peril." On March 22, 1860, the *San Francisco Bulletin* told readers of a Japanese ship docked in the harbor. What, the paper pondered, is "the difference . . . 'twixt tweedle-dum and tweedle-dee?"

Anti-Chinese Fears Go Coast-to-Coast

On May 10, 1869, the last spike was driven into the wooden tie that connected the eastern and western segments of the Transcontinental Railroad. Chinese workers constituted the vast majority of the 4,000 laborers who built the western segment.[17] The completion of the project was a milestone in the nation's industrialization and in the anti-Chinese panic—since the low-cost Chinese labor that helped build the railroad now had a low-cost means of spreading across the country.

Just over a year later, the Lowell, Massachusetts, *Daily Citizen* reported on June 14, 1870: "Seventy-five Chinamen . . . arrived in North Adams yesterday to work in the shoe factory of C. T. Sampson and Company. A large crowd assembled at the depot to witness their arrival. . . . They were followed from the depot to Sampson's factory by the crowd, amid ominous hisses and hooting." Unbeknownst to these Chinese workers, they had been provided transportation to Massachusetts to take over the jobs of white workers who were on strike. A union leader sought to enlist the arriving Chinese in the union, but before they could comprehend the situation the company whisked them into the factory, where they were also housed. With emotions raw, the union adopted a resolution within days declaring "Chinese menials . . . degrading to American labor" and calling on "all of the workingmen throughout the country to hold meetings and urge upon Congress the passage of a bill making the importation of such labor unlawful."[18]

Even before this episode, an abstract fear that the Chinese threatened the nation's future had branched throughout the country. One month prior to the completion of the Transcontinental Railroad, on April 3, 1869, an editorial in Georgia's *Macon Weekly Telegraph* warned, "They will control California probably in less than ten years, and California itself will become but a way station in the onward march of Western colonization by the Chinese." The following month, the *New York Commercial Advertiser* upped the volume. Referring to the Chinese as "the most degraded race in the world," it warned, "They are ready and anxious to step over by millions to possess the land."[19] In addition to the panic-inducing use of the absolute "most," the statement was built upon a blank to be filled in: the phrase "degraded race" left it to the reader to decide what constitutes the gradations of race. Just as panic over Catholics was premised on an implied absolute that all Catholics behave as a bloc, so too this warning asserted all Chinese immigrants were coming with the intention of possessing the land. An additional absolute resided in the wording of this claim. Its phrase, "to possess the land," suggested the Chinese sought to possess *all* the land, as opposed to the phrase "to possess land." Ominously, the editorial went on to ruminate, "It was useless to [s]hoot them in the streets, kill them in the mines, and persecute them everywhere." Concluding in a crescendo of absolutes, it warned, "If we do not rise superior and conquer it . . . it will swamp and sink us in a darker, fouler destiny than ever overwhelmed any of the lost nations of the world."

As has been seen among the works previously cited, and will continue to be seen, literary fiction (or genres, in the case of the ostensibly nonfiction *Awful Disclosures*) periodically contributes to political panic. In the panic over Chinese immigrants, so many were so blinded by emotion that their clear misinterpretation of a poem became coin of the realm in the realm of panic. Misinterpreted was the opening stanza from Bret Harte's 1870 poem, "Plain Language from Truthful James":

> Which I wish to remark,
> And my language is plain,
> That for ways that are dark

And for tricks that are vain,

The heathen Chinee is peculiar,

Which the same I would rise to explain.[20]

The "heathen Chinee," however, turned out not to be the villain in the poem, which goes on to tell of a card game between Ah Sin, a Chinese immigrant, and Bill Nye, a notorious cheater. Nye ends up losing to this seemingly naive immigrant who, it turns out, is a more skillful cheater. Nye's shocked reaction is to attack Ah Sin as he shouts, "We are ruined by Chinese cheap labor."

Though hard to imagine today, Harte's poem was a smash hit. Apparently, it was hard to imagine then, too. "The popular favor with which Bret Harte's 'Plain Language from Truthful James' has been received all over the country is somewhat marvelous," the *Boston Daily Advertiser* wrote on October 22, 1870. "In deference to numerous and oft-repeated requests, we republish the poem."

Sadly but significantly, readers who understood the poem's irony and sought to correct the misinterpretation failed. "The point of the satire lies, of course, in the virtuous indignation of the Yankee cheat," wrote one critic in 1871. "But so dull and prejudiced is the political party that opposes itself to immigration [the Know Nothing Party] . . . that a leading member of it is said to have . . . written to Mr. Bret Harte to thank him for such a contribution to the good cause."[21] Despite this and other articles informing readers of the poem's irony, the misreading prevailed. The phrase "heathen Chinee" went on to appear more than a thousand times in American newspapers over the next fifty years.[22] The significance of this clear misinterpretation withstanding correction is that panic—being passion prevailing over reason—is immune to logic.

Bret Harte stands as further proof that alarmists—or, in this case, one who has "alarmist" thrust upon him—cannot be stereotyped. Harte stated that he wrote the poem "in an hour of idleness and threw it carelessly into his desk," retrieving it only to fill blank space in the magazine he edited.[23] But while he publicly belittled the poem, Harte never clarified that what it ridiculed was *prejudice* against the Chinese, not the Chinese themselves. As seen with politician/minister/novelist Thomas Dixon in the panic over African Americans, anti-Catholic author/later feminist Anna Ella Carroll, and socialist/later anti-Catholic author Paul Blanshard, Bret Harte had a dream toward which political panic provided an avenue. Harte's dream was to be a famous writer. A measure of recognition had recently come to him after he published, in the magazine he was hired to edit, his short story, "The Luck of Roaring Camp." When the now nationwide anti-Chinese panic raised his poem to heights so great that one phrase entered the American vernacular, Harte's desire to be a famous writer overtook any desire that his writing be understood.

As often, or more frequently, used than the phrase "heathen Chinee" was the term "inscrutable," in reference to the Chinese. While its use by Europeans predated the Gold Rush arrival of Chinese in the United States, it too became part of the American vernacular, so socially acceptable that a correspondent accompanying Ulysses S. Grant on a world tour following his presidency wrote of China, "Here you meet John, the inscrutable John, who troubles you so much in California." So long did the phrase remain socially accepted, it appeared in the government's 1940 Federal Writers' Project, *New York: A Guide to the Empire State,* which described men in New York City's Chinatown as gathering "in little clusters before shop doors, discussing in the native tongue affairs of the moment with inscrutable expressions and in modulated tones."[24] This use of "inscrutable" implied that the Chinese were mysterious, even cryptic, and in so doing the term conveyed a panic-inducing blank to be filled in. For many non-Asians, credibility was bestowed on that blank by virtue of the Chinese language being so different from those of Europe as to be incomprehensible to Westerners. Many reconceived their inability to perceive meanings from the Chinese as inscrutability of the Chinese.

Those Americans who were growing concerned about the influx of Chinese immigrants were susceptible to claims that would have been undermined by knowledge of their language. "They have their secret societies among themselves . . . by whose edicts they are governed," an article in the

August 15, 1854, issue of *United States Magazine* warned, adding that they "dare not testify against [these societies] for fear of secret death; thus rendering our very laws powerless." The charge referred to the "Six Companies," the number of which actually varied, but none of which was akin to tongs, organized crime gangs that formed later. The "Six Companies" were societies created by more established Chinese immigrants to aid newcomers from China who were themselves bewildered by America's language and customs. The accusation arose from the fact that these groups offered to arbitrate disputes between Chinese immigrants and—contrary to the claim that they enforced a separate set of laws—to help fellow Chinese avail themselves of the American judicial system.

Emerging from this misunderstanding is a significant form of blanks to be filled in. Secrecy and its siblings, mystery and inscrutability, frequently fuel political panic by virtue of being such blanks. In the panic over Chinese immigrants, the inscrutability was unintentional and the secrecy was imagined. In other instances, however, the secrecy is real. Not surprisingly, then, conspiracy theories abound regarding organizations intentionally cloaked in secrecy, such as the Central Intelligence Agency and the National Security Agency. And there are instances in which the secrecy is not only real, but exists for the sole purpose of creating fear. The secrecy that cloaks the Ku Klux Klan—quite literally in its use of robes and face-covering hoods—was implemented to create a panic-inducing blank to be filled in regarding who in the community was part of the organization's forces.

The claim that the Chinese Six Companies were a separate judicial system became a misbegotten assertion for those who believed it. Just as we saw a misbegotten assertion—that Africans were descendants of Noah's son Ham—grow to interpret three lines in the Bible as an explanation of all racial differences and inherent behaviors, so too did this misbegotten assertion grow to enormous proportions. In his 1880 book *The Last Days of the Republic,* P. W. Dooner declared the Six Companies were "treasonable associations," going on to warn, "The control of the United States would give [China] virtual control of the Western Hemisphere. . . . As the introductory act, she proceeded to transport her surplus population to the 'Six

Companies' . . . commissioned by the Emperor; and by the same authority, exercised the functions of legislative and judicial officers as well as virtual governors of the Chinese people in America."

In this climate, an ominous term began to appear, one that also appeared in the racially fueled panics over Native Americans and African Americans. "An Organization Being Perfected to Exterminate the Chinese in San Francisco," headlined a March 1, 1870, article in the *Cleveland Herald*. Anti-Chinese organizations had started to form a decade earlier, but went dormant during the Civil War. A November 13, 1861, item in the *San Francisco Bulletin* told of fifty people in an Anti-Coolie Club hearing a speaker denounce, as "a curse to all mankind . . . the disease-engendering, morals-lacking, filthy Chinese scum." The organization aimed "not only to prevent further immigration of Chinese-Tartars, but to wipe out those that are here." After the Civil War, the newly revived group put forward Thomas Mooney as its 1870 candidate for California's governor on a platform that, the Cincinnati's *Daily Enquirer* reported, vowed "to exterminate the Mongolian Race."[25] Though Mooney's candidacy ended when he fled the state amid accusations of embezzlement, the panic did not. In October 1871, a disturbance in Los Angeles' Chinatown was all the cause needed for a mob of 500 whites to attack the community, burn homes and businesses, and lynch nineteen Chinese men. In 1876, the Chinese quarter in the town of Antioch, fifty miles east of San Francisco, was burned down. While such ethnic cleansing of Chinese was not new, what was new were the endorsements they received and the genocidal tone of those kudos. "The actions of the citizens will, without doubt, meet with the hearty approval of every man, woman, and child on the Pacific coast," the *San Francisco Chronicle* declared of the pogrom at Antioch, "and will go a long way toward convincing the people of the Eastern States that the Chinese nuisance on our seaboard has assumed such vast proportions that it . . . must be wiped out."[26]

The following year, an Irish immigrant named Denis Kearney linked panic over Chinese immigrants with the now widespread panic over capitalist corporations when he formed the Workingmen's Party of California. Its slogan was "The Chinese Must Go!" Kearney, who had been active in the city's Drayman & Teamsters Union, formed his party during a year of nationwide labor unrest stemming from a strike of railroad workers. A charismatic speaker, he attracted some 10,000 listeners to a July 23, 1877, rally in San Francisco, after which a throng headed off to that city's Chinatown, where it smashed windows and set several buildings ablaze.

Kearney set off on a nationwide tour, fueling the now twinned panics by declaring at rallies, "I advise every man within the sound of my voice, if he is able to, to own a musket and a hundred rounds of ammunition."[27] He then aimed those firearms with statements such as, "I will give the Central Pacific just three months to discharge their Chinamen, and if that is not done, [company cofounder Leland] Stanford and his crowd will have to take the consequences."[28] This use of the word "consequences" functioned as a blank to be filled in and, as such, contributed to inducing panic among those who filled it in as a threat to do that which they feared. Afraid that industrialists and Chinese immigrants endangered the republic, "consequences" could be interpreted to mean endangering the republic by replacing the Constitution's guarantee of due process of law with due process of Kearney. At other times in his speaking tour, Kearney filled in this blank in precisely that way. "I want Stanford and the press to understand that if I give an order to hang [company cofounder Charles] Crocker, it will be done," he declared in one speech.[29] He then rang even larger liberty bells of panic when he advocated that the nation be saved by replacing the Constitution of the United States with the Constitution of Denis Kearney. "When I have thoroughly organized my party," he proclaimed, "I will lead you to the City Hall . . . hang the Prosecuting Attorney, burn every book that has a particle of law in it, and then enact new laws for the workingmen."[30]

Twinned Panics Beget Scapegoat

With the United States on the brink of economic and political calamity due to the turbulence surrounding the nationwide railroad strike of 1877, the linking of the panic over Chinese immigrants to the panic over capitalist corporations provided Congress an opportunity to reduce the danger of those panics by weakening their link. In 1878, it sent legislation to President Rutherford B. Hayes prohibiting further immigration of Chinese. Putting eyeglasses on the Founding Fathers, a March 1, 1879, editorial in the Portage, Wisconsin, *State Register* entered the portal to panic when it asserted, "Who can suppose that . . . the makers of the Constitution . . . saw, even in imagination, the weird form of John Chinaman, with his almond eyes, yellow skin, and pig tail, coming under that rule?" The editorial then crossed the threshold into the realm of panic when it continued, "It may be that necessity, which it is said knows no law, or which, perhaps, finds a higher law, may justify, nay, even compel us to restrain a people who may come down upon us like the frogs of ancient Egypt." The editorial then filled in the blank created by the phrase "higher law" when it concluded, "Self-preservation is the first law of nature, either for an individual or a nation." As with Denis Kearney, panic resided in the editorial advocating that which it feared—in this instance, protecting the endangered United States by replacing its Constitution with survival of the strongest. President Hayes vetoed the bill.

But he could not veto panic. Indeed, his veto added more genocidal fuel to those in panic, some of whom now employed secrecy to combat their fear of secrecy among the Chinese. "At a secret meeting last night of a [San Francisco] workingmen's club, styling itself 'The Council of Thirteen,'" the *Boston Journal* reported on February 23, 1880, "a long preamble was read, winding up by saying, 'Chemistry has placed in the hands of this generation means of removing obnoxious races in a more sure and effective manner than by firearms.'" After Denver's *Rocky Mountain News* declared on December 6, 1879, "We trust that the day is near at hand when these degraded human beings will be driven out of our country," precisely such violence followed. A mob of some 1,500 people tore down houses belonging to Chinese residents; one Chinese immigrant, after being dragged from his home by a rope around his neck, had his skull crushed by boot kicks and bricks.[31]

Panic now covered the country. Denver's riots were reported in the November 2, 1880, *New Orleans Times-Picayune* under the headline, "Broken

China—The People of Denver Express Themselves in an Emphatic Way on the Chinese." At the 1880 Republican National Convention, an anti-Chinese plank was included for the first time in the party's platform. After that convention's presidential nominee, Chester Arthur, won the election, he signed the 1882 Chinese Exclusion Act into law.

As it turned out, the law's scapegoating of the Chinese had no impact on the panic over corporations. It did, however, decrease the intensity of the panic over the Chinese. Only a single sentence appeared, under "Short Specials," in Michigan's March 30, 1898, *Jackson Daily Citizen:* "The United States Supreme Court has decided that children of Chinese parents born in this country are entitled to citizenship." What remained of the panic over Chinese Americans no longer found fuel in legal issues.

But a good deal of fuel could still be pumped from the nation's racial groundwork. Moreover, its octane could be raised by connecting racial fears to fears now emanating in the nation's industrialized cities: pollution. The 1885 book *The Chinese at Home and Abroad* asserted that Chinatowns were "the source of the most terrible pollution of the blood of the younger and rising generations among us, and that it is destined to be the source of con-tamination and hereditary diseases among those who are to come after us [is] too frightful to contemplate." As seen in the way Catholicism was linked to witchcraft, the connection was effected by describing one panic with the terminology of another—a panic-inducing technique that recurs, most nota-bly in links between the panic over homosexuals and the panic over women. In addition, this particular assertion employed a panic-inducing absolute in its use of "most terrible," and a blank to be filled in with its phrase "too frightful to contemplate." The 1908 book *Race or Mongrel* told its readers, "The Californians, having seen . . . other yellow-white mixtures, either knew that the white-yellow mongrels were among the most worthless of mongrels, or their instinct told them the same truth." More significant in this instance than the double-absolute ("most worthless") is the widening of the panic in a statement that followed. This "instinct," it asserted, explained "the clamor against the admission of the Japanese."[32]

Anti-Japanese Fears

While a number of the nation's first Japanese immigrants had pursued work in the gold mines and on the railroads, most sought agricultural work. In time, some Japanese immigrants purchased land to cultivate silk worms or grow tea, rice, or produce. The *San Francisco Call* told readers in 1870 that the Japanese "are in every respect a superior race to the Chinese."[33] But such attitudes began to change as Japanese immigration increased. A July 22, 1891, headline in the Tacoma, Washington, *Morning Olympian* told its readers, "Now It Is the Japs—California Getting More Than Her Share of the Orientals."

One might suspect politicians were behind these rumblings. The Chinese Exclusion Act would expire the following year unless Congress extended it, and the Japanese presented an added opportunity to arouse voters. San Francisco congressman Thomas Geary led the successful effort to renew the law and to add further restrictions. At no point, however, did he seek to include Japanese immigrants. Either Geary personally felt no fear of the Japanese, or he professionally felt anti-Japanese attitudes were not yet ready to detonate. Two years later they were. A mob of 150 raided the homes of Japanese residents in Vacaville, California. "They took them prisoners, drove them in front of them and in various ways maltreated them," the *Morning Olympian* reported on May 18, 1894. By 1900, the *Fort Worth Register* took note of the fact that several of those who "in 1885 drove the Chinese out of Tacoma declare that they are ready to undertake similar work in the case of the Japanese."[34] This time, however, no such mob rallied in Tacoma, quite possibly because the Chinese residents previously ousted didn't simply leave, they immediately brought charges against the mayor and other leaders of the mob, resulting in indictments and trials. While none of the perpetrators was convicted, the fact of their trials may well have caused Tacoma's anti-Japanese residents to back away from repeating this act of ethnic cleansing.

On the legislative (hence, legal) side, however, Congressman Geary was now ready to avail himself of the growing anti-Japanese panic. "We are getting frightened at the invasion of the Jap," he declared. "They are proving a far more dangerous element than Chinese."[35] Geary, however, was no longer in office when the Chinese Exclusion Act next came up for renewal. San Francisco congressman Julius Kahn introduced the bill to extend it yet again. This time, as the *Duluth News Tribune* reported on February 8, 1901, "The people of the Pacific coast are demanding that exclusion laws shall be aimed at Japanese, as well as Chinese." But Kahn did not include the Japanese in the renewal of the Chinese Exclusion Act. That November, he lost his bid for reelection. Kahn subsequently climbed onboard the anti-Japanese bandwagon. "I have always felt that the day would come when we would go to war with Japan," he declared. "I believe that every [Japanese] comes here as a spy for his government."[36] In 1905, San Francisco voters returned Julius Kahn to the House of Representatives. Next time around, Congress broadened its exclusion of Chinese immigrants, in the Immigration Act of 1917, to exclude the Japanese as well.

Similar to the raging fire that erupted in the 1906 San Francisco earthquake, panic over Japanese Americans and immigrants also spread in the wake of that same earthquake. In rebuilding their city, San Franciscans took the opportunity to construct separate schools for students of Japanese descent. As one member of the state legislature explained, "Japanese youths of sixteen to eighteen years, with their characteristic disregard for the virtue of women, should not be permitted to sit beside our own children. They are a menace to the girlhood of the state."[37] Panic resided in the statement's misbegotten assertion, ostensibly based in genetics, regarding the behavior of Japanese youth while filtering out white youths with comparable disregard for the virtue of women. Among those Americans who disagreed was President Theodore Roosevelt. In his 1906 State of the Union message, he declared, "Here and there a most unworthy feeling has manifested itself toward the Japanese—the feeling that has been shown in shutting them out from the common schools in San Francisco . . . We have as much to learn from Japan as Japan has to learn from us; and no nation is fit to teach unless it is also willing to learn."[38] As with efforts to correct the misreading of Bret Harte's "heathen Chinee," this effort by Theodore Roosevelt demonstrated that reason is not welcome in the realm of panic. "Denounced—Mass

Meeting in San Francisco Resents President's Japanese Message," headlined a December 24, 1906, article in Illinois's *Belleville News Democrat*. Newspapers across the country were now attuned to the anti-Japanese movement gathering force in the West. As in the anti-Chinese panic, far more foreboding words now began to appear. A January 14, 1909, headline in the *Baltimore American*—"Bitter Against the Japanese—California Legislators Plan To Oust Or Herd Them"—pertained to proposals to prohibit Japanese immigrants from owning land in California and to define regions in which the Japanese must live. Neither measure passed, but restrictions on land ownership were enacted in 1913.

Connecting fear of the Japanese to fear of the Chinese, California governor George Pardee told the legislature in 1909, "Neither the Japanese nor the Chinese appear to be capable of absorption and assimilation in the mass of our people."[39] The governor's assertion filtered out that, precisely because he and his legislature feared absorption, the state had just amended its 1850 law banning "all marriages between white persons with negroes" by adding "mongolians" [*sic*] to the prohibition. Widespread panic over the Chinese, however, was beginning to show its first signs of diminishing when other alarmists sought to fuel their anti-Japanese warnings by *disconnecting* them from the Chinese. "San Francisco Hates The Japs—Chinese Are Liked Much Better—Japanese Are Too Aggressive," headlined a July 31, 1908, article in North Dakota's *Grand Forks Herald*. The *Dallas Morning News* told readers on April 29, 1913, that the Chinese "are well liked but Japanese, individually or collectively, are cordially disliked, not only by the white people of California, but by the Chinese as well."

An element of political panic surfacing here amid the diverging views toward Japanese as opposed to Chinese is the impact of foreign affairs. It is an element that will recur in the panics over communist subversion and Muslim Americans. In this instance, aggressive acts by the Japanese government raised concern in the United States. As that aggression came to include expansion into Manchuria, China came to be favorably perceived by Americans by virtue of its opposition to Japan. By the time the United States entered World War I, newspapers were running headlines such as that in

Idaho's April 1, 1919, *Twin Falls News:* "Think Japanese Want Territory—California Senator Declares Nipponese Are Like Kaiser in Ambition to Conquer." That same year, Congressman Albert Johnson amplified the alarm when the October 5 *Dallas Morning News* quoted his warning: "I charge the Japanese with deliberately entering upon a plan of American colonization."

Any remaining embers of panic regarding Chinese Americans were blown to smithereens on December 7, 1941, when Japan bombed the American military installation at Pearl Harbor, Hawaii. Tens of thousands of Chinese Americans served in the military during World War II. To eliminate its potential as a propaganda wedge for Japan, the Chinese Exclusion Act was repealed in 1943. The extent to which attitudes about Chinese Americans changed, even as racial slurs remained, can be seen in an item in the September 1, 1946, *Los Angeles Times.* "They go chop-chopping at the maple sticks today and tomorrow," it sports section reported. "The occasion is the first annual Pacific Coast Chinese bowling tournament. Bowlers from San Francisco, Sacramento, Fresno, and San Diego, as well as local teams, will compete."

Panic over Japanese Americans, needless to say, intensified and spread exponentially after Pearl Harbor, though not as immediately as one might expect. The day after the attack, Attorney General Francis Biddle assured the public regarding FBI investigations of Japanese in the United States, but stressed, "It would be unwise to treat all Japanese living in the United States as enemies."[40] First Lady Eleanor Roosevelt, following a visit to the West Coast after the attack, told interviewers, "The amount of concern for the loyal, American-born Japanese in that vicinity was encouraging. One of our obligations . . . is to live up to the things we have established as the rights of human beings."[41]

It was the calm before the storm. On February 12, the highly respected columnist Walter Lippmann warned, "The Pacific Coast is in imminent danger of a combined attack from within and without."[42] Lippmann buttressed his argument for internment of the region's Japanese residents by invoking the nation's preeminent Founding Father. "Think of the lineal descendant, if there happened to be such a person, of George Washington," he wrote, pointing out that "if he decides he would like to visit the warship, or take a walk in the airplane plant . . . he has to register, sign papers, and wear an identification button. . . . Have Mr. Washington's constitutional rights been abridged? . . . Everyone should be compelled to prove that he has a good reason for being there." Thus far, Lippmann's remarks do not convey panic. Indeed, they demonstrate that references to the Founding Fathers are not necessarily indicative of panic, just as other elements that recur in political panics do not automatically mean the speaker is panicked. Where Lippmann entered the portal to panic was in his remarks that followed. "The Pacific Coast is officially a combat zone," he continued, asserting an unverified claim, since there had been no official designation of the Pacific Coast as a combat zone. It had, however, been described by government officials as a *potential* combat zone. The significance of the distinction surfaced when Lippmann concluded, "Nobody's constitutional rights include the right to reside and do business on a battlefield." Panic resided here in filtering out the word "potential" and in his use of the absolute, "nobody." This absolute filters out those whose constitutional rights did enable them to live and reside in the region. Had Lippmann's hypothetical descendant of George Washington resided on the Pacific Coast in 1942, he would not have been forced to move to an inland detention camp.

If Walter Lippmann had held off writing this column for one week, his arguments would have had a more solid basis since, seven days later, Franklin Roosevelt authorized the secretary of war "to prescribe military areas . . . from which any or all persons may be excluded."[43] On the other hand, had influential voices such as Lippmann's not added fuel to the panic, the more reasoned voices of Eleanor Roosevelt and Attorney General Biddle may have persuaded the president to resist such wholesale government participation in the panic. "All Japanese Persons, Both Alien and Non-Alien, Will Be Evacuated from the Above Designated Area by 12:00 O'clock Noon Tuesday, April 7, 1942," a U.S. Army proclamation read on flyers posted throughout San Francisco and, during the ensuing days, throughout the Pacific Coast.[44] Restrictions were also placed on German aliens and selected naturalized German citizens, along the lines Attorney General Biddle had initially urged for the Japanese. But coming amid an ongoing panic over people of Japanese descent in the United States, the relocation was applied to *all* Japanese in the designated zones. A total of 120,313 Japanese were interned during World War II, compared with 11,507 Germans.[45]

Many Americans were not so panicked over Japanese loyalty and, likewise, many Japanese Americans remained loyal despite the panic. Nearly 21,000 Japanese Americans served in the armed forces during World War II, in addition to some 6,000 Japanese Americans who served as linguists in the Military Intelligence Service. The 442nd Regiment Combat Team, comprised entirely of Japanese Americans, became the most highly decorated unit in American history. But the single-biggest factor in ending the anti-Japanese panic was, as with the end of the anti-Chinese panic, a bombing—in this case, the atomic bombs that fell on Hiroshima and Nagasaki. The fear that Japan planned to invade the United States evaporated in a mushroom cloud.

What remained, however, was a phase of predatory opportunism. "Judge Clark Clement has ordered restored to California the title of land assertedly owned by . . . Sogataro and Kozue Fujita, husband and wife and natives of Japan, and their daughter, Tomoye Fujita, an American citizen," the *Los Angeles Times* reported on December 16, 1946. "Judge Clement held Sogataro and Kozue Fujita illegally obtained two parcels of farm lands . . . in violation of the California alien land law." Five days earlier, the *Times* had reported a similar case involving the California Lettuce Growers, "a concern that took over many Japanese land leases . . . when the Japanese were interned." The organization sought to invalidate the land claim of a Japanese American upon his release from internment. In this instance, however, a different judge upheld the Japanese American's claim. Hundreds, if not thousands, of similar incidents greeted Japanese Americans when they returned to their homes. By 1948, the first such case to reach the Supreme Court resulted in a ruling that voided California's 1913 restrictions on land ownership, a law aimed at Asians in general and Japanese in particular.

Attitudes toward Japanese Americans began shifting around 1950. "Henry Ohye, prominent in Los Angles Nisei circles . . . won high honors recently when he became a member of Chevrolet Motor Division's famed

100 car club," the February 26, 1950, *Los Angeles Times* stated, citing Ohye's achievements as a car salesman. Just as racial slurs remained when widespread panic over Chinese had passed, so too did an element of condescension toward the Japanese after that panic had passed, too. "Sue Mira . . . is a very Japanese girl at the very Kawafuku Café, or sukiyaki house," a Los Angeles columnist told readers on August 23, 1950, when describing his visit to a Japanese restaurant. "She asked me if I wanted some *unagi donburi*. She said that is eel on steamed rice. 'No.' She asked if I would like some *sashimi*. That's fresh raw fish. 'No.' So she brought *sukiyaki*. . . . I ate it. *Sukiyaki* sure gets you in the mood."

For a century, however, vast numbers of Americans were not in the mood for Japanese or Chinese immigrants. Why did they stay? Undoubtedly, there are many answers, but what is significant in terms of political panic in America is that they did stay, that the quest of the United States prevailed over its panic.

Six

"WHEREVER THE JEW IS AL-
LOWED TO ESTABLISH HIM-
SELF dishonesty takes the place of
honesty; immorality, of virtue; disease, of health; sluttishness, of cleanliness; anarchy, of order.... He is now
carrying out his work of deterioration
and destruction in the United States."

—Telemachus Timayenis, THE AMERICAN JEW (1888)

For centuries, Jews have faced persecution in every land in which they've lived with few exceptions—one of which, and the largest of which, is the United States. Not, however, for lack of trying on the part of numerous alarmists. While there have been discriminatory and violent acts against Jews in the United States, the fears which led to them have never coalesced into a widespread panic. The absence of mass hysteria regarding Jews raises the single most important question regarding political panic: Can it be avoided?

The Jewish Question v. The Jewish Equation

As early as 1728, Europeans discussed what they termed the "Jewish Question," which pertained to the role of Jews in Christian nations. So too did those founders of the new United States in eleven of the first thirteen states, which prohibited Jews from holding elective office (twelve, when Vermont soon became the fourteenth state).[1] This fear was expressed in a September 24, 1776, letter to the editor of the *Pennsylvania Post*. After urging that citizenship be limited to Christians, the reader warned, "Jews and Turks may become in time not only our greatest landholders, but principal officers in the legislative or executive part of our government, so as to render it not only uncomfortable but unsafe for Christians." This alarmist, like so many others, did not see himself as biased. "Nor can I think that such a measure would be any restraint upon the freedom of any one of whatever sect," he asserted, since it "would only be confined to those who are to become possessed with the powers of government, in order to prevent . . . our acting as a state contrary to or in opposition to the general doctrines and laws of Christianity." Panic resided in his advocating that which he feared. Fearful that Jews and Turks, if elected to public office, could endanger freedom of religion, he urged that religious freedom be limited.

Prohibitions on Jews holding elective office fell by the wayside very quickly, in part because Jewish Americans, few though they were, participated in the American Revolution. But American Catholics also fought in the Revolution, yet their participation availed little in averting the panic that rose up against them. Jews, however, had no equivalent of a pope—no chief rabbi to arouse fears that they would act as a unified bloc. After the Revolution, when President Washington visited Newport, Rhode Island, in 1790, its small Jewish community formally expressed its welcome and loyalty. "Deprived, as we have hitherto been of invaluable rights of free citizens," their rabbi declared, "we now . . . behold a government erected by the majesty of the people, a government which gives no sanction to bigotry and no assistance to persecution."[2] In responding, Washington echoed these words, thereby endowing American Jews with the endorsement of the nation's preeminent

Founding Father: "The Government of the United States . . . gives to bigotry no sanction, to persecution no assistance. . . . May the children of the stock of Abraham who dwell in this land continue to merit and enjoy the good will of the other inhabitants, while everyone shall sit in safety under his own vine and fig tree, and there shall be none to make him afraid."[3]

Washington underscored his acceptance of Jews in similar declarations to the Jewish communities of Philadelphia and Savannah. But the Chinese too participated in patriotic events after arriving in the United States and it did not avert persecution. Unlike the Chinese, however (and later Japanese), the Jews had no homeland at that time to which they could be accused of being loyal. Moreover, most Jews loathed the nations from which they or their ancestors had fled persecution. That singular devotion to the new United States likely made George Washington more comfortable in writing to the Jews of Newport a sentence that contained a key phrase: "The citizens of the United States of America have the right *to applaud themselves* for having given to mankind . . . liberty of conscience." (Italics added.) Rejecting anti-Semitism enabled Americans to applaud their new nation as being different from the monarchies of Europe, where anti-Semitism had long found fertile ground. George Washington's initiation of that ovation was widely published. Carrying the weight that it did, his viewpoint undermined the incipient panic over Jews holding elective office. In addition, American "anti-anti-Semitism" further served the nation for an opposite reason. It helped the nation filter from its self-perception its persecution of other groups. The "Jewish Question" thus became, in the new United States, what one might call the "Jewish Equation."

Not until the mid-nineteenth century was there a resurgence of anti-Semitism. Political and economic upheavals in Germany, leading to full-scale revolution in 1848, resulted in a wave of German immigrants, many of whom were Jews. As with similar sudden influxes of Irish Catholics and Chinese, many Americans' attitudes toward Jews began to alter, though not nearly to the same degree of fear and panic. An item in the May 1858 issue of *Harper's New Monthly Magazine* began, "Rarely have we any shrewder specimens of modern financing," and went on to tell of a Jewish merchant who, to satisfy an unpaid bill from a customer, acquired possession of the impoverished customer's home. "Sharp practice this," the item concluded, "and very Jewish."[4] Three frequently seen aspects of panic are packed into that last phrase. The first is its reliance on an absolute: that all Jews are avaricious. The second is an element that often adheres to absolutes, filtered facts, as the phrase filtered out non-Jews who are avaricious. Thirdly, "very Jewish" functioned as an accusation of divided loyalty. Since there was no homeland at the time to which Jews could be accused of remaining loyal, it expressed the fear long familiar in Europe that Jews were loyal to money over neighbors or nation. Such attitudes strained America's Jewish Equation. But by the mid-nineteenth century the strain was countered in the opposite direction, as European nations increasingly looked upon the slave-holding United States as *less* progressive than their governments.

When the Civil War commenced, New York's *Albany Journal* noted on November 9, 1861, that "a Committee of Ladies representing the Jewish population of our city has signified its willingness to cooperate with the [Army Relief] Association in soliciting donations among their number. The Jews have not been backward in their devotion and loyalty to the Government, as the muster-rolls of our regiments attest." Meanwhile, on May 3 of that year, Virginia's *Alexandria Gazette* similarly noted, "Eight Jewish ladies in Lynchburg contributed one hundred dollars to the volunteer companies of that city. The Jews in Charlottesville have been more liberal, in proportion to their means, in their contributions to aid the soldiers and their families than any other class of our citizens." Virtually all American Jews, as with virtually all Americans, remained loyal to their regions during the Civil War.

For Southern Jews, however, loyalty to the Confederacy required coping with the fact that the Torah repeatedly references the importance of their liberation from slavery in Egypt. Rabbi Morris Raphall pointed the way to sidestep these references when, hoping to forestall the imminent Civil War, he urged the congregants of a New York synagogue to remember that Abraham, Isaac, and Jacob were slaveholders. Rabbi Raphall then approached the portal to panic when he employed a keyword in asking, "When, and by what *authority* . . . slaveholding ceased to be permitted and became sinful?"

(Italics added.) In defining that authority, he zipped through the portal and directly entered the realm of panic by advocating that which he feared: "If they [abolitionists] truly and honestly desire to save our country, let them believe in God . . . and then, when the authority of the Constitution is to be set aside for a higher Law, they will be able to appeal to the highest Law of all, the revealed Law and Word of God."[5] Panic resided in his seeking to save the United States by destroying one of its fundamental pillars, the First Amendment's freedom of religion, and replacing it with the Torah.

While Rabbi Raphall rooted his defense of slavery in the Torah, the Nature-based justification of slavery was employed by some in an effort to preserve both slavery and the nation's Jewish Equation. In his 1854 book *Sociology for the South,* George Fitzhugh pointed out, "The Jewish slaves were not negroes," and went on to assert, "We presume the maddest abolitionist does not think the negro's providence of habits and money-making capacity at all compare to those of the whites." Combining these assertions, he concluded, "Although the Jews were scattered in after times . . . downtrodden, hated, persecuted, oppressed . . . they are today a great, numerous and prosperous people."

In announcing his state's secession from the Union, Louisiana senator Judah Benjamin (a Jew who would go on to become the Confederacy's secretary of state) declared, "You can never subjugate us; you can never convert the free sons of the soil into vassals . . . and you never, never can degrade them to the level of an inferior and servile race."[6] American Jews, like their fellow countrymen, were not immune to racism, nor, as Rabbi Raphall demonstrated, were they immune to political panic.

During the war, Jews were periodically the objects of panic. In 1862, General Ulysses S. Grant issued an order declaring, "The Jews, as a class violating every regulation of trade . . . are hereby expelled from the Department [of the Tennessee] within twenty-four hours."[7] The Department of the Tennessee embraced the swath of land surrounding the Tennessee River, which flows through Tennessee, Alabama, Mississippi, and Kentucky. As worded, the order applied to all Jews in that vast corridor. Questions later arose as to whether Grant, preoccupied with difficult battles, actually or carefully read the order, which was written by his adjutant before he put his signature to it.

Whether worded by Grant or not, others were panicked as well. "A recent order of Gen. Grant, banishing all Jews from his department, has created intense excitement . . . as many of that class are very rich, and the money power has resisted the blow," the *National Intelligencer* told readers on January 6, 1863. But others felt Grant had gone too far. "The great injustice and unpopularity of Gen. Grant's recent order expelling the Jews from his lines is daily becoming more apparent," the *Wisconsin Patriot* declared on January 17, adding that "among the condemned class there are good and bad, as in all classes." The *Philadelphia Inquirer* agreed, then speculated as to why Grant would have issued such an order: "Certain adventurous and keen speculators may have annoyed him and embarrassed his military operations . . . in their eager pursuit of bargains and trade . . . . [but] they should have been arrested and punished as offenders . . . not denounced and expatriated in their relation as religionists."[8] The phrase "embarrassed his military operations" suggests the *Inquirer* may have known that one of the illegal speculators, working with a Jewish partner, was General Grant's father. If Jesse Grant were to be arrested, it would indeed embarrass General Grant. President Lincoln, if he knew, likewise opted not to bring scandal on his most effective general. He did, however, countermand the order,

Ulysses S. Grant went on to demonstrate that alarmists cannot be stereotyped. Other than at that time and place, nothing in his life indicated hostility toward Jews. As president, he spoke out strongly against atrocities being committed against Jews in Russia and Romania, and was the first president to attend a religious service in a synagogue. These actions may reflect a politician mending fences rather than attitudes toward Jews, or they may reveal that attitudes are rooted in circumstances as much, if not more, than any fixed beliefs.

In the South, too, the view that Jews were more loyal to money than to their aspiring nation increased with the danger confronting the Confederacy. When the Union army, after capturing Norfolk, Virginia, in 1862, required its merchants to take an oath of loyalty or close their stores, Georgia's *Augusta*

Chronicle wrote on March 18, 1863, "All stores have been closed except a few shops kept by Yankees and Jews." Yet, as with Grant's order in the North, anti-Semitic attitudes were not widespread. Even in 1864, as financial speculators began to prey upon property-owning Southerners in dire need of cash, Confederate general Howell Cobb, a former governor of Georgia, sought to tamp down an anti-Semitic brushfire sparked by the fact that Jews were among these financial predators. "In the ranks of speculators and extortioners there are to be found no small number of '*uncircumcised* Jews,'" he declared. (Italics in original.) General Cobb's emphasizing the phrase, "uncircumcised Jews," highlighted his reference to Christians who acted like Jews—an oxymoron likely aimed at having greater effect on anti-Semites whose vehemence he sought to mitigate. But Cobb employed no such paradoxes when he added, "Many of this much abused sect have done their duty, both in the field and at home."[9]

After the Civil War, instances of anti-Semitism continued as they had before and during the war, but the Jewish Equation continued. "The anti-Semitic feeling in Europe is growing stronger every day," a May 4, 1881, editorial in the *St. Louis Globe-Democrat* stated, then asserted, "In our country the anti-Semitic movement is almost entirely confined to hotel keepers for advertising purposes. The American people, as a whole, will have nothing to do with it." The equation, however, was facing new strains at the time this editorial appeared. Those strains emanated from political events abroad that were causing a new and far more massive influx of Jews into the United States. That their arrival did not spark the kind of widespread panic that accompanied previous influxes of Irish Catholics and Chinese can be attributed, in part, to endurance of the nation's Jewish Equation; it is also because those who did become panicked undermined each other's alarms by connecting their panic over Jews to two contradictory panics: the panic over communists and the panic over capitalists.

Fear of Jews as Communistic Subversives

Beginning in the 1870s, political upheavals in Russia triggered a massive flight of Jews from Eastern Europe who fled intensified persecution and ethnic cleansing in the form of murderous pogroms. Among the many who made their way to the United States were some who had been involved in those revolutionary upheavals. Moreover, some of their revolutionary founding fathers were of Jewish descent, including Karl Marx, author of *The Communist Manifesto;* another, though less remembered today, was Ferdinand Lasalle. In 1878, Lasalle was sufficiently well known that American missionary Joseph Cook, invoking the recurring fear of danger to the nation via the family unit, warned that Lasalle "adopts false doctrines concerning the family . . . [and] after having abolished the family in his scheme of thought . . . plunges onward with his followers into the abyss of Communism." Cook then connected the fear of communism to the fear of Jews. "In Lasalle you find the eloquence of a cultivated Jew, and also in Karl Marx."[10]

After the communists seized power in Russia in 1917, fear of Jews as revolutionaries increased markedly in the United States. Just as in the panic over Japanese Americans in events leading up to World War I and culminating in World War II, and just as we currently see in panic over Muslim Americans, foreign affairs can fuel intense (but not necessarily false) domestic fears. "Renegade Jews Lead Bolshevik Apostasy," headlined a March 10, 1918, article in the *Idaho Statesman.* In his 1918 book *Russia's Agony,* Robert Wilton employed the panic-inducing element of secrecy to fuel alarm when he wrote, "They [Jews] studiously concealed their identity under assumed Russian and Polish names. It became known that the principal ones were . . . Apfelbaum-Zinoviev, Rosenfeldt-Kamenev, Goldmann-Gorev . . . Trotsky, whose real name was Bronstein, and Feldmann, *alias* Chernov."

A far more influential figure, Henry Ford, published *The International Jew* in the early 1920s. It too sounded the alarm over Jews as revolutionaries. "The Soviet is not a Russian but a Jewish institution," he declared in one of a series of articles in the newspaper he owned, the *Dearborn Independent,* and later published in booklet form. Cloaking his identity by the absence of any statement indicating authorship, Ford went further than accusing Jews of being communists. "Bolshevism, which is now known to be merely the outer cloak of a long-planned coup to establish the domination of a race," he asserted, "immediately set up the Soviet form of government because the

Jews of all countries who contributed to Russian Bolshevism had long been schooled in the nature and structure of the Soviet."[11]

Henry Ford's certitude about Jews was also reflected in his certitude about lifestyle, which led to lifelong contention between himself and his only child, Edsel. Though purely speculation, one might suspect that Henry Ford possessed not great certitude, but rather a great *need* for certitude. In terms of political panic, this speculation is supported by the fact that all the elements of political panic that have surfaced so far function to enhance certitude. What we are beginning to see is that, while alarmists cannot be stereotyped, to the extent that they are alarmed (as opposed to using alarm) they have a *need for certitude*.

Irrespective of Henry Ford's needs, he possessed such influence that the possibility of widespread panic over Jews was greater than ever before. Not only was he the nation's preeminent industrialist of the time, he aspired to become more. In 1916 he announced that he would run for president "if the people wanted him."[12] They didn't. Nor did the people want him when he made overtures for the nomination in 1923 and 1936. His anti-Semitism, being so connected to his panic over communism, met resistance not only from those alarmed over capitalist corporations such as the Ford Motor Company, but also from those appalled by the violent physical attacks on labor-organizing workers by squads his company hired.

Still, an increasing array of influential Americans added their alarm to that of Henry Ford. In the 1930s, Father Charles Coughlin achieved fame through his nationwide radio broadcasts that frequently included statements such as, "If Jews persist in supporting communism directly or indirectly, that will be regrettable." At one mass rally Coughlin went further. "When we get through with the Jews in America," he declared, "they'll think the treatment they received in Germany was nothing."[13]

Fear of Jews as Capitalists

In 1891, the Marxist newspaper *People* warned of capitalist Jews controlling the press when it asserted, "Joseph Pulitzer is the worst kind of Jew."[14]

Working people, it went on to say, "all have a right to indict for treachery Joe Pulitzer, the present proprietor and editor of the *New York World*. . . . Incest, rape, adultery, and even unmentionable crimes are now exploited [in his newspaper, but] . . . for the labor movement, it has almost been banished from the columns of the *World*." Recurring elements of panic permeate these statements, which begin with a *double* blank to be filled in: "the worst kind of Jew." The phrase left it to the reader to determine the kinds of Jews and the scale to determine the best from the worst. Filtering resided in ascribing Pulitzer's brand of journalism to his Jewishness—though, in this instance, we discover how finely woven a filter can be when the article goes on to state, "Nothing shows better the contempt in which the working class is held by plutocrats than the present attitude of the notorious multimillionaire [William Randolph] Hearst, proprietor of the *New York Journal*." The finely woven filtering surfaces in the absence of any reference to Hearst being the worst kind of Episcopalian. A misbegotten assertion was employed in stating that Pulitzer should be indicted for treachery, as treachery is not a crime. A similar sounding word, *treason, is* a crime, but publishing offensive articles or opting not to publish other articles does not constitute treason. If the newspaper *People* sought to overthrow the United States government (as it may have), it cannot be said that the statements advocated that which they feared. But if it feared Pulitzer endangered the United States, then the statements were panicked by advocating the protection of the United States by eliminating the First Amendment's freedom of the press.

The fear of Jews controlling the news media has continued unabated. In 1974, the chairman of the Joint Chiefs of Staff, General George S. Brown, asserted that Jews "own the banks in this country [and] the newspapers." In 2002, author Kevin McDonald wrote, "A quarter of the Washington press corps were found to be Jewish in a 1976 study, and fifty-eight percent of the television news producers and editors at the ABC television network in a 1973 study were Jewish."[15] McDonald used this data to support his assertion that "Judaism must be understood as exhibiting universal human tendencies for self-interest, ethnocentrism, and competition for resources and economic success."[16] This claim, McDonald immediately pointed out, applies to all humanity ("universal human tendency"). Still, panic-inducing elements hover over two aspects of his data on Jews in the news media. The first, which is built into his theory of ethnocentric tendencies, is that correlation implies causation. The second is the implication of an absolute, namely that *all* Jews in the news media report events the same way. A parallel fear of Jews was and continues to be expressed in regard to the nation's entertainment media. In 1922, Episcopal minister William Sheafe Chase published *Catechism on Motion Pictures,* in which he stated, "The few Hebrews who control the motion picture business . . . [are using it] for selfish commercial and unpatriotic purposes. . . . It has been prostituted to corrupt government, to demoralize youth, and break down the Christian religion." The assertion remained an unverified claim in Chase's book, one that simultaneously filtered out non-Jewish-owned studios whose productions featured similar content. Moreover, it filtered out films from Jewish-owned studios that featured patriotic, moral, and even pro-Christian content, such as the top-grossing film of the year before Chase published his book: *The Four Horsemen of the Apocalypse,* produced by Metro Pictures Corporation under the ownership of Jewish American Marcus Loew.

More influential than Reverend Chase was aviation hero Charles Lindbergh, who warned in a nationally broadcast speech in September 1941, "The greatest danger to this country, lies in their [Jews'] large ownership and influence in our motion pictures, our press, our radio, and our Government."[17] The panic-inducing elements in Lindbergh's statements consisted of a blank to be filled in, "large," leaving it to his listeners to determine how large, and in his use of two absolutes—one explicit ("greatest") and the other the implicit assumption that all Jews think and act as a bloc.

In some instances, the same people alarmed about Jews as anti-capitalists also voiced alarm about Jews as capitalists. Henry Ford, who had declared that the Soviet Union "is not a Russian but a Jewish institution," also warned, "To make a list of the lines of business controlled by the Jews of the United States would be to touch most of the vital industries of the country."[18] That these conflicting bases undermined each other, and that the

Jewish Equation still exerted its influence, can be seen in responses to these eminent anti-Semites. "Ex-Editor Says Ford Directed Attacks on Jews—Presidential Ambitions Are Alleged Cause," headlined a July 12, 1927, *Chicago Tribune* article. A December 12, 1938, headline in the same paper declared, "Cardinal Issues Stern Rebuke to Father Coughlin." As Charles Lindbergh commenced a speaking tour on the heels of his 1941 radio address, the *Washington Post* topped a September 19 article with "Texas House Asks Lindbergh to Stay Away."

With these types of accusations regarding Jews, we see that fear of a group acting as a bloc occurs more frequently in nonracially rooted panics. Accusations of a plot by Jews or Catholics, Wall Street or communists, and equivalent accusations of a homosexual agenda or feminist agenda, far outnumber accusations of political conspiracy leveled at Native Americans, African Americans, or Latinos. In all political panics, fear emanates from uncertainties as to the future of one's freedom. But in racially based panics, the fear is powerfully buttressed by virtue of its emanating from genetic, and therefore sexual, uncertainties.

Private Restrictions

An additional reason the flood of Eastern European Jews did not trigger widespread panic is that this wave of immigrants (which also included vast numbers of Italian Catholics, who also did not trigger widespread panic) arrived at a time when their presence did not result in job competition. During this era, technological advancements created a need for labor in new industries. One such industry, already mentioned, was motion pictures. Far larger, however, was the mass-produced garment industry, made possible by advances in the sewing machine. "Our national interests are . . . found concurrent with the interests of European sufferers," a November 10, 1877, editorial in the *New Orleans Times-Picayune* observed, going on to say that the nation had "good reason to welcome" these Jews. This new garment industry soon demonstrated to the nation that Jews were not a unified political bloc. As it came to be plagued by labor-management conflicts, both sides in garment industry strikes were predominantly Jewish (with significant numbers of Italian workers as well).

As the first generation of American-born Jews entered the workplace, employment competition did arise in white-collar occupations, at which point anti-Semitism in that realm appeared. "TYPISTS—Rapid, accurate. Gentiles only. Apply 9 A.M., 904. Walnut St.," read a classified ad in the April 19, 1916, *Philadelphia Inquirer*. In their study of Jews in the Protestant establishment, researchers Richard Zweigenhaft and G. William Domhoff found that in the early decades of the twentieth century, "Jews were almost totally absent from commercial banking . . . public utilities, and manufacturing, and, contrary to popular belief at the time, they were . . . a tiny minority in newspapers and radio . . . [and] virtually absent from magazines, book publishing, and advertising."[19] Such restrictions also arose in many of the clubs and resorts where white-collar Americans socialized, and in the nation's elite universities.

That these restrictions were new can be seen in a widely reported incident in 1877. The *Cincinnati Gazette*'s June 19 coverage stated, "On Wednesday last, Joseph Seligman, the well-known banker . . . visited Saratoga with his family. For ten years he has spent the summer at the Grand Union Hotel . . . . The manager [told him], 'Mr. Hilton has given instructions that no Israelites shall be permitted.'" A generation later, Seligman's nephew, Theodore, was denied membership in New York's tony Union League Club, despite the fact that his father had been a member for twenty-five years. Such restrictions had rapidly spread and were becoming deep-rooted. By 1949, Wisconsin's *Capital Times* was reporting on "a drive to discourage Wisconsin resort owners from using such phrases as 'restricted clientele' and 'gentiles only' in their resort advertising."[20]

Within these professional ranks, anti-Semitism was voiced with greater elegance, but the underlying elements of panic were the same as those that fueled the fears of less educated alarmists. Harvard University president A. Lawrence Lowell lamented in 1922 not only that "gentile clubs are excluding Jews" but also that "private schools are excluding Jews, I believe, and so, we know, are hotels."[21] In his capacity as the leader of so prestigious a university,

Lowell went on to state, "The question for those of us who deplore such a state of things is how it can be combated, and especially for those of us who are connected with colleges." Lowell's answer to his question was to combat anti-Semitism by limiting the number of Jews admitted to Harvard. "If their number should become forty percent of the student body," he explained, "the race feeling would become intense. When, on the other hand, the number of Jews was small, the race antagonism was small also." The elegance that cloaks the elements of panic in Lowell's statement resides in his ability to convey all those elements implicitly rather than explicitly. Filtered from his key phrase, "race antagonism" is the cause for the antagonism. The absence of any explanation is a blank to be filled in. Those who fill it in with the fear that Jews constitute a danger to the nation, and subscribe to Lowell's solution, have thus been induced into the realm of panic by advocating that which they fear. Fearing Jews are a danger to the nation, they seek to protect the nation by limiting, where legally possible, freedom of religion. Lowell's legerdemain worked. Soon after its implementation at Harvard, Jewish enrollment at Columbia University was cut in half; other universities followed suit. In cities such as Minneapolis, the number of Jewish doctors permitted to rent space in downtown office buildings was limited. The federal government similarly imposed selective quotas on immigration in 1921, closing the gates on the flood of Jews seeking to escape persecution in Eastern Europe and, not long after, Nazi Germany. In the years following World War II, however, restrictions aimed at Jews began to recede, as Americans came to learn the horrors of the Holocaust and the nation's perception of the United States as "not Europe" was renewed.

Intersecting Panics: African Americans and Jews

During the era of massive immigration by Eastern European Jews, a few in panic over Jews connected their alarm to the nation's preeminent political panic over African Americans—a connection that would grow in the years to come. In his 1910 book, *The Jew a Negro,* Arthur T. Abernethy began with what is now the familiar assertion and possibly genuine self-perception:

"This work must not be interpreted into an attack upon the Hebrew race." His claim, he said, was simply "that the Jew of today, as well as his ancestors in other times, is the kinsman and descendant of the Negro." Abernethy told his readers that intermarriages "have elevated the Jewish people to a condition where they control vast commercial enterprises . . . yet thousands of years of effort to throw off their nigrescence have failed to eradicate those race characteristics, and the Jew of today is essentially Negro in habits, physical peculiarities and tendencies." Those characteristics, he declared—not to be misinterpreted as an attack on the Hebrew race, remember—are "cunning and susceptibility to bribery" and "their pitiable disregard, especially among the men . . . for the regularities restricting sexual indulgencies [*sic*] . . . whom this mania often drives to crimes against womanhood. But what the Negro may accomplish only by brute force and crime, the Jew . . . artfully effects by the gentler process of blandishment, ingenuity and gold." Touching upon that aspect of the connection that later grew into a more widespread fear of black-Jewish relations, Abernethy asserted, "Like the Negroes, they have foisted race riots on countries wherever they have lived." Arthur T. Abernethy was later elected to the American Association for the Advancement of Science and became the poet laureate of North Carolina. And indeed, his book's conclusion was very prescient when it stated, "The overshadowing predominance of the Negro question has alone kept the American people at peace with the Hebrews."[22]

The following year, Henry Suksdorf also connected panic over Jews with panic over African Americans, but in a very different way. In *Our Race Problems,* he wrote of the Jew, "His race is in its dotage," in contrast to his view that "the African race is in its infancy." While Suksdorf's premise was the opposite of Abernethy's, it led to the same conclusion. A person of African heritage was, he wrote, "indolent . . . submissive, credulous . . . all characteristics of a race in its childhood." Of the Jews, he concluded, "Anti-Semitism is but the spasmodic effort of a sound organism to eject an indigestible morsel from the system."

Filtered from both books was any mention of the single most obvious connection between African Americans and Jews: their shared history of enslavement and persecution. Filtering this connection enhanced certitude because the connection so clearly *complicated* black-Jewish relations, making certitude more difficult. Many American Jews adopted the racism that (as seen in the success of *The Birth of a Nation*) offered immigrants a path to mainstream America. Vividly illustrating the complicated relationship, W. H. Council, a leader in African American education, urged African Americans in 1894 to emulate Jews by being "honest and industrious . . . patient and thrifty. . . . We must learn lessons on that line from the Jews, whose grip is on the pocket book of the world."[23]

Nevertheless, there were blacks and Jews who did connect via their shared heritage of slavery and persecution. In the context of working-class solidarity, the defense attorney provided by the Communist Party to take up the case of the previously mentioned Scottsboro Boys was an American Jew, Joseph Brodsky. So too was the noncommunist attorney who took over from the controversial Brodsky, Samuel Leibowitz. Black-Jewish solidarity also emanated from wealthy capitalists who were Jews. Julius Rosenwald, a co-owner of Sears, Roebuck and Co., endowed the Tuskegee Institute and, at the behest of its director, Booker T. Washington, provided millions to improve the educational facilities of African Americans in the South. Arthur Spingarn, a descendant of a wealthy Jewish American millinery and real estate family, disagreed with the nonconfrontational views of Booker T. Washington. He joined with African American leaders W. E. B. Du Bois, Mary Church Terrell, and others to form the National Association for the Advancement of Colored People (NAACP), whose founders also included prominent white Americans who were not Jewish, such as Jane Addams, William Dean Howells, and Lincoln Steffens.

An act of political panic emanating from the intersecting fear of Jews and of African Americans made nationwide headlines in August 1915 when a mob lynched Leo Frank, a Jewish resident of Atlanta. The body of fifteen-year-old Mary Phagan had been discovered in the basement of the city's National Pencil Company; her torn clothing indicated she had been sexually assaulted and murdered. Initially, both the factory superintendent, Leo Frank, and its African American night watchman were taken to police headquarters for questioning. With the night watchman having an alibi, suspicion shifted to another African American at the factory, while Leo Frank continued to remain a suspect. The press reported heated conflict behind the scenes of the investigation, the details suggesting a three-way tug-of-war involving anti-Semites, racists, and those seeking truth.[24] Whether or not anti-Semitism ultimately determined that Frank would be charged remains a matter of conjecture. Not conjecture, however, and most significant in terms of political panic, was the nature of Frank's trial, in which he was convicted. "I very seriously doubt if the petitioner has had due process of law because of his trial taking place in the presence of a hostile demonstration and seemingly dangerous crowd," Supreme Court justice Oliver Wendell Holmes later wrote.[25] Precisely the same could have been said of countless trials of African American defendants.

Having been accused for so long of persecuting African Americans, the similar treatment of Leo Frank represented a racist recalculation of the Jewish Equation. The recalculated equation demonstrated equal mistreatment of Jews and blacks. Many Southerners, however, did not adopt this newly calculated equation. After Leo Frank was sentenced to death, Georgia governor John Slaton, having doubts regarding the trial and its verdict, commuted Frank's death sentence to life imprisonment. Soon after, a group of men abducted Frank from prison. The following morning, Georgia's *Columbus Ledger-Enquirer* reported, "The body of Leo M. Frank, found hanging from the limb of a tree two miles east of Marietta . . . was cut down at 10:15 o'clock this morning in the presence of a crowd estimated at several thousand people."[26]

The connection between blacks and Jews in the minds of those alarmed about both further developed with the Civil Rights Movement. In the 1950s, flyers appeared in parts of the South declaring, "Jews Behind Race Mixing," the same phrase serving as the title of a booklet published by Edward R. Fields in the 1960s. During this era, more instances occurred demonstrating the recalculated Jewish Equation. In 1964, civil rights workers James Chaney, Mickey Schwerner, and Andrew Goodman were abducted and shot to death in Neshoba County, Mississippi. Chaney was African American;

his fellow activists were Jews. Headlines of bombings at black churches were interspersed with headlines such as "Students Find Bomb Beneath Steps of Synagogue" in the October 13 *Atlanta Daily World*. While that incident, which took place in Miami, was foiled, as was another that year in North Carolina, bombs were detonated at synagogues in Skokie, Illinois (1956); Peoria, Illinois (1958); Jacksonville, Florida (1958); Atlanta, Georgia (1958); Kansas City, Missouri (1960); Gadsden, Alabama (1960); Chicago, Illinois (1961); Jackson, Mississippi (1967); Meridian, Mississippi (1968); Temple Hills, Maryland (1969); and Wilmington, North Carolina (1973).[27] As panic over African Americans began to abate, so too did the bombing of synagogues. Alongside the post–World War II upheaval over civil rights, the original Jewish Equation continued to function, though still strained by competition in professional ranks. Concern over foreign affairs added more strain to the equation with the creation of Israel in 1948 and the resulting upheavals in the Middle East, a region of great significance to American economic and political security. Evidence of both the continued functioning of the equation and the strains upon it can be seen in the use of code words to mask anti-Semitism. On April 15, 1972, the *Washington Post* reported that Congressman John Dowdy, after being convicted for bribery, "would identify the 'they' and 'them' who wanted to 'get' him only as the 'Eastern liberal establishment.'" By not defining "Eastern liberal establishment," Dowdy created a blank to be filled in—a blank likely filled in with "Jews" by those who feared Jews. Vice presidential candidate Dan Quayle employed a similar panic-inducing blank in 1992 when he said, "I know exactly who the cultural elite, the media elite, and the Hollywood elite are."[28]

That Congressman Dowdy and candidate Quayle employed coded blanks does not indicate either man was necessarily anti-Semitic. It does, however, demonstrate that both sought the support of anti-Semites. In some instances, phrases that can be used as codes are not a version of blanks to be filled in. When syndicated columnist Charley Reese wrote on July 23, 2007, "The Israeli lobby likes to boast about defeating candidates who don't toe the Israel-right-or-wrong line," he did not use "Israeli lobby" as a code for Jews, even though the phrase has often been used in that way. Reese's column had already filled in the blank that phrase might otherwise create by having commenced, "One of the myths created by the Israeli lobby is that Jews . . . are unanimous in their support of Israel. That's not true and never has been true."[29]

Rarely but occasionally after the Holocaust, Americans have expressed anti-Semitism without codes. When White House correspondent Helen Thomas declared in 2010, "Congress, the White House and Hollywood, Wall Street, are owned by the Zionists," there was little doubt that Zionists meant Jews.[30] Thomas's statement did, however, include a blank to be filled in with her use of the word "owned," as it left it to others to determine what constitutes ownership of Congress, the White House, Wall Street, and Hollywood. Neither codes nor blanks were used when movie star Mel Gibson declared, "The Jews are responsible for all the wars in the world."[31] The statement did employ an absolute, "all," which made his claim so clearly false it had little impact in spreading panic and more likely served to diminish whatever panic existed. Indeed, a former president of the 16 million member Southern Baptist Convention, James Merritt, called Gibson's remark, "reprehensible and . . . shameful."[32] Ted Haggard, at the time the pastor of Colorado's 14,000-member New Life Church, rejected Gibson's defense that his outburst resulted from drunkenness. "My view of alcohol is that it lowers inhibitions," Haggard stated, "and . . . [people] say what they really think."[33]

The reaction to Gibson's remark by columnist Charley Reese stands as a striking example that alarmists cannot be stereotyped. In contrast to Reese's nonpanicked statement about the "Israel lobby," he wrote on August 9, 2006, "Whether Gibson is an anti-Semite or not, I don't know and frankly don't care."[34] What Reese did claim to know was that "an anti-Semite in today's America . . . is not a person who hates Jews, but a person Jews hate." Panic resided in the statement's filtering of facts and use of an absolute. It asserted the absolute that *all* American Jews share the same view as to who is anti-Semitic. It filtered out individuals whom many Jews do not consider anti-Semitic even though they revile that individual. (As present-day examples, many Jews revile Sarah Palin or Ted Cruz, but few, if any, Jews consider either to be anti-Semitic.)

Among the political panics that have erupted throughout American history, the limited panic over Jews reflects the fact that the history of American Jews has been a perfect non-storm of panic-inducing elements. At the nation's birth, its efforts to distinguish the new United States from the old monarchies of Europe included widespread rejection of anti-Semitism, as articulated by George Washington. During the nation's greatest internal crisis, the Civil War, sparks of anti-Semitism failed to ignite in part because Jews remained loyal to their respective regions. In the late nineteenth century, the arrival of massive numbers of Jewish immigrants did not ignite widespread panic due largely to technological advances, particularly in the garment industry, which created vast numbers of jobs that minimized economic competition with other groups. As the American-born offspring of those immigrants began to compete with other Americans for professional positions in the first half of the twentieth century, efforts to ignite anti-Semitism were doused by American reactions to the genocidal horrors of Nazi Germany. At the present time, efforts to ignite anti-Semitism on the basis of Israeli domination of Palestinians have been delimited by terrorist acts committed by Arabs. By being a perfect non-storm, however, the lack of widespread panic toward Jews yields no instruction as to how to avoid or minimize panic.

Still, one aspect of American Jewish history yields hope. So long as Americans continue to view the United States as different from other nations, there is hope that the nation's Jewish Equation will change from a "Jewish" variable to a "minority" variable. We may already, in fact, be beginning to see this evolution of the equation. The arcs of the political panics in the United States, most of which have abated (though new ones have emerged), lend tenuous credence to the hope that the Jewish Equation is evolving into a "Minority Equation" that may someday further evolve from equation to equality. As the ensuing chapters show, should that day come, it will be far in the future.

Seven

"THE COMMUNIST PARTY, USA, works day and night ... virtually invisible to the non-communist eye ... for its objective, the ultimate seizure of power in America."

—J. Edgar Hoover, MASTERS OF DECEIT (1958)

Technological advances, which set in motion massive industrialization in the nineteenth century, changed the nation's (indeed, much of the world's) social landscape in ways that fueled numerous political panics. The two preeminent panics that resulted from this tectonic economic shift were fear of capitalist corporations and its twin, fear of communistic revolution. On the surface, these two panics would seem to be the opposite of twins, as the fundamental philosophy of communism is that government should own industries and the fundamental philosophy of capitalism is that individuals should own industries. But the elements that created panic over communism and panic over capitalism were identical.

While the relationship between these two panics is particularly vivid, this interrelationship is not unique. In the case of industrialization, it wove

together numerous panics. As already seen, the panic over Chinese immigrants intensified with the use of their labor to construct the Transcontinental
Railroad and that panic became widespread with the subsequent availability
of Chinese labor via rail transportation. The preexisting anti-Catholic panic
was further fueled by Irish Catholics pouring into the United States in the
mid-nineteenth century, seeking jobs in the nation's burgeoning industries
and the growing cities that provided their infrastructure. Expanding into
a more complex web of interrelationships, the panic over Jews was further
fueled less by job competition than by the industrially spawned panic over
communists *and* the panic over capitalists. Both the panic over capitalists
and the panic over African Americans intensified when blacks, fleeing persecution in the South, accepted work in northern cities at companies where
white workers were on strike. In chapters to come, we will see how the panic
over women interwove with the panic over capitalists by virtue of the fact
that many women altered their traditional roles in the home to accept jobs
in factories. The unequal treatment (and often mistreatment) of women in
those jobs added fuel to the women's movement, which in turn added fuel to
the panic over women. What is significant in these examples is that political
panic often functions within a web of panics.

Birth of the Panic Over Communism

Fear of communism in the United States first flickered as early as 1840 when
the *New York Spectator* translated a report from France pertaining to turmoil
in that country. "These men were Communists," an editor's note explained,
"who openly advocate . . . the abolition of individual property . . . [and]
would carry out their principles by force . . . even if in a minority."[1] The
panic-inducing element resided in the editor's next statement, which employed the words "doctrine" and "principles" as blanks to be filled in: "We
have translated the preceding . . . as an illustration of the doctrines really
lying at the root of the principles avowed by Mr. Van Buren." Few Americans today would fill those blanks by concluding that President Martin Van
Buren was a communist.

Adoption of the philosophy of communism in the United States first surfaced in 1848 when John Humphrey Noyes founded the Oneida Society, a settlement in upstate New York where everything was shared. Virginia's *Alexandria Gazette* warned readers on February 5, 1852, that "about 150 men, women, and children live . . . with no distinction of property, family, or authority . . . [and it] is by no means confined to Oneida. In New York and Brooklyn, and in Newark, N.J., and in many other places, there are groups of practicing members . . . in boarding houses established on similar principles." But in this era preceding the Transcontinental Railroad and massive industrialization, most Americans were far more concerned with the agrarian issue of slavery and the threat of secession that it generated.

By 1870, however, with slavery gone from the land and railroads crossing it, a September 29 article in the *Chicago Tribune* posed the question, "What are the Reds?" After defining communism's fundamental principles, the article asserted, "It is the grand collective ignorance of the Cincinnati Workingmen's Congress." Panic resided in the article offering no information to verify the claim. Indeed, it was a false claim. The goal of the Cincinnati Workingmen's Congress was to organize efforts to urge workers to vote for those politicians who supported their concerns.

The unverified claim in the *Tribune*'s accusation that the Cincinnati Workingmen's Congress was communist illustrates another recurring element in political panic. The voting efforts organized by the Cincinnati Workingmen's Congress were a form of collective action. Collective action was also a tenet of communist doctrine. The *Tribune* article used these two verifiable facts to conclude that the organization was communist. But its underlying logic was a form of a classic example of fallacy:

All cats have ears.
Socrates has ears.
Therefore, Socrates is a cat.

This type of fallacy has spawned a kind of accusation made prominent in the panic over communists: guilt by association. While most of us think of guilt by association involving people associated with other people, the accusation leveled at the Cincinnati Workingmen's Congress demonstrated that it can also involve people associated with methods. Indeed, such instances of the accusation occur more frequently than one might think. In 2012, Sarah Palin told viewers of Fox News, "Barack Obama is a socialist." Explaining her claim she stated, "He believes in socialism, in redistributing, in confiscating hard-earned dollars of our small businessmen and women so that they cannot reinvest their dollars and hire more people and grow and expand."[2] In this instance, the fallacious syllogism was:

> *Socialists want government to confiscate businesses.*
> *Barack Obama wants the government to confiscate money (taxes) from*
> *   businesses.*
> *Therefore, Barack Obama is a socialist.*

Just as the fallacy *correlation implies causation* enables conclusions that filter facts, this form of fallacy does likewise. In this instance, Palin's logic filters out the fact that every president since the enactment of the Sixteenth Amendment has confiscated hard-earned dollars from businesses and individuals via the wealth-redistributing income tax.

Valid Alarm Versus Panic

Another recurring element of political panic vividly illuminated in panic over communists is the use of verified claims to lend credence to panic-inducing claims. "The Communists of this city . . . [are] under the protectorate of the Society of International, which has branches in every prominent city in the world," the *Chicago Tribune* told readers on November 23, 1875. This statement was indeed a verified claim. When the article stated, "they have been organizing military companies in nearly all the large cities," its claim was somewhat inaccurate but verified in terms of some radicals organizing squads armed with (another recent technological development) dynamite. Treading further into the portal to panic, the article then ventured an unverified claim when it warned, "These fanatics are maturing plans to burn the principle cities in this and the old country at the same time." Proceeding into the realm of panic with the panic-inducing element of secrecy, the *Tribune* article told readers that "a secret meeting in this regard . . . was held yesterday . . . at which time plans were laid to reduce Chicago to a heap of smoldering ruins whenever the signal is given by the Central Committee of the Internationals." Unreported was where the meeting was held or who was in attendance or even how the *Tribune* acquired this information. The *Tribune* thus did that which it feared by engaging in secrecy as to the basis of its warning about secrecy. A follow-up article the next day emanated entirely from the realm of panic, as it explicitly—and more ominously—advocated that which it feared. Fearing communists threatened the nation's constitutional foundations, it declared, "If the Communists in this country are counting upon . . . the American tendency to proceed against criminals by due process of law . . . they have ignored some of the most significant episodes in American history . . . Judge Lynch is an American by birth and character."[3]

Urging that which one fears can now be seen as a hallmark of political panic. It appeared in the witchcraft panic when a "witch cake" was prepared to cast a spell that would break the spell of the devil. It surfaced when the founders of New Hampshire, New Jersey, both Carolinas, and Georgia, fearing Catholic theocracy, allowed only Protestants to hold public office. It recurred when Americans, fearing Jesuits and convents were secretive groups that threatened the nation, reacted by joining the Know Nothing Party— the name referring to its members' oaths of secrecy. And it recurred when Americans who believed Jews were toxic to the nation's way of life by virtue of being clannish and ill-mannered, sought to preserve that way of life by restricting Jews from hotels, clubs, resorts, colleges, and communities, thereby acting clannish and, in snubbing people, ill-mannered.[4]

The extent to which the aforementioned *Tribune* articles induced panic over communistic radicals was enhanced by verified claims in the articles lending credence to the less verified and unverified claims. By the same token, however, unverified claims that turn out to be false can undermine the credibility of claims that are true, as Aesop's fable "The Boy Who Cried

Wolf" depicts. In this instance, the *Tribune* warning of imminent coordinated attacks proved false. No such event ever took place.

In addition to the *Tribune* using verified claims to lend credence to unverified claims, these two news reports also sought to induce panic by filtering facts. Filtered out was any reference to the reasons other than allegiance to the Communist International that these radicals were preparing for violence. No mention was made of working conditions in factories as contributing to such rage. In Chicago itself, for example, workers at the Chicago, Burlington & Quincy Railroad were required to rent company-owned housing, to be in their housing at specified times, and to make purchases of any kind at company-owned stores unless given special permission. Throughout the country, laborers typically were required to work ten to sixteen hours a day, six days a week. The struggle for an eight-hour day led to nationwide strikes in 1875. In Chicago, as in many other cities, workers striking for an eight-hour day increasingly clashed with police in skirmishes that turned increasingly violent. "A Storm of Strikes," headlined an article in the May 2, 1896, *Chicago Tribune.* The escalation of violence can be seen from a headline two days later in the *St. Louis Globe-Democrat:* "Labor Riots—A Battle Between Chicago Police and Striking Socialists."

Widening Fear of Radicals

In December 1885, Chicago police found a bomb in the executive offices of the Chicago, Burlington & Quincy Railroad. Only a few days earlier, San Francisco police had caught four radicals in the act of making bombs. These verifiable facts lent credence to a report in the *San Francisco Bulletin* by its Chicago correspondent that told readers, "The Socialists boast that they have over nine thousand bombs loaded and distributed in the hands of trusty persons."[5] This report would soon turn out to be particularly significant, most notably when it said these socialists "have been going to the country to practice the throwing of bombs."

Its significance occurred shortly afterward, on May 3, 1886, when Chicago police arrived at a picket line of strikers outside the McCormick

Harvester Company with a "wagon-load of men armed with rifles [who] scattered the crowd four different times," as the *Milwaukee Journal* reported.[6] That same day, Chicago police fired into the ranks of striking workers at a nearby strike by the Lumber Shovers' Union. In the clamor that followed, the *Milwaukee Journal* article went on to state, "No one, whether he looked like a rough or a respectable citizen, was allowed to stop for a moment." Chicago's radical activists issued a flier for a rally the following day, May 4, 1886, at Haymarket Square. Some 3,000 were listening to speakers at the rally when 400 police approached, marching in formation with their clubs drawn and ready. But the police were not ready for what descended upon them, hissing from the roof of a nearby building. A bomb detonated in their ranks, with injury, death, and panic ensuing as the mass of uninjured police reacted by charging into the crowd and firing their weapons indiscriminately, despite the fact that the bomb did not come from that direction and that shots were not being fired in return. While no official tally was made, the death toll from all who died on the scene or later from their wounds has been estimated to be fourteen.[7]

Eight men were soon arrested and tried for conspiracy to commit murder. At their trial, the degree to which panic existed corresponded to the degree to which verified facts lent credence to unverified facts. Considerable evidence was presented verifying that a number of the defendants had conspired to create and transport bombs. But testimony placing the bomb and the accused bomb thrower at the scene was shown to be dubious, at best, if not demonstrably false. Some police officers testified that, a moment before the bomb was thrown, the speaker, defendant Samuel Fielden, declared, "Here come the bloodhounds! Do your duty now and I'll do mine!" then pulled a pistol and fired point blank at the police as the bomb sailed overhead. But two newspaper reporters near the speaker stand and other police officers testified that Fielden called out, "We are peaceable!" The previously mentioned journalist who had written the article revealing that Chicago radicals were amassing bombs and practicing throwing them testified that two of the other defendants were his sources and had shown him the bombs. But his earlier article, in the July 15, 1886, *San Francisco Bulletin,* had reported only that they "boasted" and "claimed" they possessed bombs. An onlooker not acquainted with the defendants testified that he saw two of them go into an alley and, deciding to follow them, saw a package exchanged and overheard them talking about pistols. In addition to the question of why this man did not notify any of the nearby police, his account maintained that, within earshot of a stranger, two of the defendants risked being overheard and seen engaging in a highly incriminating act. Nevertheless, these unverified claims were so sufficiently bestowed with validity by the verified claims that the defendants were convicted and sentenced to death—all but one, who was sentenced to fifteen years.[8]

The Haymarket bombing detonated more widespread panic. Less than two weeks after the defendants were convicted, an August 23, 1886, editorial in the *Chicago Tribune* declared of an individual in no way connected with the Haymarket bombing, "It is a shame that such as person as Joe Gruenhut is retained in the public employment. His Communistic leanings and affiliations are well known." The editorial went on to assert that Gruenhut "was aware of the dynamite preparations . . . and he failed to properly warn the authorities" and that he "had something to do with the arrangement for the Haymarket meeting, and probably knew its purpose." In this instance, panic resided in what the editorial filtered out. It did not say that, four months prior to the bombing, a January 15, 1886, article in the *San Francisco Bulletin* stated, "About the only man in Chicago who thinks the Socialists may find an opportunity for incendiary work through an association with labor unions is Joseph Gruenhut." Most likely written by the same correspondent who had previously reported on unnamed radicals boasting of their bombs, this article quoted Gruenhut publicly and accurately warning, "I think the great crisis will come on the first of May or very soon after." It came on May 4.

Panic and Pathology

Verifiable facts, such as a bomb being thrown on police at Haymarket Square, enlarge the number of those whose alarm enters the realm of panic, and not infrequently single individuals perpetrate such verifiable facts. One such instance in the panic over communistic subversion occurred on July 23, 1892. "Frick Shot Down in His Office by an Anarchist—Attempt to Assassinate the Chairman of Carnegie Steel," read the next day's headline in the *New York Herald*. The assassination attempt occurred during a strike at the Carnegie Steel Company's plant in Homewood, Pennsylvania. Earlier that month, company chairman Henry Clay Frick had arranged for the hiring of a brigade of 300 men armed with rifles to attack striking workers. While this action fueled panic over capitalists, the assassination attempt that followed fueled panic over communist radicals. "'I am now satisfied that there was an organized movement against Frick,'" the *Herald* quoted the lead police investigator two days later. "'In a few days there will be some developments that will startle the community.'"[9] As it turned out, the anonymous police investigator's unverified claim did not materialize. Other than the would-be assassin arrested at the scene, a militant radical named Alexander Berkman, no "organized movement" to kill Frick was ever uncovered.

Alexander Berkman single-handedly intensified the panic over communistic subversion. He also serves as yet another example of why alarmists cannot be stereotyped, but as such represents an element in political panic not yet discussed. Though Berkman had acquired renown among his fellow radicals as the lover of the charismatic and prominent anarchist Emma Goldman, in his more personal life he appears to have been subject to depression and suicidal thoughts. His plan to kill Frick, for example, included then martyring himself. But he bungled his effort at murder, injuring but not killing Frick before others rushed into the room and subdued him. After serving fourteen years in prison, the now more renowned Berkman went on a lecture tour during which he was driven by depression to purchase a pistol with the intention of killing himself—though, again, he could not pull it off. When Berkman died in 1936, it was from suicide. Significant in terms of political panic is that Berkman found a place for his pathology in the terrain of political panic.

Alexander Berkman was not alone in having such an impact by finding a nest in political panic for personal pathology. The waning panic over Native

Americans received a shot in the arm eight days after the convulsive massacre of the Sioux at Wounded Knee, when a member of that tribe named Plenty Horses shot a friendly army lieutenant in the head, at point blank range, without provocation. Plenty Horses too turned out to be a troubled soul. As a young boy, he had been taken from his parents by whites who sent him from the reservation in South Dakota to an Indian school in Carlisle, Pennsylvania. There his long hair was cut, a sacred token given to him by his grieving mother was taken and discarded, and he was forbidden to speak his native language. When he returned to his reservation five years later, Plenty Horses found himself not fully accepted by his tribe nor by whites. Rage and a desperate need for acceptance drove him to murder Lieutenant Edward Casey, a man he did not know. In this instance, acceptance did not follow, as his fellow Sioux abhorred such murder. What did follow was another burst of panic over Native Americans. Despite the fact that the Sioux had been clearly decimated at Wounded Knee, the killing of Lieutenant Casey sparked a resolution in Congress to send South Dakota's militia 1,000 additional rifles, each supplied with 200 rounds of ammunition.[10]

Personal pathology finding a home in political panic continues to this day. In 2011, panic over the Tea Party movement intensified when Jared Lee Loughner shot Gabrielle Giffords, a Democratic congresswoman whom conservative organizations opposed. Loughner had a documented history of paranoid schizophrenia but, as *New York Times* correspondent Matt Bai pointed out, his paranoia found a home among those alarmists who, at the time, were warning that we may soon need to shoot members of Congress. One such alarmist, Bai pointed out, was Sharron Angle, the Republican candidate for Senate in Arizona's northern neighbor, Nevada. This "Tea Party favorite," Bai stated, "talked about 'domestic enemies' in the Congress and said, 'I hope we're not getting to Second Amendment remedies.'"[11]

Government Participation in Panic

An 1894 House Judiciary report referred specifically to individuals such as Alexander Berkman, an immigrant from Russia, when it stated, "The United

States will soon be the rendezvous of these human monsters" and urged leg-islation to assure "that no alien Anarchist shall be permitted to land at any port in the United States."[12] The proposal was ultimately enacted in 1901, weeks after another anarchist, Leon Czolgosz, assassinated President William McKinley. The Anarchist Exclusion Act marked the first time immigration would be mandatorily denied on the basis of political beliefs. It also marked the federal government's entry into the realm of panic to the degree that it filtered such facts as Leon Czolgosz not being an immigrant. He was born and raised in Michigan and, like his parents, was a registered Republican. Whatever personal issues caused him to associate with anarchists also caused anarchists to distrust him to the point that one of their publications, *Free Society,* alerted its readers to be on the lookout for Czolgosz, whom the magazine suspected of being a spy "pretending to be greatly interested in the cause, asking for names or soliciting aid for acts of contemplated violence."[13]

The Anarchist Exclusion Act did not salve those in panic. "There is an undercurrent of political thought today in the United States which drifts toward Socialism, and this unconscious drift . . . creates a danger to our in-stitutions," Edward F. Browne wrote in *Socialism or Empire.* His 1906 book echoed the recurring fear that the nation was straying from the vision of the Founding Fathers when he warned, "Our Constitution was framed with the creditable object of allowing absolute freedom in business conduct." Here Browne has employed an absolute (in this instance literally, "absolute") to fil-ter out the only section of the Constitution that deals with business conduct: Article I, Section 8, which in fact absolutely authorizes Congress to regulate interstate commerce.

In warning of government regulations, Browne voiced a new concern that would be echoed up to the present day by commentators such as Rush Limbaugh and Bill O'Reilly, who say such things as, "This agitation in fa-vor of the government . . . taking control of business ventures or regulating them . . . is Un-American and wrong. It is but the froth escaping from the seething pot of socialism." But neither O'Reilly nor Limbaugh made this statement; it was Browne in his 1906 book. The element of panic resides in the same fallacy that led to the conclusion that Socrates was a cat. Socialists do seek government regulation and ownership of industries. Sometimes non-socialists do, too. This does not mean nonsocialists are socialists.

Browne's fears were fueled by the creation, one year earlier, of the Industrial Workers of the World (IWW). Unlike labor unions organized by craft, the IWW sought to create one big union whose size and unity would "put the working-class in possession of the economic power . . . in control of the machinery of production and distribution, without regard to capitalist masters." So said William "Big Bill" Haywood in the opening address at the IWW's founding convention.[14] The creation of the IWW doubly unnerved Americans such as Browne by providing Haywood with a national platform.

Big Bill Haywood was the leader of the Western Federation of Miners. During an 1899 strike by his union, the miners hijacked a train, loaded it with 3,000 pounds of explosives, took it to the company's mining mill, and blew up the structure. In response, Idaho governor Frank Steunenberg declared the mining region to be "in a state of insurrection" and imposed martial law.[15] Five years later, ex-governor Steunenberg was assassinated when a bomb exploded at his home. Police arrested a miner named Harry Orchard, who confessed. Orchard's confession grew to include other acts of violence that had occurred, and it included Haywood. "Inner Circle's Secrets Told— How Dynamiters Control Federation," the front page of the February 25, 1906, *Portland Oregonian* declared in reporting on Haywood and Orchard's trial. Haywood, however, was acquitted. Orchard, who was sentenced to life in prison, turned out to be a troubled soul who found a place for his problems in the realm of political panic. His real name was Alfred Horsley. Before taking up the cause of the miners, he had left behind him a trail of aliases and police records for fraud, thefts, and bigamy.

Panic over communists spread further in November 1916 when the IWW was again at the center of a violent battle in Everett, Washington. In this instance, the striking workers were not members of the IWW but of a union affiliated with the anti-communist American Federation of Labor (the AFL of the later confederated AFL-CIO). The IWW took the opportunity to send 250 of its members to support the strikers. In response, the local sheriff assembled a posse of 150 men and attacked the IWW members when they arrived, resulting in five deaths and scores of injuries. The elements of panic that this event spread can be seen in a November 8, 1916, editorial in the *Portland Oregonian*. "Something more than the right of free speech is involved in the . . . murderous affray at Everett, Washington last Sunday," it justifiably stated before asserting, "It is the right of a citizen, or anybody, in a free country, to go about his business without molestation from hecklers, or heelers, or hoboes." These statements enter the portal to panic when the verifiable claim—that speech seeking to incite a riot is not protected by the First Amendment—lends credence to the unverifiable claim that the First Amendment guarantees freedom from "hecklers or heelers or hoboes." The editorial then entered the realm of panic when it advocated that which it feared by remarking with approval that the "disorder and lawlessness [was] incited by the I.W.W., and they were finally expelled from the town by the local authorities, aided by citizens." Fearing that the communistic IWW endangered the Constitution, the editorial applauded the violent expulsion of IWW members without the constitutionally mandated due process of law: arrest and trial by a jury of one's peers. While more Americans were then falling prey to such panic, far more would succumb the following year when communists seized control of Russia.

Foreign Fears and Domestic Panic

Panic over the connection between American communists and Russia first surfaced in 1917, when the United States joined England, France, and Russia in fighting Germany and its allies in World War I. Later that year, the communists took over Russia, renamed it the Soviet Union, and withdrew from the war, declaring it to be "Capitalism and Imperialism which have drenched the country in blood in this, most criminal of all wars."[16] IWW leaders in the United States joined their Soviet comrades in opposing the war. "Why be a soldier?" Big Bill Haywood told workers. "Join the I.W.W. and fight on the job for yourself and your class." When Haywood later declared, "It is better to be a traitor to a country than to your class," he was arrested.[17]

Thus began the widening fear, but not initially a panic, as the fear in this instance was based on a verified assertion, at least by Haywood. Less verifiable were claims that led to headlines such as, "55 Indicted on Sedition Charges—Stunning Blow Lands on I.W.W. Activities," in the *Portland Oregonian* on February 9, 1918. Ultimately, over a hundred IWW members were convicted of sedition. Those who were American-born were imprisoned; those who had come as immigrants were deported. When the United States and its allies won the war, the new Soviet Union was plagued by civil war and famine. One might therefore expect that fear over communist subversion would subside. It did not.

Within months of the November 1918 armistice, a nationwide steel strike was described by the publisher of the *Pittsburgh Leader* as "the first blow of the radical labor leaders in the revolution they are seeking."[18] Panic resided in filtering out the fact, reported in the *Philadelphia Inquirer* and elsewhere, that the strike was in danger of collapse precisely because of opposition by many of the workers to undemocratic methods used by communists in the union to declare the strike.[19] The filtering of such facts paved the way for 10,000 "deputies" to be sworn in and assembled in preparation for battle with the presumably revolutionary strikers. Acts of panic soon commenced. Fifty "deputies" rounded up 186 suspected revolutionaries and, as the *Baltimore American* reported on October 8, 1919, "marched them to the public square, forced them to kneel and kiss the American flag. After this, 180 of the men were released and driven out of town." The many ways in which these defenders of democracy did that which they feared need hardly be enumerated. By the time the nationwide steel strike collapsed at year's end, twenty people had been killed and hundreds injured.[20]

During the strike, raids by law enforcement on suspected subversives also commenced on the federal level. Attorney General A. Mitchell Palmer deployed agents of the Justice Department's Bureau of Investigation (soon to be renamed the Federal Bureau of Investigation) to assist local law enforcement and to conduct their own raids on the offices of strike leaders. In addition, the attorney general urged the enactment of laws aimed at making the belief in communism illegal. In June 1919, a bomb exploded outside Palmer's

Washington home. The man who planted the bomb was killed; Palmer, un-injured, emerged with the potency of his warnings greatly enhanced.

Such bombings and attempted bombings of government and industrial leaders had become a frequent occurrence, but for Palmer it was a mile-stone moment. He stepped up to become the preeminent antiradical of his era. "Palmer Declares Russian Workers' Union More Radical and Secretive Than Bolsheviki," the *Duluth News* reported in a November 16, 1919, article on federal raids in which 360 radicals were arrested in a single day. Palmer, however, raided more than radicals. "Seize Books in Cambridge Raid," the *Boston Globe* announced that same month in a report on a federal raid on a company printing books by Soviet leaders Leon Trotsky and Vladimir Lenin.[21]

Though the steel strike collapsed in December, Palmer's raids contin-ued. "3966 Reds Jailed in Nationwide Raids—Crushing Blow Is Dealt Rad-icalism," bannered the front page of Montana's *Billings Gazette* on January 3, 1920. In all, federal agents arrested some 10,000 people feared as being revolutionaries during the month of January, with 4,000 arrested soon after. Palmer intensified his efforts after anti-communism among workers in the steel strike revealed how weak—and then, how further weakened—was the threat; this suggests that panic over communists was valuable to Palmer. That value soon became evident. "Palmer After Presidency, He Admits," the *Chicago Tribune* told readers on February 6, 1920.

On April 30, 1920, the *Tulsa World* reported "Plots against the lives of more than a score of federal and state officials have been discovered by the Department of Justice as a part of radical May Day demonstrations." The department's warning demonstrated the use of a paradox analogous to doing that which one fears. It unsettled Americans by ostensibly reas-suring them with a panic-inducing blank to be filled in. It did so by com-municating to the public in ways that newspapers conveyed, as in this *Tulsa World* article, "State officials marked as 'victims' have been notified by the department." By not naming any of the officials who had been warned, the statement left it to others to imagine who, and how many, public offi-cials faced imminent danger. That such panic-inducing elements emanated from Palmer became evident when the *Tulsa World* article continued, "Mr. Palmer said that . . . he could not disclose the nature of the communist labor party's plans." The article did report, however, "The assassinations and assaults, Mr. Palmer said, were included in the May Day program organized by the communist labor party and other radical elements." No such assaults took place on May Day.

Palmer's quest for the presidency illustrates how crying wolf undermines panic. Shortly after his mass roundup of suspected subversives, the secretary of labor canceled 71 percent of more than 2,000 deportation orders issued by Palmer. At that summer's Democratic convention, Palmer's chances quickly faded. With Palmer's exit from the stage, federal raids ceased for the rest of the era between World War I and World War II. Even as Palmer's fortunes and those of his generation of anti-communists faded, however, the fortunes of the next generation were already on the horizon. "J. Edgar Hoover, special assistant to the Attorney General, said that 'the American Communist party . . . is an integral part of an international conspiracy,'" an Associated Press report had stated during the Palmer raids.[22]

For the rest of the 1920s, alarm over communistic subversion surfaced only in isolated incidents. One such incident illustrated the comparative extent, at this point in time, of the nation's panic over communists and other anti-capitalists and its panic over capitalists. In May 1920, two Italian immigrants who espoused anarchist views, Nicola Sacco and Bartolomeo Vanzetti, were charged with murder in connection with a robbery in South Braintree, Massachusetts. Uncertainties regarding the evidence necessitated a second trial, but ultimately those uncertainties were swept aside when their convictions resulted in death sentences. Many Americans who were panicked over radicals shared views such as those expressed in an October 8, 1925, editorial in Massachusetts's *Lowell Sun*. Commenting on the size of the defense funds raised for the long legal battle, the paper asserted, "If an oil magnate or a steel magnate or some other kind of capitalist were on trial . . . the very people who urge contributions for Sacco and Vanzetti would denounce what they would regard as the use of money to obstruct justice." Being a plausible argument, it lent credence to panic-inducing assertions that followed. The editorial not only employed but highlighted a blank to be filled in when it wrote in regard to the hundreds of thousands of dollars donated, "Where it went is not answered." It then proceeded further into the portal to panic with an unverified claim that it underscored with certitude. "We have no doubt," the editorial concluded, "that one object of the agitation for Sacco and Vanzetti has been the collection of money from radicals and others whose sympathies have been aroused."

Among those alarmed about capitalists, on the other hand, many shared the view expressed in the August 1921 issue of the IWW journal, *Industrial Pioneer*, which declared, "American workers are getting hardened to the prostitution of capitalist courts." Not all, however, were hardened. Ten thousand who feared capitalists were gaining legislative and judicial control gathered in Madison Square Garden in November 1926 to protest the conviction of Sacco and Vanzetti. Twenty thousand assembled in Philadelphia in July 1927. One measure as to which of these contesting panics—fear of capitalists or fear of communists—prevailed at the time is in the outcome. Sacco and Vanzetti were executed on August 23, 1927. Fear of communistic radicals prevailed.

With the onset of the Great Depression in 1929, Americans became even less susceptible to panic over communism as the collapse of the economy presented capitalism with its greatest challenge in the nation's history. The temper of the times was reflected when the March 7, 1930, *Baltimore Sun* reported on protection provided for communist demonstrators: "900 Policeman Aid 150 Radicals' March—Spectators Laugh." As the Depression dragged on, however, fewer laughed at radicals and more joined them.

Those alarmed by the increasingly large, and increasingly open, number of communists sought to add impact to their warnings by connecting them with other panics. "J. Edgar Hoover, director of investigation of the [Justice] department . . . charged the Communist party of America has organized a special committee to incite revolutionary activities among the Negroes," the *Washington Post* reported on June 11, 1930. A March 16, 1935, headline in the *Chicago Defender* announced, "Tennessee Passes Bill to Keep Communist Party Off Ballot—Says 'Too Many Negroes Are Taught to Aspire for

Executive Positions.'" With the economy in shambles, however, the connection did less to fuel panic over communists than panic over African Americans by enabling those in fear of blacks to brand white civil rights advocates as communists. Similarly, it was in this era that Henry Ford, Father Coughlin, and Charles Lindbergh connected their fears of communists to their fears of Jews. That this connection found traction can be seen in a July 29, 1930, article in the *New York Times* reporting on a claim that an unnamed Chicago elementary school principal had asserted that "six or eight Communist sympathizers, children of Jewish origin, were found in the schoolyard with circulars." Here again, however, the effort to connect fear of communists to other fears failed to reignite widespread fear of communism amid the widespread economic debacle.

A new effort that employed an old element of political panic was launched in 1934 when Elizabeth Dilling published *The Red Network*. Her book was a directory of subversives, based on the approach used to conclude that Socrates was a cat: guilt by association. It listed over 1,300 individuals whom Dilling deemed subversive by virtue of their connection to people or organizations she deemed subversive. Its ineffectiveness during the Depression is suggested by the negative reviews it received, while at the same time its prominence can be seen in the *Washington Post* dedicating an editorial to the book headlined, "Wolf! Wolf!" Dilling's book was not totally ineffective, however. A letter to the editor in the June 26, 1934, *Washington Post* criticized the paper's editorial: "Many prominent [people] . . . have given substantial aid to the revolutionary cause. Their names are frequently used by promoters of strikes and riots to gain recruits."

Were anti-communists crying wolf in the years of the Great Depression? Clearly Elizabeth Dilling was when her list of subversives included Eleanor Roosevelt, Albert Einstein, New York mayor Fiorello LaGuardia, future Supreme Court justice Felix Frankfurter, women's suffrage advocate Jane Addams, and birth control advocate Margaret Sanger. Panic likewise was clearly present when, in 1938, a witness before the newly created House Un-American Activities Committee named movie star Shirley Temple, age ten, as subversive.[23] But warning that the ranks of the nation's Communist

Party were swelling was not crying wolf; it was a verified fact. Rallies by communists increasingly drew crowds of thousands.

In response, anti-communist rallies drew commensurately increasing crowds. Four thousand anti-communists gathered in New York in April 1937 at a rally cosponsored by the American Association against Communists and the International Catholic Truth Association—both of which were founded by Edward Lodge Curran, a priest who, like Charles Coughlin, had a radio program on which he broadcast his political alarm. One month later, the May 3 *New York Times* reported, "13,000 Anti-Reds Rally in Brooklyn." By June 7, the *Times* was reporting, "A throng estimated at half of the more than 300,000 residents of Jersey City joined tonight in an 'Americanism' parade and rally designed by the Mayor to show . . . his city is solidly behind him in his fight on what he calls 'the Reds.'"

This crescendo of competing rallies quickly turned into a trickle with the onset of World War II, as the United States now found itself uneasily allied with the Soviet Union in fighting Nazi Germany. Following the war, however, the warnings returned. The Depression, however, did not. Indeed, the United States emerged from the war as the most powerful nation on earth—a mantle that most of its citizens prized highly, feared ever losing, and continue to do so to this day. Only one nation at that time posed a threat to the United States' continuing to be the world's most powerful nation: the Soviet Union.

Postwar Panic

"I have in my hand fifty-seven cases of individuals who would appear to be either card carrying members or certainly loyal to the Communist Party," Senator Joseph McCarthy declared on February 9, 1950.[24] Those fifty-seven unnamed State Department employees were just the tip of the iceberg, he warned, further asserting that the State Department "is thoroughly infested with Communists." Americans' fear of losing their newly acquired military supremacy was so intense at the time that McCarthy's unverified claims ignited his meteoric ascent to becoming the nation's preeminent anti-communist. To this day, the post–World War II Red Scare remains known as the McCarthy Era.

Ironically, Joseph McCarthy was one of the last to gain prominence as an anti-communist, and reigned supreme in that role relatively briefly. In the years leading up to World War II, Congressman Martin Dies had become the nation's leading anti-communist, a position he achieved by creating the long active House Un-American Activities Committee.[25] Dies also preceded McCarthy in alleging communist infiltration of government, and in 1939 *surpassed* McCarthy by dispatching his committee's legislative aides to raid the offices of communists. That same year, however, Americans were leaving the Communist Party in droves, feeling betrayed by the Soviet Union's recent nonaggression pact with Nazi Germany. This pact, moreover, had been preceded by a wave of treason trials in the Soviet Union, whose clearly controlled proceedings followed by massive numbers of executions disenchanted many Americans communists. So widely known was this exodus of members of Americans from the Communist Party that in 1939 the *Washington Post* ran a series of six articles detailing "The Red Collapse."[26] Those who continued to sound alarms that communist subversion represented a danger to the nation now had to rely far more on the elements of panic to fuel their warnings.

After the war, several prominent figures sought the spotlight on this re-erected stage that featured fear of domestic subversion by communists. J. Edgar Hoover, now director of the Federal Bureau of Investigation, declared in January 1947 that the Communist Party in the United States had "power and influence out of proportion to its membership" and advised that "patriotic Americans everywhere purge un-American agents from organizations."[27] Hoover offered no facts to verify his claim, which was governed by a blank to be filled in: "un-American." Syndicated columnist Westbrook Pegler, who had also sounded alarms over communists prior to the war, did provide specifics in a 1948 column headlined, "Harvard Teacher Fellow Traveler." The professor Pegler openly accused of communist ties was Arthur Schlesinger Jr., a Pulitzer Prize–winning historian who would go on to win another Pulitzer and serve in the administration of President John F. Kennedy. What had been called the "Dies Committee," now under the chairmanship of J. Parnell Thomas, also resumed making headlines. "Un-American Committee to Probe Influences in Hollywood," the *Baltimore Sun* reported on January 23, 1947. This investigation would soon send ten filmmakers to prison for refusing to answer the committee's questions.

Filtered out by those in panic over the "Hollywood Ten" was the fact that most had drifted away from the Communist Party, and the fact that only one of the films these men helped make was cited as subversive (*Counter-Attack*). Indeed, during the thirty-plus-year existence of the House Un-American Activities Committee, only six Hollywood films were characterized as subversive, and even these claims entailed panic-inducing filtering. All six—*Mission to Moscow* (1941), *Three Russian Girls* (1943), *The North Star* (1943), *Song of Russia* (1944), *The Boy from Stalingrad* (1943), and *Counter-Attack* (1945)—were made at the urging of the Roosevelt administration, and under the supervision of the Office of War Information, to promote the military alliance between the United States and the Soviet Union during World War II.

Two new verified facts in foreign affairs, however, lent credibility to filtered and unverified claims. In 1949, China came under communist rule. That same year, the Soviet Union detonated its first atomic bomb. Less verifiable claims, aspects of which were sufficiently verifiable to raise suspicion, also lent comparable degrees of credibility to unverified claims and statements that filtered facts. Joe McCarthy's 1950 claim regarding fifty-seven unnamed communists in the State Department was buttressed by a partially verified claim in 1948 when a young congressman named Richard Nixon accused a former State Department official, Alger Hiss, of having been a spy for the Soviet Union. Hiss had assisted at the 1945 Yalta Conference, during which Franklin Roosevelt, Winston Churchill, and Joseph Stalin negotiated the future of Europe after the imminent defeat of Germany. Many Americans felt the agreement was a sell-out, as it relinquished Bulgaria, Romania, Czechoslovakia, Yugoslavia, Albania, Hungary, Poland, and the eastern region of Germany to the Soviet Union's sphere of influence. Nixon based his claim of Hiss's unspecified role in this alleged sell-out on the testimony of Whittaker Chambers, a former communist who claimed he had known Alger Hiss in the 1930s as a fellow member of the party.

Though Hiss denied having ever been a communist or having ever known Chambers, suspicion mounted when Chambers produced microfilm of government documents he claimed Hiss had given him.[28] Many Americans now believed Alger Hiss had been a Soviet spy. Unknown by the public was that Whittaker Chambers was a deeply troubled man. A closeted homosexual, Chambers stated that when he first read the writings of Lenin he saw in its analysis of capitalism's failures the failures of his parents and the family from which he came. As Chambers's biographer, Sam Tanenhaus, aptly put it, "He had at last found his church."[29] Also unknown by the public—indeed, kept classified for decades—was that the allegedly incriminating microfilm contained no secret information of any sort. Congressman Nixon's role in this panic-inducing charade catapulted him to the Senate in the 1950 election, during which he told Californians that if his opponent, Congresswoman Helen Gahagan Douglas, was elected, "the Communist *Daily Worker* will have one of its heroes in the body of Congress which passes on the national foreign policy."[30]

The arrest of verified spies in a ring that included accusations against some whose participation was less verified followed closely on the heels of the suspicion that Alger Hiss was a communist spy. Among the less verified was the purported head of the ring, Julius Rosenberg, who was charged with passing secret information to the Soviet Union that was essential to their recent success in creating an atomic bomb. Rosenberg's wife, Ethel, was also arrested for typing the information Julius was accused of giving the Soviets, information that came from members of the ring who were employed at the Los Alamos nuclear research facility in New Mexico.

Despite considerable uncertainties at the time as to Julius and Ethel Rosenberg's participation, verified claims lent credibility to less verified claims. Evidence regarding accused ring member Klaus Fuchs, a German physicist, was verifiably true. In addition, accused ring member David Greenglass confessed. As when Harry Orchard's 1906 confession grew to include Big Bill Haywood, uncertainties arose as to the extent of the truth in Greenglass's confession as it grew to include his sister and brother-in-law: Ethel and Julius Rosenberg. And as in the 1886 Haymarket bombing trial, those uncertainties were swept aside when both Julius Rosenberg and his wife were convicted and executed, leaving their two young sons orphans. Under the law, capital punishment is not to be imposed so long as there is uncertainty—the proverbial "shadow of a doubt." This maxim, however, does not apply in terms of political panic nor, it should be noted, does uncertainty necessarily mean falsehood. In this instance, suspicions regarding the Rosenberg's participation were validated decades later when their names appeared in classified Soviet documents from that era that were made public after the collapse of Russia's communist regime.[31]

In this atmosphere, the government increased its participation in the panic when it enacted the 1950 McCarran Act, which required communist organizations to register with the Justice Department and authorized the president to approve the detention of anyone the government suspected "will engage in, or probably will conspire with others to engage in, acts of espionage or sabotage."[32] Seeking to prevent subversion of American principles, the bill subverted the constitutional principle of due process of law. President Truman vetoed it. So widespread was the panic, however, that Congress overrode his veto with a three-fifths majority.

That same year, syndicated columnist Ed Sullivan, soon to become host of one of television's most successful shows, wrote, "A bombshell will be dropped in the offices of radio-TV networks, advertising agencies, and sponsors this week with the publication of 'Red Channels.'"[33] This book, following in the footsteps of Elizabeth Dilling's 1934 The Red Network, listed over 150 people in film and television deemed to be subversive. In the atmosphere of the 1950s, Red Channels proved far more effective than Dilling's Depression-era book. As with Dilling's book, Red Channels was predicated on guilt by association. The handful of verified communists in the entertainment industry listed in the book lent credibility to the far larger list of unverified subversives such as Leonard Bernstein (composer whose works include On the Town and West Side Story), Dashiell Hammett (novelist whose works include The Maltese Falcon and The Thin Man), Judy Holliday (noted for starring in the film comedies *Born Yesterday* and *The Solid Gold Cadillac*), Orson Welles (noted for the films *Citizen Kane* and *The Magnificent Ambersons*), and Gypsy Rose Lee (noted striptease dancer, later celebrated in the musical *Gypsy*). An overarching filtered fact functioned as the second fundamental element of panic in *Red Channels.* In its introduction, its anonymous authors asked, "Can you conceive of anyone more potent when an emergency strikes than the man at the mike—the network mike?"[34] Filtered from this warning was the fact that actors, directors, movie producers, screenwriters, composers, and striptease artists would not be the person at the mike broadcasting vital information in the event of a national emergency. But in the early 1950s, panic was so widespread that Ed Sullivan accurately predicted in his newspaper column that "'Red Channels' listing of performers who . . . are affiliated with Commie-front organizations will be a reference book in preparing any program." As he noted, "Sponsors, sensitive in the extreme . . . want no part of Commies or their sympathizers."[35] Following publication of the book, more than 300 Americans who worked in radio, television, and film were blacklisted.

Sullivan's column also revealed an additional element symptomatic of political panic. Referring to the man who was later revealed to be the (or one of the) anonymous contributors to *Red Channels,* former FBI agent Theodore C. Kirkpatrick, Sullivan wrote, "Kirkpatrick has sat in my living room on several occasions and listened attentively to performers [who had been associated with organizations listed in *Red Channels*] eager to secure a certification of loyalty. On some occasions, after interviewing them, he has given them the green light; on other occasions he has told them, 'Veterans organizations will insist on further proof.'" Such proof of the sincerity of one's loyalty entailed naming others the accused knew to be or had been connected with organizations listed in *Red Channels.* This procedure mirrored the Salem witch hunt, where only by confessing the names of others involved in sorcery could the accused be absolved. Not only was the accused redeemed by naming others in one's confession, the accuser's credibility was also enhanced by virtue of the confession. Such enhanced credibility then lent added weight to other unverified claims on the part of the accuser.

In *Red Channels,* as in much of this wave of panic over communists, unverified claims and blanks to be filled in ran rampant. *Red Channels,* for example, asserted, "Those who know radio can recite dozens of examples of anti-Communists who, for mysterious reasons, are *persona non grata* on numerous programs." Unnamed were any of the "dozens of examples of anti-Communists" who, by virtue of their anti-communism, had experienced blacklisting. In then going on to state, "Communists and Communist sympathizers have no place on our air," *Red Channels* urged that which it decried: blacklisting.

As with the wartime films (for which the Hollywood Ten became the first to be blacklisted) that were made in cooperation with U.S. government policy, Hollywood did likewise with postwar films that promoted the government's anti-communist foreign policy—and cashed in on the public's panic over domestic subversion by communists. These years saw the release of *The Red Menace* (1949), *I Married a Communist* (1949), *Walk a Crooked Mile* (1949), *I Was a Communist for the FBI* (1951), *Atomic City* (1952), *Big Jim McLean* (1952), *The Steel Fist* (1952), *Walk East on Beacon Street* (1952), and *My Son John* (1953). By 1953, however, 43 percent of American homes had acquired a television set. Television now also functioned as a medium of persuasion, and its producers patriotically joined in—and economically cashed in, as well. One of the first panic-inducing television programs was lent credence by being based on a best-selling nonfiction book, *I Led 3 Lives: Citizen, Communist, Counterspy.* From 1953 to 1956, actor Richard Carlson portrayed the book's author, Herbert A. Philbrick, in episodes that took viewers into its depictions of secret communist cells.

While both television and film remain persuasive media, the more recent profusion of television networks made possible by the development of cable and satellite broadcasts has enabled its blades of persuasion to be sharpened by networks dedicated to particular points of view. But another difference between television in the 1950s and today is that, with the blacklist no longer in place, panic-inducing programming such as that currently featured on the Fox News network is countered by programming on other networks that undermines panic, such as *The Daily Show with Jon Stewart* and *The Colbert Report,* neither of which could have aired during the era of the blacklist.

The Decline of the Panic

As actual events increasingly pertained to communist nations rather than domestic communist subversion, the panic over American communists began to decline. An influential model for making this distinction was President John F. Kennedy. In 1962, he risked war to force the Soviet Union to remove its nuclear missiles from Cuba. But Kennedy was so little concerned about domestic communist subversion—and so little concerned about the number of voters still panicked about such subversion—that he attended the 1961 film *Spartacus,* despite American Legion picketers protesting that its screenwriter, Dalton Trumbo, had been a member of the Communist Party. When it premiered, *Spartacus* was much more than a big-budget spectacle featuring superstars Kirk Douglas and Laurence Olivier confronting one another in an epic slave rebellion set in ancient Rome. As notably at the time, it was the first film to break the Hollywood blacklist by openly crediting Dalton Trumbo as its screenwriter.

This decrease in panic might, at first, seem to be at odds with the way in which foreign policy conflicts can fuel domestic panic. During the years following Kennedy's attendance at *Spartacus,* not only did the nation sense danger in the Cuban missile crisis, but also in the 1961 erection of the Berlin Wall, China's tyrannical Cultural Revolution, and communist inroads into Vietnam, Laos, Cambodia, and Nicaragua. The virtual absence of panic over American communists, however, was not contradictory; it reflected the virtual absence by then of American communists—though a new wave of communistic radicals would soon organize.

Anti-communist alarms also resumed—and also seemingly contradictorily—following the fall of the Soviet Union in 1991. Fox News commentator Bill O'Reilly asserted in 2007 that government regulations "bring corporations under stakeholders' control, not just stockholder control . . . [and are] another top ten hit from the socialism playlist," echoing

Edward F. Browne's 1906 statements regarding government regulation of business being socialism.[36] Journalist Aaron Klein wrote of President Barack Obama's "ties to communists, socialist, Marxists . . . and former 1960s radicals," echoing the 1840 warning that President Van Buren was in league with communists.[37] In 2012, Congressman Allen West declared that in the House of Representatives "there's about seventy-eight to eighty-one members of the Democratic Party that are members of the Communist Party," echoing Joe McCarthy's 1950 warning of communist infiltration of government.[38] All these warnings mirror the timing of Attorney General A. Mitchell Palmer in 1920, when the Soviet Union was prostrate with civil war, American communists were prostrate from their failure in the 1919 steel strike, and the primary purpose of Palmer's alarms was the advancement of his career.

Eight

"CORPORATIONS HAVE BEEN ENTHRONED ... and the money power of the country will endeavor to prolong its reign ... until all the wealth is aggregated in a few hands and the Republic is destroyed."

—Abraham Lincoln, letter to William Elkin, November 21, 1864.[1]

At first glance, panic over capitalists might appear to be the sibling of the panic over communists in a dysfunctional national family, but the two are only distantly related. Their relationship, moreover, is not that they emanate from opposite fears, but rather from the same fear: tyranny. Americans who feared capitalists predated those who feared communists by nearly a century. And where fear of communists has all but evaporated, widespread fear of capitalists continues to this day.

American fear of capitalists predates the creation of the United States and, to a considerable extent, accounts for it. Complaining of the political influence of the British East India Company, an October 21, 1773, letter to the editor of the *New York Journal* declared, "If the East India Company can once establish a monopoly in this country in the article of tea, they may do it with equal facility in every other article of their trade. . . . Our posterity [will be] subjected to a state of vassalage." Two months later in Boston, protesters boarded three ships laden with East India Company tea and jettisoned the cargo—an event commemorated in American history as the Boston Tea Party and a prelude to the American Revolution.

The first corporations in the young United States were not capitalist enterprises but rather educational and religious institutions that, having constitutionally protected status, were granted the ability to incorporate. Fears arose, however, when Congress approved Alexander Hamilton's proposal to create a capitalistic corporation, the Bank of the United States. Thomas Jefferson wrote to President Washington on September 9, 1792, that Hamilton's "system flowed from principles adverse to liberty, and was calculated to undermine and demolish the Republic." Urging the nation's first president to veto the bill, Jefferson continued, "I saw this influence by the votes of the very persons who, having swallowed his bait, were laying themselves out to profit by his plans."[2] Though Jefferson failed to persuade President Washington, indeed shortly after the creation of the Bank of the United States speculators sought to profit by buying and selling its shares. In 1792, two speculators secretly joined forces in an effort to corner the market on the bank's shares. In so doing, the price of the shares rose, but reached a tipping point as it was increasingly perceived to be beyond its worth, then plummeted. As a result, lending by banks froze, and the fledgling nation's economy came to a standstill. In terms of political panic, two blanks to be filled in triggered panic over corporations—blanks that continue to fuel such panic even now: the mysteriousness of economics for many Americans (this author included), and the secrecy that often attends speculation in securities.

Fear and distrust soon spread beyond the incorporation of a federal bank as incorporation spread into the other realms. In 1834, prominent orator and abolitionist Paul Brown wrote in *The Radical,* "We shall find in every state enactment . . . [of] banking companies, manufacturing companies, trading companies, land companies, bridge companies, road companies, canal companies, etc. . . . What manner of government is that? . . . It is sheer aristocracy." One reason Congress allowed capitalists to form corporations to build and operate interstate canals, bridges, and roadways was the Constitution prohibits Congress from doing so for purposes other than military and postal transportation.

Soon, however, Congress allowed capitalists to incorporate in an endeavor the Founding Fathers had not foreseen: railroads. So vital were railroads to the nation's economy that the relationship between their corporate leaders and the nation's political leaders became one that remains familiar, and feared, to this day. When President Franklin Pierce authorized James Gadsden, a railroad president, to purchase land from Mexico to enable a railroad to be built through present-day New Mexico and Arizona, the *New York Herald* called it "that magnificent railroad swindle."[3] Today we call it the Gadsden Purchase. But a dual view of these mighty corporations commenced with the onset of the Civil War, a dual view that has recurred during times of war. The *Cleveland Herald* wrote on August 1, 1862, "The railroad companies, in this crisis, have it in their power to become the most mighty of all instruments in the putting down of this rebellion." Still, wartime pride in the nation's manufacturing muscle did not supplant the fear of corporations.

Lincoln's forebodings, cited in this chapter's title, that "corporations have been enthroned" likewise occurred during the war. Events soon after the Civil War proved Lincoln's fears were not without foundation. "Under a law passed last winter," the *Cleveland Herald* reported on May 1, 1867, Ohio granted "railroad policemen jurisdiction in every county in the state through which the road extends." Such laws led labor activist Horace H. Day to declare two years later, "A consolidation of [rail] roads exists . . . in the hands of a few capitalists whose influence controls a certain radius of country each side of said roads, thus . . . belting the country with iron bands."[4]

As railroads and, in their tracks, other corporations grew increasingly large, so too did the nation's alarm. But alarm itself is not necessarily panic. It was a verifiable fact, for example, that entire communities were being created and owned by private corporations that often required their workers to live in their housing and shop in their stores using company-issued currency

called scrip. In some cases, the companies endowed these towns with libraries, schools, and churches, though not always for altruistic reasons. "Where
does the church stand on the . . . company town?" asked an article in the
September 5, 1914, issue of *The Survey,* a social service journal. "If it accepts
the subsidy of the company it must pay with loss of liberty of speech. . . .
If it stands by the workers, its lease will not be renewed."[5] But the ultimate
element of control provided by company towns was the threat that, if the
workers went on strike, they and their families would be summarily evicted
from their homes. "From thirty to forty families, tenants of the Carnegie
company's houses . . . were evicted by the sheriff and his deputies," the *Harrisburg Patriot* reported on August 1, 1892. "The sight of a long line of wag-
ons filled with household goods passing down Eighth Avenue in the driving
rain brought out many expressions of condemnation from spectators on the
street." This particular, but not unusual, sight occurred at the Homestead
plant of Carnegie Steel Company, the strike in which Alexander Berkman
attempted to assassinate Henry Clay Frick. While Berkman's act fueled fears
of anti-capitalist radicals, for the tens of thousands who dwelled in the communities built and owned by capitalist corporations, the enthronement of
corporations that Lincoln feared was now a fact.

Less than a decade after Lincoln sounded his alarm regarding the future
of corporations, a *San Francisco Bulletin* editorial rephrased it in the present tense. "The plutocrat of modern times . . . sits in his back office, bereft
of human sympathy," it declared in a January 7, 1873, editorial. "When he
locks up money he does not see the individual ruin which he creates, nor
does he care for it." Panic resided in the use of an absolute, "bereft of human
sympathy"; a blank to be filled in, "plutocrat," which left it to readers to
determine which businessmen are or are not plutocrats; and in filtering out
any "plutocrats" who do care about the well-being of their workers. Two such
men were chocolate magnate Milton S. Hershey and lumber baron Frank
R. Gilchrist, both of whom built company towns and offered them to their
workers as *options* for living, not requirements. The town Hershey built in
central Pennsylvania included a department store operated as a cooperative
owned by the workers and also an amusement park of considerable size for

the children. Hershey Park continues to operate to this day as an attraction open to the general public.

The Panic Turns Violent

Hershey and Gilchrist were at one extreme end of capitalists who constructed company towns. Striking miners in Ludlow, Colorado, faced capitalists at the opposite extreme. After being evicted from company homes, they set up a tent community to which the mining company responded by extending itself beyond the realm of law enforcement and into the military realm of declaring war with a privately hired army. "Machine Gun Mows Down Strikers in Pitched Battle at Forbes Mining Camp," headlined Colorado Springs's *Gazette* on October 18, 1913. Only the arrival of U.S. Army troops, dispatched by President Wilson to disarm both sides, brought an end to the bloodshed. By then, over seventy men, women, and children had died.

In the run-up to this episode, panic over capitalists was stoked by imprecations from an unlikely looking activist, Mary Harris "Mother" Jones, a grandmotherly figure who, in a grandmotherly way, imparted ungrandmotherly maxims such as "A 'lady' is the parasitical outgrowth of the system we live under."[6] During the mining strike in Colorado, Mother Jones traveled to Ludlow to address the miners but was prevented from doing so by being arrested and jailed en route on trumped up charges. Nevertheless her message arrived simply by virtue of her attempt to arrive. Moreover, by preventing her from speaking, the authorities rendered her message a blank to be filled in. Those alarmed over corporations likely filled it in with knowledge or lore of her earlier declarations, such as "The power is not in the government, but in Wall Street. The president who is elected is named two years before election by the banks on Wall Street. The press is controlled by that power and it molds public opinion."[7] While one hesitates to criticize a grandmother, and even with all the verifiable wrongdoing by corporations in her day, such remarks were draped with panic-inducing elements. Her claim that the president is selected by Wall Street two years before each election was an unverified claim predicated on secrecy. Likewise, her use of the term "Wall Street" functioned as a blank to be filled in, not unlike those dating to panic over witches in Salem, as it left it to her listeners to decide which corporations constituted this secret coven of capitalists. Panic further draped this remark by filtering out the fact that President Wilson sought, and ultimately succeeded, in having an amendment added to the Constitution that created a permanent income tax, thereby fundamentally changing the nation's economic landscape through this massive redistribution of wealth. Wilson also oversaw the passage of laws requiring railroads to implement labor's long-sought eight-hour day. While Rockefeller's Standard Oil Company had just been revealed to have pumped hundreds of thousands of dollars into electing their preferred presidential candidates, clearly Woodrow Wilson was not their preference.[8] Jones's claim that the press was controlled by the same coterie of capitalists that secretly selected the president filtered out the fact that many newspapers not only were supportive of labor's struggles but also supportive of Mother Jones. The *Duluth Tribune* declared in an editorial on March 30, 1914, "It is hard to believe that there is any condition that justifies or warrants the arrest and imprisonment of 'Mother' Jones. . . . She carries no weapons but her brain and her tongue."

Panic in the Farm Fields

Fear of corporate oligarchy was not limited to Americans in industrialized regions. As early as 1869, an Iowa farmer wrote, "The bondholders are eating out the sustenance of all our common little Western farmers . . . worse than leeches on blood, grasshoppers on grain, or locusts in scriptural days . . . under the present sectional laws and money-bought laws."[9] While vehement, the only hint of panic was the unverified claim that bribery was involved in passing laws that enabled predatory land speculation (though other verified instances involving money and legislation lent credence to the claim). By comparison, Southern Farm Alliance leader Harry Tracy did enter the portal to panic when he referred to corporations as "a monied aristocracy more potent than that of any monarchy," a statement that filtered out monarchies still ruling at the time in Spain, Japan, and the Middle East that exerted far more control of their people than any American corporation.[10]

A spate of books now appeared bearing titles such as *The American Plutocracy* (1895), *The New Plutocracy* (1903), *The Railroad a Public Servant* (1908), and *The People's Law* (1914). This last book was authored by William Jennings Bryan, the era's most widely known voice of warning that large corporations endangered democracy. Believing banks and corporate trusts maintained a tyranny over farmers, laborers, and small businesses by their influence in the government's use of gold to secure the value of the nation's money, Bryan and his supporters sought a switch to more plentiful silver. Organizers of an 1896 "Free Silver" rally in Washington, D.C., anticipated a turnout of under a thousand but had to make last-minute adjustments to cope with far larger numbers converging on the event. Similar rallies sprung up throughout the nation. At one such gathering, Bryan declared, "We have to choose between throwing overboard those who have been millstones about the necks of democracy and throwing overboard democracy itself."[11] His invocation to action employed a not-yet-seen form of absolute—one might call it a bifurcated absolute—in the either/or choice that governed his statement. Additionally, Bryan used a blank to be filled in as to what constituted "throwing overboard." To this day, numerous Americans echo the views expressed by William Jennings Bryan and Mother Jones that corporate power has trumped American democracy. In an effort to explain the Occupy Movement that began in 2011 with an encampment on Wall Street and then spread to cities nationwide, Kalle Lasn and Micah White wrote of "the pervasive corruption at the heart of our political system, in which corporate money wins elections, drafts laws, and trumps citizen desires."[12]

In Bryan's era, fear of capitalists was so widespread that the Democratic Party nominated him for president three times. In his quest for the White House, Bryan coined this panic's most famous phrase. "Having behind us the commercial interests and the laboring interests and all the toiling masses," he told delegates to the 1896 Democratic convention, "we shall answer their demands for a gold standard by saying to them, you shall not

press down upon the brow of labor this crown of thorns. You shall not cru-
cify mankind upon a cross of gold."[13] Bryan's now legendary reference to the
"cross of gold" demonstrates that not all metaphors are blanks to be filled in,
as the meaning of Bryan's metaphor is crystal clear.

Peak of the Panic

Panic over capitalist corporations crested in the era that spanned the late
nineteenth-century labor violence and the Great Depression in the 1930s.
In the earliest of these years, one of its preeminent voices was a man little remembered today, Johann Most. A German immigrant who had periodically
been imprisoned in his homeland for his revolutionary views, Most arrived
in the United States in 1882 and quickly became both a leading voice in the
panic over capitalists and a lightning rod for those voicing panic over communists and other anti-capitalists. "Hang Most Too" headlined an August
23, 1886, *Milwaukee Journal* editorial on the sentencing of the alleged Haymarket bombers. Its view was based on the belief that speeches by Johann
Most had inflamed the violence. Most did employ panic-inducing words,
as when, in his 1903 book *The Social Monster,* he declared, "The power of a
privileged class has never yet been broken by peaceable means." The statement was predicated by an absolute ("never") that filtered out such events as
the 1890 Sherman Anti-Trust Law or the history of England.

In the footsteps of Johann Most came others, such as "Big Bill" Haywood, whose anti-capitalist alarms also, as previously seen, triggered panic
over communists. In a 1911 coauthored book, *Industrial Socialism,* Haywood spread panic not only through its now increasingly familiar rhetori-
cal elements, but also, and most significantly, by advocating that which he
feared. "The industrial oligarchs are now attempting to destroy freedom of
speech and of the press," the book stated, going on to detail this fear by asserting, "Professors in the universities and colleges and teachers in the public
schools do not attempt to tell the truth about government. . . . Clergymen
and priests do not dare preach the truth about the working class." But the
political system the book went on to propose would do that which Haywood

feared. "College professors, preachers, authors, and business men," the book stated, "must take the working class point of view before they can understand Socialism."

Panic-inducing alarms, such as those sounded by Big Bill Haywood and Johann Most, contributed in some degree to a lengthy epidemic of bombings aimed at capitalists and those perceived as government warriors for capitalists. In addition to the 1886 bombing at Haymarket and the 1919 bombing at the home of Attorney General Palmer, other targets included John D. Rockefeller, J. P. Morgan Jr., Secretary of Labor Will B. Wilson, Supreme Court justice Oliver Wendell Holmes, Mississippi governor Theodore Bilbo, Pennsylvania governor William Sproul, and New York mayor John F. Hyland. A bomb exploded on Wall Street in September 1920, killing thirty-six pedestrians and injuring more than 140 others.

The most widespread alarm over capitalist corporations resulted less from fear that they endangered the nation's democracy than from fear that they endangered the nation's economy. The collapse of the stock market in October 1929 and the Great Depression that followed drove multitudes of Americans in the direction of, and many into, the Communist Party. In 1932, party leader William Z. Foster wrote in *Toward Soviet America,* "The present government of the United States . . . is dominated by the Morgans, Mellons, and other big bankers and industrialists. . . . All the current talk about democracy are only so many screens to hide the capitalist autocracy."

As seen with other alarmists, Foster commenced with claims that were sufficiently verifiable as to lend credence to later unverified claims when he first asserted, "The capitalist industrial system is paralyzed as never before. Tremendous masses of workers are thrown into unemployment and destitution." When he then warned that "capitalists everywhere are increasingly developing their dictatorship from its masked form . . . into open systems of fascist terrorism," his unverified claim was nevertheless supportable by the fact that Germany and Italy had become such dictatorships. Foster then led readers into the portal to panic with the use of absolutes when he continued, "*Every* piece of legislation, *every* strike, *every* demonstration of the unemployed illustrates . . . [that] the American government is as much the property of the capitalists as their mills, mines, factories, and land." (Italics added.)

Once within the portal, Foster coaxed readers to cross into the realm of panic by asserting that which he feared. Attacking traditional labor unions, he evoked the fear that "union leaders have developed their movement into an organ of the bosses for the fascist repression . . . of the working class. They have practically grafted . . . unions on the capitalist state." But Foster later advocated that which he professed to fear when he wrote that, under communism, "the trade unions play a fundamental role. . . . Their representatives occupy key positions in every stage of the economic, political, and social organization." Elsewhere in the book, he wrote, "When workers have struck against actual starvation conditions, they have to face troops, as well as armies of police, gunmen, etc.," then later declared, "In order to defeat the class enemies of the revolution . . . the proletarian dictatorship must be supported by the organized armed might of the workers, soldiers, local militia, etc." Most dramatically, he expressed fear not over that which he later advocated but that which he earlier had done. "Union elections are a farce," he told his readers. "Conventions are packed with administrative henchmen." He filtered out the fact that the 1919 steel strike, which Foster had led, collapsed largely because the strike vote meetings had not included all the workers and had been packed with Foster's allies.

Still, because so much of what Foster said of capitalist corporations was verifiably true in 1932, Communist Party rallies routinely attracted crowds of 10,000 to over 23,000. In a single day in 1931, communist rallies were held in New York, Chicago, Washington, Boston, Hartford, Baltimore, St. Paul, Kansas City, Austin, Dallas, Oklahoma City, Los Angeles, San Francisco, Oakland, Sacramento, and Seattle. In the 1932 presidential election, over 12,000 voters in Illinois cast their ballots for William Z. Foster.

Alongside the rise of the Communist Party in the United States, the Socialist Party also grew in numbers. In the same 1932 presidential election, its candidate, Norman Thomas, received nearly 900,000 votes. What is notable about the alarms sounded by the nation's socialists is that, in comparison to those of communists, they relied far less on panic-inducing elements. The

1928 Socialist Party Platform declared, "The Republican and Democratic parties . . . belong to the landlords, bankers, oil speculators, coal and power barons—in short, to the capitalist class which finances them . . . [and] makes our alleged democracy largely an illusion." The governing adjective in the statement, "largely," was explicitly *not* an absolute. The platform then proceeded to advocate the enactment by Congress of socialist remedies that included nationalization of coal mines, electrical utilities, and railroads, along with the creation of federally funded unemployment insurance, old age pensions, health insurance, flood control, and natural disaster relief. The degree to which the Socialist Party advocated acts that weakened the Constitution out of fear that capitalists threatened the Constitution can be approximated by speculating as to which of these programs might have been ruled unconstitutional—if one assumes Supreme Court rulings are an accurate gauge.

With America's entry into World War II, two key elements contributed to a decline in the panic over capitalist corporations. Economically, the war ended the Great Depression by virtue of its tremendous need for manpower and production in defense industries. Politically, pride in the nation's industrial muscle offset fear of industrial corporations, just as it had among northerners during the Civil War. Less than a month after Pearl Harbor, an Associated Press report declared, "The economic might of America begins a new year swiftly forming itself into a modern military phalanx of puissance to span oceans, envelop continents, and strike with a cyclonic force never before made by man."[14]

Also as during the Civil War, pride in the nation's corporate muscle did not supplant fears of corporate power. "[Franklin] Roosevelt started out the great champion of the underdog. All the big companies feared him, hated him, fought him," syndicated columnist Drew Pearson wrote on January 25, 1943. "Then came the war, and they moved back like homing pigeons. They had the big lobbies in Washington already organized . . . and pretty soon the country woke to find that during the first defense period, one-third of all the orders went to exactly six companies."[15]

With the Cold War that followed World War II, the equation that offset pride and fear regarding the nation's corporations continued. But with the

Cold War's resurgence of the anti-communist panic, voicing fears of capitalist corporations risked being branded a communist. These elements are all present in the 1946 film *It's a Wonderful Life.* The character of banker Henry Potter evoked the fear that unfettered capitalists threatened the nation, as depicted in a nightmarish vision of the film's homespun town of Bedford Falls having become Pottersville, in which shops such as the beloved pharmacy where children enjoyed ice cream are now saloons and striptease joints. Voicing fear of capitalists, the film's hero, George Bailey, says of Potter, "He's already got charge of the bank. He's got the bus line. He's got the department stores." Evoking the oligarchy of company towns, the speech to his neighbors went on to say, "Joe, you had one of those Potter houses, didn't you? Well, have you forgotten? Have you forgotten what he charged for that broken-down shack?" Pride in the nation's corporately produced military might was presented hand-in-hand with pride in collective action when George Bailey's brother, a Medal of Honor–winning army pilot, arrives despite a blizzard to join the townspeople in contributing cash to save the Bailey's Building and Loan from being acquired by Potter's bank. But such collective action against capitalist domination was camouflaged in a distinction (mysterious to most viewers) between a bank and a building and loan. Even the risk of being branded a communist was present with this film, as it was later revealed that the FBI had secretly noted it as purveying communist propaganda.[16]

During the resurgence of anti-communist panic that followed World War II, alarm over corporations more typically morphed into alarm that capitalist corporations were a threat to American individualism, as opposed to democracy. In 1955, Sloan Wilson published *The Man in the Grey Flannel Suit,* a novel depicting this danger. The word choices of *New York Times* reviewer John McNulty stand out in his stating that the novel "succeeds in imparting the panicky quality of the lives of so many of the commuters in gray flannel who battle daily . . . in Madison Avenue and Rockefeller Center, then go home to Connecticut."[17] Soon after, William H. Whyte, Jr. published *The Organization Man.*[18] Also a best seller, it was a nonfiction work regarding individual values versus those to which one must subscribe as part of a corporation. "This is a chiller. A diagnosis of our cancerous society," Ohio's *Hamilton Journal-News* wrote on November 7, 1957. "This is a contagious malignant disease sought after by those who stand on the shoulders of the workers, and pull at the coattails of the leaders." In this instance, the use of metaphors ("contagious malignant disease," "stand on the shoulders," "pull at the coattails") functioned to camouflage their serving as blanks to be filled in.

The Organization Man and *The Man in the Gray Flannel Suit* emanate from both a political fear regarding corporations and from a spiritual fear regarding wealth and happiness. In the United States, the spiritual fear was voiced in terms of capitalists as far back as 1897 in Edward Arlington Robinson's poem, "Richard Cory"—more widely recognized today in Simon and Garfunkle's 1966 relyricized song by the same name. Both versions tell of the title character, his town's wealthiest and most powerful resident, committing suicide—thereby conveying the fear that the cost of such wealth and power is spiritual bankruptcy. In "Richard Cory" the spiritual conflict is a cautionary tale for individuals, but *The Organization Man* and *The Man in the Gray Flannel Suit* warn that such vast segments of the population face that spiritual risk from corporations that it endangers the nation itself.

Both the phrases "man in the gray flannel suit" and "organization man" went on to become part of the American lexicon, conveying to future generations the enduring fear of capitalist corporations. Among many subsequent references, both terms surfaced in an April 7, 2003, *Chicago Herald* column that said, "The boomers rebelled against their parents, their government, 'The Man in the Gray Flannel Suit' and 'The Organization Man.'"

Resurgence of the Panic

Fear that corporations endangered the United States reignited during the Vietnam War, due in no small part to an alarm that had been sounded by a former army general so influential he had gone on to become the nation's thirty-fourth president. Dwight D. Eisenhower, in his 1961 Farewell

Address, warned, "We must guard against the acquisition of unwarranted influence, whether sought or unsought, by the military-industrial complex. The potential for the disastrous rise of misplaced power exists and will persist. We must never let the weight of this combination endanger our liberties or democratic processes."[19] As the opposition to the Vietnam War grew, the phrase gained currency. For example, after noting it had become "common parlance to complain that Vietnam is tearing the country apart," a 1967 article in *The Antioch Review* declared, "More basic is the problem of our military-industrial complex."[20] Though in this instance the phrase functioned as a panic-inducing blank to be filled in, students at the University of Wisconsin were filling it with the verifiable fact that the military-industrial complex included the Dow Chemical Company. Dow manufactured napalm (a gelatinous incendiary that inflicts devastating, often lethal, burns), which American forces were using in Vietnam. Its product also inflicted the first outbreak of antiwar violence specifically resulting from alarm over the military-industrial complex. On October 18, 1967, police clubbed some 200 University of Wisconsin students to disperse their sit-in against the presence of Dow recruiters on campus. As with violence in early labor struggles, witnesses maintained that the police initiated the violence, in this instance by sweeping through the building from all directions, ostensibly to clear it of protesters but blocking every exit for escape. While the police appear to have acted with far more vehemence than necessary, neither they nor the protesters can be shown to have acted in panic. Not only was it a verified fact that Dow produced napalm, it was also a verified fact that the students were blocking access to the recruiters. These facts, however, would go on to lend credence to less verified claims on the part of those panicked over capitalists and those panicked over antiwar protesters.

Violence emanating from panic soon escalated. In 1970, capitalist corporations were the target of violence when a bomb exploded on July 27 in the entrance to the Wall Street headquarters of Bank of America. Minutes later, the militant antiwar group known as the Weathermen declared they had detonated the device, validating the claim by revealing knowledge of a communist Viet Cong flag left at the scene. In this instance, the Viet Cong flag, in and of itself, functioned as a blank to be filled in, leaving it to others to determine how, and the extent to which, the Bank of America was responsible for the war in Vietnam.

Panic expressed explicitly followed one month later when, again at the University of Wisconsin, a vehicle packed with explosives destroyed Sterling Hall in the early morning hours of August 24, killing a postdoctoral physicist working late at night. In addition to the physics department, the building housed the Army Mathematics Research Center, a think tank that earned profits for the university by providing the army with mathematical solutions to military objectives. While a number of University of Wisconsin students were alarmed by the presence of this institution on campus, the point at which those whose alarm entered the realm of panic was expressed by the bombers, who styled themselves the "New Year's Gang." The group issued a statement in the immediate aftermath of the bombing that declared the Army Math Research Center "bears full responsibility for amerikan military genocide throughout the world."[21] No instances were cited of the United States military currently undertaking the extinction of an entire group of people. The extent to which the members of the "New Year's Gang" were panicked over corporations surfaces when their statement continued, "We see our achievement as more than just the destruction of one building. We see it as part of a worldwide struggle to defeat amerikan imperialism, that monster which is responsible for the starvation and oppression of millions over the globe, that monster which is a direct outgrowth of corporate capitalism." In addition to unverified claims, a different form of blank to be filled in is "amerikan," a term frequently employed by left-wing radicals in this era. The term left it to readers to define its precise meaning, while at the same time suggesting a diminishment of America's stature by replacing the capital "A" with a lowercase "a." Subtextually, replacing the "c" with a "k," a letter that replicates the sound of a hard "c" but not that of a soft "c," suggested a hardening of the nation's soul. Visually, this switch to "k" also enabled the use of a letter that can be seen as a figure standing ramrod straight with one leg forward and an arm thrust upward, not unlike a Nazi salute. To those who remained panicked over Germans, America is spelled "Amerika" in German. As blanks to be filled in go, it is among the more creative.

More recently, violence spinning out of panic over capitalist corporations was seen in 1999 during a World Trade Organization (WTO) conference in Seattle. Protesters gathered to sound their alarm that WTO efforts to expand trade with impoverished nations put, in the words of the *Chicago Herald* coverage on December 1, 1999, "profits for multinational corporations over other concerns, forcing nations to engage in a 'race to the bottom' to compete . . . with low wages and lax environmental standards." During the protest, windows were smashed and WTO participants were assaulted. Still, not all the protesters can be said to have been panicked. The *Herald* reported, "Black-garbed young men in ski masks were behind some of the vandalism and got into shouting matches with more peacefully inclined protesters." One point at which those alarmed over the WTO crossed into panic is revealed in an article on the protests in the December 4, 1999, issue of *People's World.* "The WTO is an instrument of that greed, centered on Wall Street and Washington, D.C. . . . [which] sets policies that squeeze trillions of dollars in profits from workers while inflicting hunger, poverty, unemployment, and environmental ruin around the world." Impassioned and debatable as these words are, no elements of panic are employed. Yet again, however, nonpanicked statements lent credence to panic-inducing statements when the article continued, "The Pentagon is its enforcer. The media spinmeisters tell us that there is no alternative to this system." The absence of any examples of the Pentagon enforcing WTO actions renders the remark an unverified claim. It is then joined by a claim about the media that filters out numerous instances of newspapers arguing for alternatives to the WTO. As far back as the creation of the WTO in 1995, many Americans expressed concern over the organization's ability to increase corporate influence. During the planning of the WTO, union leader Jack Sheinkman warned in an August 9, 1994, *New York Times* opinion column, "If the current accord is approved . . . [the WTO] should also include mechanisms to enforce internationally recognized workers' rights, including outlawing child labor, and set environmental standards."

The point at which alarm over the WTO crossed into panic is seen all the more vividly by comparison with statements that were alarmed but not panicked. "The WTO must be shut down because it is unelected, un-accountable, and has the power to undermine local laws that protect the environment and labor from exploitation," declared the December 31, 1999, issue of *Earth First!* While the statement approached the portal to panic in its use of the absolute "must," the *Earth First!* article stopped at that threshold and, in a January 31, 2000, article on the violence in Seattle, stated, "One of the most striking elements of the WTO protests was the level of conflict between adherents of 'nonviolent' protest methods and those who preferred to more concretely express their feelings toward global capitalism. . . . If the Left activist community is to be united and strong, more communica-tion and internal discussion around strategic issues is necessary." Advocating nonviolence is not what rendered these remarks nonpanicked. They were not panicked because what they advocated—discussion—is not that which they feared: neocolonial oligarchy.

The resurgence of alarm over capitalist corporations that commenced during the Vietnam War has continued into the twenty-first century, spreading from left-wing radicals to mainstream Democrats. In 2001, Con-gressman John Lewis cited figures showing increasingly huge donations to political campaigns and warned, "More than ninety percent of these big contributions came from corporations and wealthy individuals."[22] The fol-lowing year, the still-widening extent of alarm over corporations was re-vealed when Republican strategist Kevin Phillips warned, "Will modern Republicans be painted as courtiers of the new Robber Baronage? . . . The unprecedented size of American fortunes built up in the 1990s . . . plus rev-elations of corporate misdeeds, are setting up U.S. politics for a historically unduckable issue: too much money in too few hands." Philips wrote these words shortly after Congress had enacted the bipartisan McCain-Feingold Campaign Finance Reform Act, which he applauded. Still, he concluded, "The danger remains."[23]

A new generation of books again sounded alarms about corporate power, including *Colossus: How the Corporation Changed America* (2001),

Confessions of an Economic Hit Man (2004), *When Corporations Rule the World* (2005), and *State-Corporate Crime* (2006). Their warnings acquired increased credibility following the international economic collapse in 2008. Some of America's largest corporations received bailouts totaling trillions of dollars in federal loans and investments. "The top dogs prospered and their national government either sat by passively or intervened to help the 'haves,'" Princeton University professor Alan S. Blinder wrote in the November 9, 2008, *New York Times.* Not one who tended to agree with the intellectual elite or what she called the "lamestream" media, former Alaska governor and vice presidential candidate Sarah Palin declared, "While people on Main Street look for jobs, people on Wall Street, they're collecting billions and billions in your bailout bonuses."[24] *It's a Wonderful Life* served as a blank to be filled in when the *Portland Oregonian* said of bankers and corporate executives, "They live in Pottersville. The rest of us live in Bedford Falls."[25]

Alarm over corporations threatening the nation's democracy intensified in 2010 when a Supreme Court ruling in *Citizens United v. Federal Election Commission* enabled corporations to make undisclosed donations to groups indirectly campaigning for political candidates. The element of secrecy permitted by the court's ruling added considerable fuel to the alarm of many Americans—though not enough, according to *Washington Post* columnist E. J. Dionne, among his colleagues in the press. "They ought to be asking . . . what these secret donors expect for their money," he told readers on October 25, 2010. "You can be sure the benefactors will not keep their identities hidden from the members of Congress they help elect. Only the voters will be in the dark."

One year later, the nation's increasingly widespread alarm formed into a visible mass. "In the eleven days since they arrived, a few hundred activists protesting American capitalism have turned a New York City park into an urban campground," the *Wall Street Journal* reported on September 11, 2011. On October 4, the *New York Times* reported, "A loose-knit populist campaign that started on Wall Street three weeks ago has spread to dozens of cities across the country." The movement, initially dubbed "Occupy Wall Street," was now being called the "Occupy movement."

In seeking to camp indefinitely outside financial institutions, and with some participants clad in various costumes, the Occupy movement might give the impression of political panic. But was it? And if so, where did it cross the threshold? Panic can be detected in a September 30, 2011 article by Occupy cofounder Arun Gupta in a rally-based publication called the *Occupied Wall Street Journal.* "The Wall Street occupation has succeeded in revealing how corporations, politicians, media, and police have failed us as institutions," he stated, employing an absolute—"failed"—that filtered out instances where these institutions did not fail those who identified with the Occupy movement. In the news media, scores of articles, editorials, and columns had reported the actions and views of the Occupy movement to the public and, in some cases, endorsed them. The failures attributed to politicians filtered out the fact that Congress had recently enacted the most comprehensive health care guarantees in history, halved the interest rates on student loans, and enacted legislation that sought to enable more restructuring of home mortgages in default. At the same time, Gupta revealed an overarching absence of panic when he concluded, "It is only through common struggle, debate, and popular democracy that we will create genuine solutions which have legitimacy." What he advocated ultimately was not that which he feared—domination by an elite group—but precisely the opposite: democracy.

Gupta's remarks further illuminate political panic. They reveal that panic-inducing elements can be employed to advocate nonpanicked actions. Alarm, like alarmists, cannot be stereotyped.

Nine

"WOMAN SUFFRAGE ... revolutionizes society ... revolutionizes religion
... revolutionizes the Constitution and
... the legitimate and proper sphere of
woman."

—Speech in U.S. Senate by George Vest
(D-MO), December 16, 1881[1]

At first glance, many may find it difficult to perceive that women
have ever been feared as a danger to the nation—let alone the cause
of widespread panic over that fear. Though the proverbial "battle of the
sexes," which included resistance to giving women the vote, has been fought
throughout American political history, has there actually been panic? When
one considers that no other group has had as many legal restrictions for as
long as women; that wives did not begin to acquire property rights or any
rights regarding child custody until the mid-nineteenth century; and that
not until 1920 did the Constitution provide that women had the right to
vote, an outline begins to surface that resembles the other panics discussed.
Clearly, there has been concern regarding women as a danger to the nation.

As we unearth those past concerns, we will discover that whenever women have openly sought to confront them, there has been panic. While the elements of the panic are the same in this instance as in others, in this instance widespread panic has surfaced *solely* as backlash. So particular is this aspect that Pulitzer Prize–winning journalist Susan Faludi explored it in her 1981 book *Backlash: The Undeclared War Against American Women.* It is not, however, unique to women, as will shortly be seen in the panic over homosexuals.

"I desire you would remember the ladies and be more generous and favorable to them than your ancestors," Abigail Adams wrote her husband in 1776. As John Adams joined with other American colonists to declare a new and independent nation, his wife entreated, "Do not put such unlimited power into the hands of husbands. . . . If particular care and attention is not paid to the ladies, we are determined to foment a rebellion, and will not hold ourselves bound by any laws in which we have no voice or representation."[2] The future second president of the United States responded, "You are so saucy." Adams then admitted to his wife, "We know better than to repeal our masculine systems . . . which would completely subject us to the despotism of the petticoat."[3]

The limitations against which Abigail Adams was pushing were articulated one decade earlier in *Sermons to Young Women,* a two-volume collection of homilies by Reverend James Fordyce. Though Fordyce was Scottish, Americans so highly regarded him that his book was published, and repeatedly republished, in the United States. In it, he advised the ladies, "Your business chiefly is to read men, in order to make yourselves agreeable and useful."[4] While Abigail Adams displayed political insight as keen as that possessed by the men who signed the Declaration of Independence, she confined herself to the prescript Fordyce advised—"reading" her husband and making herself "useful"—but never went public with her very non-Fordycian feminist views. In pushing those boundaries, however, she did share her political views in correspondence with other women, as in her letters to Dolley Madison, wife of the nation's fourth president.

Abigail Adams was not the only American woman of her era to express feminist thoughts, but none sought to organize women to attain equality.

Women and men in the new United States faced more immediate—and often potentially fatal—obstacles from those who opposed them. One woman in this era who did publicly ring a liberty bell for women was British. In 1792, Mary Wollstonecraft published *A Vindication of the Rights of Woman,* a work so influential it quickly spread to and through the United States. "Much has been said lately concerning the works and character of Mrs. Wollstonecraft," a March 22, 1803, feature in the *Boston Weekly Messenger* stated as preface to reprinting a British article on the then deceased Wollstonecraft. The article began with a defense of Wollstonecraft that lent credence to its ultimate condemnation of her. Its British author, John Evans (like Fordyce, a widely published minister), began by refuting the accusation that Wollstonecraft's ideas were un-Christian based on her having ceased to attend church. "Let it be remembered that Mrs. Wollstonecraft has written decidedly in favor of public worship . . . at an uncontaminated period of her life," Evans reminded his readers, citing examples from earlier published works. But in his use of "uncontaminated," Evans employed a potent blank to be filled in. Some readers may have filled in the blank with the onset of illness, leading not only to Wollstonecraft's death but altering what had been healthy perspectives. Those who knew she died suddenly following childbirth may have filled it in with sexual escapades in the not-so-private lives of England's intellectual elite. For others, contamination may have triggered associations with urban pollution and implied that urbanity contributed to Wollstonecraft's view. The particular potency in Evan's use of "uncontaminated" was that it simultaneously functioned as an absolute by conveying the notion of purity. Unless one refused to fill in the blank, whatever one used to fill it deposited that person in the portal to panic via a brilliantly dizzying use of the fallacy that correlation implies causation. The fallacious syllogism in this instance spins:

[FILL IN THE BLANK] = *contamination.*

Before her contamination, Mary Wollstonecraft espoused pure (religious) views.

Ergo, contamination caused her to espouse feminism over religion.

Once so cognitively spun, one is understandably more apt to latch on to the offering of a view that has the stability of certitude.

Roots of the Panic

"Every widespread demonical movement has been inaugurated by a woman," an August 1912 article declared in the magazine *Leaves of Healing*. As examples of female-inaugurated demonical movements, the article cited Spiritualism, Christian Science, and Theosophy. Its use of an absolute ("every") filtered out male-inaugurated (and presumably, in its view, demonical) movements, such as Islam, Buddhism, Communism, and Mormonism. Likely penned by the magazine's publisher, religious leader John Alexander Dowie, the article went on to "account for it on the very same basis that I account for the temptation of Eve. . . . It is far easier for her to be tempted by the devil." As in the panic over African Americans, many of those alarmed about women had beliefs rooted in (or that they attributed to) the Bible. In Fordyce's *Sermons to Young Women,* he too based his claims regarding the role of women on the Bible—claims that the soon-to-become-public feminist, Mary Wollstonecraft, challenged. "I will use the preacher's own words," she began, then quoted Fordyce: "'Let it be observed that in your sex manly exercises are never graceful . . . that men of sensibility desire in every woman soft features and a flowing voice, a form not robust, and demeanor delicate and gentle.'" To which Wollstonecaft then asked, "Is [this] not the . . . portrait of a house slave?"[5]

Numerous women's rights advocates noted the similarities between slavery and the legal status of women. Nature was also invoked, either alongside or in lieu of the Bible, as the basis of claims regarding character. "The condition of women is very miserable among barbarous nations; they are slaves," Johann Spurzheim wrote in his 1821 book *Education: Its Elementary Principles Founded in the Nature of Man.* Spurzheim, a German physician whose works were published throughout Europe and in the United States, mirrored those scientists in the panic over African Americans who presented themselves as unbiased, and therefore trustworthy, experts. Spurzheim even cited

Mary Wollstonecraft and agreed with her that abilities typically considered superior in males "exist in some women stronger than in many men." But in other respects, he wrote, "Mary Wollstonecraft is very wrong." As examples of her errors, this ostensibly unbiased expert wrote, "There are . . . feelings more active in women than in men. . . . They are constantly desirous of knowing what others say of them; they are fond of distinctions of every kind, of decorations and external show. . . . They wish to enjoy immediately; are moved by momentary impressions; do not like to work for a future period." Spurzheim's claims entered the portal to panic by filtering out men who are fond of distinctions (such as *Sir* Isaac Newton, *Lord* Baltimore, or *Dr.* Spurzheim), men who are fond of decorations (such as award medals or lapel pins), men who are desirous of knowing what others say of them, and men who seek instant gratification rather than work for a future period.

Spurzheim entered the realm of panic when he went on to do that which he feared. "More girls than boys learn music, drawing and painting. . . . Why then, we may ask, do their compositions so rarely equal those of men?" he asked, and then answered, "Whenever great combinations, deep reflections, discrimination, and general abstraction are required, when principle and laws are to be established, females in general remain behind." These claims could have been tested by providing identical education and career opportunities to randomly selected males and females, then measuring to see if these differences resulted. Spurzheim, however, sought instant gratification and opted (to borrow his words) to engage in shallow reflection rather than great combination and discrimination by which principles are to be established. "No education will change the nature of the innate dispositions," he concluded, thereby wrapping his entire book in an unverified claim.

A new scientific approach that did entail the collection of data was put forward in *Women Physiologically Considered* (1840). Its author, Alexander Walker, claimed to have proven "that the natural inferiority of intellect in woman . . . and her politics, requiring the exercise of reason, are so feeble as to be worthless." Walker measured the heads of twins in which one was male and the other female. Indeed, his research discovered differences, though he admitted these differences in head size were very slight and decreased as the children grew older. Nevertheless he concluded, "Here, then, is a striking anatomical and physiological distinction between the mind of man and that of woman." More striking is that Walker, a renowned physiologist in his day, did not then compare the "intellect" of these subjects to see if even a correlation existed. He did note, however, that there were exceptions. "When a woman, indeed, is notorious for her mind," he explained, "she is in general frightfully ugly." Walker thus demonstrated his panic by doing that which he feared by putting forth scientific assertions "so feeble as to be worthless."

In one key respect, the panic over women differed from other panics in that those panicked over women included women. Elizabeth Griffith wrote in her 1782 book *Essays Addressed to Young Married Women,* "A love of power and authority is natural to men, and . . . every man ought to be the principal object of attention in his family." With this unverified claim that Nature endowed males more than females with a love of power and authority, Griffith set her toe in the portal to panic. No sooner had she done so than suddenly her own "love of power and authority" swept her across the threshold to panic, from which she tossed other women a bouquet of absolutes. "Patiently submit to his *all-wife* decrees," she declared. "It is *doubtless* the great business of a woman's life to render his home pleasing to her husband . . . It is the *duty* of a wife not only to regulate her own temper towards her husband, but also to pay such an attention to his as may prevent it from *ever* appearing in a disagreeable light." Griffith employed another absolute to underscore her advice when, referring to herself in the third person, she told her readers that "after thirty years of *uninterrupted* happiness in the marriage-state, she may be deemed qualified." (All italics added.)

Many may wonder why a woman would hold such beliefs. Among many possible explanations, one emanates from the recurring element in political panic that alarmists cannot be stereotyped. Quite possibly, Elizabeth Griffith was not panicked, nor even genuinely concerned, about wives behaving deferentially to their husbands. Her statement regarding thirty years of uninterrupted happiness in her marriage filtered out the fact that financial stress, and the ascendance of her career as a writer over her husband's, contributed to repeated separations.[6] By writing this book, Griffith could well have been availing herself of panic to further her career. She may have done so for financial reasons or, as a former actress turned playwright, out of a need to be on the public stage.

Even if Griffith's alarm was more role than real, other women appear to have been genuinely alarmed about women. One such woman was Jane West, whose 1806 book *Letters to a Young Lady* warned that too many young women were becoming "enthusiastically attached to visions of independence, philanthropy, energy, and perfection." In ways that would be echoed over the next two centuries, West ascribed this activism and ambition among women to "the effects of subverting doctrines." Her book, then, was a form of backlash in response to "activism and ambition among women." In it, she attributed her views to biblical beliefs. But her need for certitude in her beliefs led her into the portal to panic when she sought to foist them on others through the use of absolutes: "The peculiar path of each sex is marked by those nice shades of approbation which *only* an all-wise Being, intent on the general benefit of the *whole* human race, could impose." (Italics added.) West entered the realm of panic by doing that which she feared. Becoming "enthusiastically attached to visions of independence . . . and perfection," she appointed herself God's authorized agent when she told wives, "In the conjugal state we are designed to be the helpmates," and later insisted, "The duties that it requires are of such hourly, such momentary recurrence, that the impropriety of our engaging in public concerns becomes evident." She declared that the same strictures apply to women who were not wives when she told them, "As daughters, sisters, neighbors, and friends, the active duties of female usefulness may be happily exerted." Allowing no exceptions, West added, "Even the insulated spinster has no right to consider herself exempt from the generation obligation." West's entire book emanated from the realm of panic since she responded to her alarm—that too many women were neglecting "obligations . . . of such hourly, such momentary recurrence, that the impropriety of our engaging in public concerns becomes evident"— by setting aside those obligations in order to engage in public concerns by writing a book.

The First Wave of Panic

Panic that women were beginning to endanger the nation began to spread in reaction to those women who became politically involved via the abolitionist and temperance movements. Even among men in these movements, a considerable number were panicked that women were joining their ranks. Reporting on the May 1840 election of officers for the American Anti-Slavery Society, the *Philadelphia Enquirer* noted of the one female candidate, Abby Kelley: "The male members were all chosen unanimously, but to her election the negative answer was so loud that it was found necessary to try the vote by rising."[7]

Three years later, the October 30, 1843, *National Intelligencer* told readers, "Among the young women in Rochester, New York, there are in existence forty secret societies." Panic surfaced in the article doing that which it feared (secrecy) by not identifying the groups—thereby maintaining their secrecy—since these allegedly secret groups were no longer secret to the author of the article. Still, the alarm was not spun from thin air. Something was abuzz among women, and not at all secretly. "A convention of indignant women was held at Seneca Falls, New York," Connecticut's *New London Democrat* reported on August 5, 1848. "The object of the convention was the declaration and protection of woman's rights . . . drawn up very much after the style of the Declaration of Independence." The resolution was actually entitled a "Declaration of Sentiments," but it did commence, "When in the course of human events, it becomes necessary for one portion of the family of man . . ."[8] The *Democrat,* paraphrasing rather than quoting the document, told readers that the woman's rights resolution protested their having been "trampled on, abused, sucked in, cheated, made slaves of, and received more cuffs than kisses." Filtered from the news report was the fact that the resolution did not actually include the words "trampled on," "abused," "sucked in," "cheated," "slaves," "cuffs," or "kisses." By filtering out the actual wording, the report enabled itself to fill in the resulting blank with words suggestive of a temper tantrum. In so doing, it did that which it feared. The article itself was a tantrum.

Two novels that appeared shortly after the Seneca Falls Convention reveal that these intense expressions of panic were a backlash in response to the 1848 launching the women's rights movement. In 1850, Nathaniel Hawthorne published *The Scarlet Letter,* a novel that frankly depicted the struggles of a woman who committed adultery. While some criticized the book's flirtation with indecency, none expressed outrage. Soon after, Mary Gove Nichols published a novel about a woman tempted to commit adultery entitled *Mary Lyndon* (1855). "Its whole undercurrent is one of poison," the *Sandusky Register* declared. "Its philosophy [is] fatal to all social purity." The *New York Times* wrote of the book "having been written with the special purpose of recommending adultery as a personal right and a social duty." Filtering out the fact that the title character did *not* commit adultery— indeed, she repeatedly resisted it—the *Times* went on to accuse Nichols of being part of a conspiracy. "This book is not an isolated performance. . . . Its publication is part of a plan. . . . The disgusting and detestable Free Love system which is openly advocated in *Mary Lyndon* . . . is obtaining a wide and alarming currency throughout the country."[9]

That Nathaniel Hawthorne was not accused of participating in this conspiracy may suggest that vehemence was directed at Mary Gove Nichols because she was a woman; yet other women published novels in this era that were not received with vehemence. Since, in Nichols's novel, Mary Lyndon did not commit adultery, why such rage? What sparked the rage was that, in the story of Mary Lyndon's struggles to resist sexual temptations, she came to acquire control of her own life, emotionally and financially, to the same degree as a man. Her achievement produced profound fear among men such as these reviewers, whose need for certitude regarding their own autonomy (ability to govern oneself) was so great they felt that autonomy was endangered unless they also controlled the lives of women. "It is an abuse of liberty of the press to publish such a book as *Mary Lyndon,*" the Sandusky reviewer declared, and in so doing revealed panic. Fearing that a woman such as the one depicted in the novel endangered American liberty, he advocated denying author Mary Gove Nichols the liberty guaranteed to all Americans under the First Amendment.

The women's rights movement paused during the Civil War, but afterward returned, reinforced by values emanating from the emancipation of the slaves. "The question now is, have we the wisdom and conscience . . . to reconstruct a government on the enduring basis that has never yet been tried—equal rights for all," Elizabeth Cady Stanton declared, keynoting a shift in the women's rights movement that once again paralleled that among African Americans. With this shift, the sexual crossroad encountered in the abolitionist movement expanded to become a major political intersection at which many of that movement's men joined legions of others alarmed at the prospect of political equality for women. Wendell Phillips, a leading voice in the abolitionist movement, declared in an 1866 speech that "when you come to the Woman Question, the first great abiding difficulty is that woman is herself the obstacle—that she fills the chair most potent and irresistible in this discussion, that of popular opinion, and she utters her verdict against us."[10] Phillips's statement was governed by an absolute in his use of the word, "woman," which in this context asserted that all women oppose voting rights for their sex. For those who granted the orator a measure of artistic license, "woman" in this context went from being an absolute to being a blank to be filled in, leaving it to those listeners to determine what percentage of women opposed voting rights for their sex.

That same year, Congress passed the Fourteenth Amendment, extending voting rights to African American men. During debate in the House and the Senate, there was virtually no discussion about the amendment including women. One year later, however, the women's rights movement was sufficiently awakened from its hibernation during the Civil War that the issue dominated much of New York's 1867 Constitutional Convention. Delegate Horace Smith recited a poem celebrating motherhood before packing absolutes into his warning: "Change her, transfer her to another sphere, and you have *no* such mother; you have robbed her of her influence, *bereft* of her power, and *blotted out* that home forever!" (Italics added.) Delegate John Gould asked, "What sort of children will raise up when they see the father and mother . . . constantly quarreling with each other with regard to political affairs?"[11] Gould's question filtered out those families in which the parents already fought over politics, such as that of John and Abigail Adams—one of whose children grew up to become the sixth president of the United States. Ironically, given this example of John Quincy Adams, Gould's statement hinged on the blank to be filled in: "what sort of children will raise up."

Founding Father anxiety entered a new realm during the debate over women at this New York convention when Abraham Conger said of women's rights advocates, "I would like to ask them . . . whether the dignity of her who is known as the mother of Washington would have been advanced at all in their judgment, had she . . . had the power of voting?"[12] The statement illuminates why references to the Founding Fathers recur in political panic. Conger probably knew little of Mary Ball Washington other than that she was the mother of George Washington. If he did know more, he filtered out that George Washington had a very strained relationship with his mother. She disapproved of his military career, complained to the Virginia government that the money he provided her was inadequate, and opposed the American Revolution. The women (and men) who knew her spoke little of her views out of respect for both her advanced age and her illustrious son.[13] Conger's absence of facts resulted in a blank that he filled with his ideal Mother of the Father of Our Country. Likewise, others have idealized the Founding Fathers. Idealization of the Founding Fathers also requires filtering, as in fact the nation's founders agreed on little other than not wanting their colonies to remain part of England. The idealization resulting from such filtering is an absolute, one that runs along the lines that *the Founding Fathers knew*. Absolutes provide comfort to a person to the extent that he or she is troubled by a need for certitude. At New York's 1867 constitutional convention, the proposal to extend voting rights to women was defeated.

Two years later, however, the Wyoming Territory granted women the right to vote. New York's *Troy Weekly* downplayed this landmark moment by noting on December 25, 1869, "There are said to be but seven women in Wyoming." In fact, as census figures would show, there were approximately 1,000 white women in Wyoming at the time. Those same figures revealed some 6,000 white men, leading historians to speculate that attracting women to the remote territory may have been one of the unstated reasons for granting them the right to vote.[14] Other news coverage of Wyoming's action revealed that many men's attitudes were beginning to shift. A December 23, 1869, editorial in New Hampshire's *Farmer's Cabinet* conveyed mixed emotions when it began, either seemingly supportive of, or sarcastically acceding to, women's rights, "The long night of woman's total obscuration as a political member of society begins to wear away." Tipping toward approval it continued, "Indeed, the dawn of her enfranchisement has actually begun—," then tipped toward disapproval by ending the sentence, "only reversing the order of the natural world, the new light breaks in the West." The majority of the nation's newspapers also provide evidence of these shifting, uncertain attitudes by virtue of the absence of any comment; most simply presented the text of Wyoming's new statute.

As seen in other panics, the waning of opposition to women's suffrage intensified the panic among some who remained opposed. "Wyoming's Experiment of Fourteen Years Results in an Increase in Bribery and Corruption," the *New York Times* headlined a November 19, 1883, report. The article cited verified facts regarding gambling, prostitution, political corruption, and election fraud in Wyoming, lending a degree of credence to claims that were unverified or entailed other elements of panic. One such element was present in the headline itself. By stating that giving women the right to vote in Wyoming had resulted in these problems, it asserted that correlation is causation. The correlation itself was governed by an unverified claim in the headline that political wrongdoing and prostitution had increased, since the article that followed presented no information on these problems in Wyoming prior to its women being able to vote. While the intensity of the article's panic was not so great as to urge the lynching of Wyoming's women, it was sufficient to blame them for one. Recounting the lynching of a man accused of murder, the *Times* told its readers, "Prominent citizens pleaded with the mob to release the man and let him be tried by process of law." That these good citizens were male became evident when the article asked, "But what is to be said of that other body of Cheyenne's citizens? . . . The women citizens of Cheyenne were enacting woman's nature . . . trembling, shivering, and crying behind window shutters, peeping at a scene most dreadful to them." In assigning a portion of blame for the lynching to women, the article employed an unverified claim and two filtered facts. Unverified was the claim that the town's women were trembling and peeping out at the scene. Filtered out were men who may have similarly watched from a distance. Also filtered were women who had no view of the scene.

As panic intensified among those who perceived widespread panic waning, alarmists sought to fuel their warnings by tapping into other panics. In Georgia, *Macon Telegraph* columnist James Callaway referred to the women's rights movement as a "conspiracy" that united its "affiliates with the most anti-South and negro-loving" organizations. Callaway warned his readers that voting rights for women would "add two million negro women" to the electorate. He then connected his alarm to the panic over corporations, adding octane with idealization of their Confederate forefathers, when he wrote, "Georgia is celebrating the new emancipation from the slavery of Eastern education and from Wall Street tyranny."[15] In like fashion, the March 1910 issue of *Pearson's* magazine sought to tap other panics in an article entitled "Why Women Oppose Woman's Suffrage" when it declared, "Woman's Suffrage is the child of Rationalistic Communism, and the suffragette is the natural exponent of that philosophy." The assertion filtered out the fact that voting rights for anyone was not a component of communism's dictatorship of the proletariat. Arguments based on Nature also tapped into other panics. In the September 1895 issue of *American Naturalist,* physiologist James Weir, Jr., connected his warnings regarding women to the newly burgeoning panic over homosexuals. Dr. Weir filtered out doubt through the use of absolutes when he wrote, "I think that I am *perfectly safe in saying* that *every* woman who has been *at all* prominent in advancing the cause of equality rights in its *entirety,* has either given evidence of masculo-feminity or has shown, *conclusively,* that she was the victim of psycho-sexual aberrancy." (Italics added.)

A particularly influential voice that revealed the diminishment of widespread panic was that of Woodrow Wilson. Previously seen to be an influential voice in spreading panic over African Americans, Wilson too stands as an example that alarmists cannot be stereotyped, by virtue of declaring during his 1913 campaign, "When the women come into politics, they come in to show us all those little contacts between life and politics, on account of which I, for myself, rejoice."[16] While Wilson did not say if his rejoicing included waving his pen across a constitutional amendment guaranteeing voting rights to women, women's rights leaders opted to assume it did. At his inaugural parade, a women's pageant was included for the first time in history. The presence of the pageant further demonstrated the waning of widespread panic, thereby intensifying the fear of some who remained opposed to women's rights. "[Men] tried to tear the flowers from our coats," one participant recounted, "and one man stuck his foot out and tried to trip up my daughter."[17] Others told of "surging crowds of men and boys."[18] Reporting on a Senate investigation of these incidents, Georgia's *Augusta Chronicle* noted on March 13, 1913, "Bursts of laughter came frequently as women told of their experiences." Such physical reactions to women's actions soon expanded into the realm of law enforcement. The *Washington Post* reported the arrest of a women's rights advocate for making a suffrage speech to farm laborers. Its September 30, 1914, article revealed that, when this activist asked to see the law she was charged with violating, "She was informed that the statutes were locked up in a safe, and so could not be produced."

When the United States entered World War I in 1917, those opposing women's rights sought to fuel their alarms by tapping into this foreign conflict. "Members of the National Woman's Party again yesterday endeavored to demonstrate the fitness of women for the ballot by displaying unpatriotic banners at the gates of the White House," the *Washington Post* told readers on June 21 of that year—a date that would mark the commencement of months of violence toward, and arrests of, women picketing for the vote. The unpatriotic words on their banner were: "America Is Not a Democracy. Twenty Million American Women Are Denied the Right to Vote." Describing the onset of this first attack by a mob, the *Post* reported, "D. J. Dunigan, a local builder . . . stopped and read, and as he read his patriotism blazed. 'Let's tear the d—n thing down,' he shouted. 'It's treasonable, and I'm with you,' said Joseph Browne Montgomery, Jr., of New York . . . 'Come on,' shouted Walter S. Timmins, a consulting engineer. . . . Mr. Dunigan reached the banner first. He gave it a vigorous yank." The mob's panic was demonstrated in its defending the nation built with a pillar guaranteeing free speech by destroying the words of the picketers. For its part, the *Washington Post* entered the portal to panic through a filtering phrase that governed its description of the event. Its constitutionally dubious premise, "the fitness of women for the ballot," filtered out women who opposed such protests during war—most notably the publicly stated opposition of the larger and more established National American Woman Suffrage Association.

Since the war was not about women, it failed to provide sufficient fuel to reignite widespread panic. North Dakota congressman John M. Baer demanded an investigation of the vandalism and of the repeated arrests of the women picketers in the days that followed this first assault. Reporting on Baer's call for an investigation, the *Washington Post* filtered (indeed, reversed) facts regarding who attacked whom, when it told readers that the congressman was "evidently of the opinion that the crowds were responsible for the disgraceful scenes of the last five days and that the women who flaunted the banners should go uncensored."[19]

Despite these confrontations, World War I contributed to further diminishment of the panic over women in the same way wars abated panics against other groups who joined side-by-side in the struggle. At the outset of the war, the May 8, 1917, *Cleveland Plain Dealer* wrote of women, "Thousands of them will be needed in office, store, and factory" where, the article quoted one executive saying, "They can do almost anything." By war's end, the impact of women having taken on these and other previously male roles can be seen in a May 15, 1919, editorial in Colorado's *Pueblo Chieftain:* "If for no other reason, the women of America ought to be given the ballot because of the splendid record of patriotism and efficient service in the world war." One month later, Congress passed the Nineteenth Amendment, which (after being ratified in 1920 by the required number of states) barred any state from denying citizens the right to vote based on sex.

The Second Wave of Panic

"Five female anti-women's libbers, waving flags and singing 'America,' . . . distributed gift-wrapped boxes of mice to [California] state senators who voted to ratify the Equal Rights Amendment to the United States Constitution," read a November 11, 1972, item in the *Chicago Tribune*. One of these women explained, "Those who voted for the amendment are mice instead of men, because a real man will fight for a woman." Her statement entered the portal to panic via a blank to be filled in, "real men," which left it to others to determine what constitutes a real man as opposed to, in some sense, an unreal man. She entered the realm of panic when her actions did that which she feared. Fearing that the Equal Rights Amendment would weaken the nation by enabling women to fight in lieu of having real men fight for them, she and her associates fought. They, after all, distributed the gift-wrapped mice as a protest rather than having men distribute the boxes for them.

The Equal Rights Amendment, first proposed in 1924, stated, "Equality of rights under the law shall not be denied or abridged by the United States or by any State on account of sex."[20] It failed to pass in every subsequent Congress, not picking up steam until this second movement of women seeking equal treatment grew to the point that Congress passed it and sent it to the states for ratification. The 1972 Equal Rights Amendment revealed the extent to which panic over women remained. During the years set for ratification, the amendment fell three states short of the thirty-eight needed in order to be included in the Constitution. But its congressional passage, and the efforts that led to that passage, sparked backlash.

Among the first men to notice this second rising tide among women was the editor of the *Salina Journal*, who wrote in a June 2, 1963, commentary: "One of the day's more popular books among the distaff set is a non-fiction—well, mostly—work called *The Feminine Mystique*." With this book, today considered a classic of its kind, author Betty Friedan keynoted her generation's quest to achieve equal treatment for women. Likewise, the editor of the *Salina Journal* led his generation's way into the portal to panic by reacting to Friedan's book with an unverified claim: "We know where women are headed with their mystiques. They're headed for domination, not only of the household but eventually of the office and, if it fits their fancy, of the political arena as well." Syndicated columnist Count Marco declared, "Femininity, to Mrs. Friedan, is pretty much of a disgraceful thing."[21]

Marco's assertion filtered out that Friedan said nothing of the sort. Rather than disgraceful ("disgrace" being a blank to be filled in that Friedan never used), she objected to the view that "the highest value and the only commitment for women is the fulfillment of their own femininity."[22]

Also in 1963, a young journalist named Gloria Steinem revealed that she had been one of the bunny-attired servers at the New York Playboy Club. Steinem took the job while researching a magazine article that appeared in two parts under the title, "A Bunny's Tale," in that year's May and June issues of *Show* magazine. Even when Steinem appeared in business attire, rather than her skimpy Playboy Club costume with its bunny ears and tail, her sense of fashion and grace further disproved that feminists viewed femininity as a "disgraceful thing." Steinem went on to demonstrate that, in addition to journalistic skill, women also could possess business acumen. In 1972, she launched *Ms.*, a highly successful magazine dedicated to women's issues. Precluded by Steinem's beauty and style from calling feminists unfeminine, columnist Ralph de Toledano characterized her as "radical chic," then attacked Steinem for attacking others. "If a woman wants to be a wife and mother," he wrote, "if she wants to be frilly and 'dependent' . . . then that is her right—and Women's Lib is denying her that right by attempting to dragoon her into another life style."[23] De Toledano's statement filtered out a spate of interviews Steinem had given in launching *Ms.*, in which she stated the opposite. In one such interview, for example, she declared of housewives: "If she's elected to become a housewife and she is happy, that's great."[24] Rooting his opposition in Nature, De Toledano entered the portal to panic when he wrote, "Superior women have a quality of mind which differs from that of superior men, and imposes a different kind of logic on their thinking." Blanks to be filled in permeated this remark. Based on their own knowledge, fears, and needs, readers were left to determine the kind of gradations that distinguish "superior women" from mediocre and inferior women, and to determine what constitutes the "different kinds" of logic. De Toledano entered the realm of panic when his own mind demonstrated neither a different kind nor, indeed, any kind of logic, when he criticized the "inconsistency in the publication of a magazine exclusively for women by Ms. Steinem and her colleagues, after they have insisted that every male sanctuary and exclusivity must be broached." The statement filtered out that *Ms.* was equally available to men and women, unlike male sanctuaries that excluded women. In so doing, his mind illogically equated that which is *exclusively about* with that which is *exclusively for.*

Like the first feminist wave in the nineteenth century, this second wave was also closely connected to African Americans. "The struggle of women to gain equality in the national economy," the *Washington Post* reported on June 26, 1963, "was compared Monday night by Assistant Secretary of Labor Esther Peterson to the Negroes' fight for civil rights." Backlash accompanied this connection, too. After Ellen Willis wrote in the September 1969 issue of *Mademoiselle,* "Just as blacks live in a world defined by whites, women live in a world defined by males," the *Wall Street Journal* cited her remark and responded, "The feminists concluded, speciously, that the complaints about society raised by black people are equally valid for women."[25] Panic resided in this statement's doing that over which it was alarmed, speciousness (the appearance of truth that is false or deceptive), by speciously asserting that *comparing* injustices is *equating* injustices. Ellen Willis never equated discrimination against women with the beatings, shootings, and lynchings visited upon African Americans.

Alarmists again sought to fuel their warnings by connecting them to other fears. When New York congresswoman Bella Abzug chaired the 1977 National Women's Conference, syndicated columnist Alice Widener asked readers, "Do you know that Bella Abzug is a radical socialist?"[26] This question—governed by a blank to be filled in as to what qualified Abzug as a "radical socialist"—was but the opening salvo in a barrage of assertions built on a foundation comprised of elements of panic. An absolute provided the foundation for Widener's next statement, "Her aim is to *destroy* the middle class." (Italics added.) The next statement, "That has been and is the aim of all dedicated Marxists," rested upon an absolute, a misbegotten assertion, and an unverified claim. The absolute ("all") modified a misbegotten fact (Marxists actually sought to destroy the upper class and eliminate the lower class by creating a classless proletarian society), and the unverified claim that

Bella Abzug was a Marxist. In a barrage of blanks to be filled in, she asserted, "They scoff at Home, Mother, and the Flag," leaving it to her readers to determine what aspects of home life, motherhood, and patriotism feminists derided. Tucked into these blanks were potential unverified claims, as whatever specifics Widener's readers used to fill the blanks, examples of feminists scoffing at those specifics were, in all likelihood, absent. To Widener's credit, however, she did not filter out the fact that the wives of three presidents also participated in this National Women's Conference. "The presence of Rosalynn Carter, Betty Ford, and Lady Bird Johnson on the podium," she wrote, ". . . shows how gullible and unsophisticated these three 'first ladies' really are." Not filtering out this fact revealed Widener's panic by her doing that over which she was alarmed. Alarmed that feminists "scoff at Home, Mother, and Flag," Widener scoffed at three first ladies who *had* opted to remain at home rather than pursue careers.

Even after ratification of the Equal Rights Amendment failed by its 1982 deadline, panic over women continued. A 1985 Heritage Foundation report on education warned, "Some radical feminist groups even received federal funding to promote their destructive sex ideology in the nation's public school classrooms." The claim employed a blank to be filled in that left it to readers to decide what constitutes an undestroyed sexuality. Tucked inside this blank was the assertion that correlation is causation. This often recurring fallacy surfaced when the report—which cited textbooks that now included "illustrations of women mining engineers, for example, and men happily tending the baby, wearing an apron, and stirring a pot during the day"—asserted that illustrations can cause a student's sexuality to be destroyed (in whatever way readers had determined). Hidden in this assertion was an unverified claim, since the report cited no instances of students who had been exposed to such illustrations becoming sexually destroyed in whatever way readers may have used to fill in the blank.[27]

Anti-feminist Phyllis Schlafly recognized this illogic when she wrote in her 2003 book *Feminist Fantasies,* "Despite all the efforts to blur gender identities by, for example, showing pictures of girls playing with snakes and boys using hairspray . . . there is no evidence that human nature is changing."

She did, however, employ two blanks to be filled in to support her unverified claim: "Feminism is incompatible with personal happiness." The statement left it to her readers to determine what constitutes feminism and what constitutes happiness. In addition, she echoed fallacy-riddled claims dating back a hundred years when she asserted, "Feminism is incompatible with human nature"; she echoed an unverified claim dating back even further when she declared with certitude, "The premise of the feminists is that God goofed." Schlafly entered the realm of panic when she told her readers, "I went to law school after I was fifty, but I'm mighty glad that I didn't try to have my six children after I was fifty. It doesn't work that way." Filtered from the book was the fact Schlafly did that over which she was alarmed. Despite urging mothers of young children to postpone their careers, Schlafly herself had not. Absent from the book was any mention of her having run for Congress three years into her marriage. Before the oldest of her children was past the age of ten, Schlafly was a frequent guest speaker on issues such as, in one news item's description, "the plan that Communists are using in swaying public opinion."[28] In addition, she conducted a weekly radio broadcast during these years, was a delegate to the 1956 Republican National Convention, spoke at gatherings throughout the country, and ran again for Congress.[29] These examples further reveal that Schlafly was not, in fact, panicked over mothers of young children entering the workplace, but rather availed herself of such panic—just as she had previously availed herself of the panic over communists—to further the career she had commenced when her children were young.

The most vivid example of the intensity reached in this second wave of panic over women occurred three days after the September 11, 2001, terrorist attacks that left some 3,000 Americans dead. In its wake, Reverend Jerry Falwell connected panic over feminists to other panics when he said, "I really believe that the pagans, and the abortionists, and the feminists, and the gays and the lesbians . . . the A.C.L.U. [American Civil Liberties Union], People for the American Way—all of them who have tried to secularize America—I point the finger in their face and say, 'You helped this happen.'"[30] Falwell's statement filtered out the fact that the United States was secularized not by those he listed but by none other than the Founding Fathers when, in the First Amendment to the Constitution, they prohibited the establishment of a state religion.

With women now having served on the Supreme Court, as Speaker of the House, as Secretary of State, in top corporate positions, and currently undertaking increasingly dangerous missions in our armed forces, widespread fear that equal rights for women are a threat to the nation is diminishing. Still, pockets of panic continue to this day. On the January 12, 2014, broadcast of *Fox News Sunday,* former ABC News correspondent Brit Hume commented on revelations of political bullying by the administration of New Jersey governor Chris Christie, "In this sort of feminized atmosphere in which we exist today, guys who are masculine and muscular like that in their private conduct, kind of old fashion tough guys, run some risk." By filtering out accusations of bullying by women politicians—such as those leveled at presidential aspirant Hillary Clinton or former Speaker of the House Nancy Pelosi—Hume lured listeners into the realm of panic.[31]

Ten

"WEAK AND EFFEMINATE Romans were powerless ... [and] the great empire ... collapsed, never to rise again ... Shall we permit ourselves to fall into this DISGRACEFUL DEGRADATION?"

—high school essay contest, first place winner, 1920[1]

As in the panic over women, panic over homosexuals occurred as a backlash to statements or actions by homosexuals. The strength of this connection between the two panics has been evidenced since the mid-nineteenth century, the time when members of both groups first began to advocate for their rights in the United States. On December 9, 1853, for example, the *Vermont Journal* characterized that year's Woman's Rights Convention as being "composed of masculine women and feminine men." Unlike the panic over women, however—or any other panic—the panic over homosexuals regards a group whose origins are uncertain, and in this respect alarm over homosexuality is rooted entirely in a blank to be filled in.

As in the panics over African Americans and women, many have filled in that underlying blank with explanations based on the Bible or Nature, these explanations being (as are all explanations used to fill blanks) tied to one's needs and fears. Also as with women, political panic—as opposed to personal panic—regards the fear that gay men and women are a threat to the nation. Regarding gay men, it emanates from fear of national effeminacy; with gay women, it emanates from fear of what one historian has called "femmocracy."[2] Their common denominator is fear of political weakness.

Early Alarm in America

During the American Revolution, Lieutenant Frederick Enslin was convicted in a court martial of attempted sodomy and sentenced by General George Washington "to be drummed out of Camp tomorrow morning by all the Drummers and Fifers in the Army, never to return."[3] Washington clearly believed that homosexuality threatened the effectiveness of the military. Was he panicked? The answer resides in questions whose answers are lost in history. Did Enslin's action involve a willing partner? Would Washington have likewise sentenced a soldier who had comparably attempted to have sex with a female? To the extent that George Washington's greatness may be tarnished by what he did in this instance, it likewise shines all the brighter for what he did not do. He did not order Enslin to be flogged, imprisoned, or executed—sentences that had been imposed even for *attempted* sodomy in colonial America. In 1625, for example, shipmaster Richard Cornish was executed in Virginia on the basis of testimony by one of his crew that his "Master would have buggered him."[4]

For the Puritans who landed at Plymouth Rock, the Bible provided their perspective on homosexuality. "Because it was sin to be punished with death," minister and jurist John Reynor (sometimes spelled Reynors) wrote in 1642, referencing Leviticus 20:13, "his sin is not mitigated wher ther is not penetration." Likewise for women, Reynor wrote, "guilty of this unnaturall sine, as well as men, 1 Romans 26–27, the same thing doth furder apeare."[5] Even among the Puritans, however, the degree of certitude they acquired from their faith failed to fill all the blanks that surround sexuality. Their leader, William Bradford, lamented that same year that, even risking the penalty of death, "sodomie and bugerie have broke forth in this land oftener than once."[6]

Panic over homosexuality emanated from more than the Bible, even in this theocratic colony, as was revealed when Reynor sidestepped the biblical command, three lines earlier in Leviticus, that heterosexual adulterers be put to death. "It is not so manyfest that the same acts were to be punished with death," he wrote to a fellow jurist. "Besides other reasons" that he cited for letting heterosexual adulterers off the hook, sodomy (as homosexuality was them termed) "is more against the light of nature than some other capitall crimes."[7]

All thirteen colonies had laws imposing the death penalty on homosexuality. While these laws suggest there was widespread panic, the number of people executed for homosexuality appears to have been very few—possibly less than ten throughout the colonial era.[8] After the Revolution, Thomas Jefferson sought to eliminate the death penalty for sexual offenses in Virginia. In 1778, he proposed castration as a more appropriate penalty. A commensurate punishment for gay women posed more of a challenge for Jefferson. For them, he proposed "cutting through the cartilage of her nose a hole of one-half inch in diameter at the least."[9] Virginians turned out to be more squeamish about mutilation than execution. Their legislature retained the death penalty until 1800. By 1829, however, all but two states had replaced the death penalty for homosexual acts with prison terms ranging from one year to life.

Not surprisingly, there were also instances in the early years of the nation of individuals and occasionally mobs assaulting homosexuals, both male and female. "Our city has been in some ferment . . . on account of a report that a female was perambulating the streets . . . in male attire," a Boston news correspondent wrote in 1832. "This morning, the person suspected was compelled by a mob of boys to take refuge in a house in Water Street. A mob of men was soon collected, and for nearly two hours from 1,500 to 2,000 persons surrounded the premises."[10] This incident, however, emanated more from *personal* than *political* panic over homosexuals, as evidenced by what happened next. Police intervened to provide safe conduct for the trapped individual, demonstrating that, as governmental authorities, they did not view the mere presence of this person as a danger. The danger was the mob.

Others, however, did fear that the very presence of homosexuals endangered the republic. Hearkening to the American flag, the *Vermont Gazette* warned on October 29, 1787, "Shall effeminate fops undermine a fabric raised by wise politicians and brave warriors?" Technically, this statement did not induce political panic by seeking to keep the nation strong by weakening the right to privacy guaranteed under Article IV of the Constitution. The reason it did not induce panic in this way is that the nation was still governed by the Articles of Confederation, which did not specify a right to privacy.

Political panic was evidenced when fear of homosexuals was connected to fear of Catholics in the book *Jesuit Juggling,* a seventeenth-century work republished in the United States in 1835. "The odious sin of sodomy was common with many of the clergy and popes themselves," author Richard Baxter declared. For Americans panicked that Catholics endangered the nation by virtue of allegiance to the pope, this connection added fuel to the fear through the claim that many of the (possibly homosexual) popes' priests were secretly homosexuals. The element of secrecy made the claim that much more potent by virtue of secrecy being a blank to be filled in, leaving readers to determine what percentage of priests were gay. Since, in all likelihood, some priests were gay, any awareness of that fact would lend credence to Baxter's unverified claims.

Connecting political fear of all homosexuals to fear of women, the *New Orleans Times-Picayune* employed panic-inducing absolutes on March 7, 1902, when it warned its readers that women's rights advocates "will *only* accomplish their purpose when the men become so *entirely* corrupt and effeminate that they can *no longer* hold the scepter of dominion." (Italics added.) The claim proceeded further through the portal to panic via its use of a blank to be filled in, "effeminate," which left it to readers to determine what characteristics are feminine or masculine. The entire statement was an unverified claim asserting that effeminate men lack the abilities necessary to govern a nation, a claim that filtered out widely known and powerful political figures such as Alexander the Great and Joan of Arc, both of whom had openly displayed homosexual characteristics.

Still, panic over homosexuals as a threat to the nation was not widespread in the nineteenth century or in the opening decades of the twentieth century. While individuals who committed or attempted to commit homosexual acts risked arrest, gays who kept their sexuality "in the closet," as such concealment came to be called, typically were not singled out as a threat to the nation. When, however, a gay person proclaimed his or her sexuality, there was backlash.

Two prominent American authors from the nineteenth century reveal these dual responses. An item in the March 31, 1866, *Boston Advertiser* began and ended, "Rev. Horatio Alger, Jr. has resigned the pastorate of the United Church at Brewster."[11] Alger, who later achieved fame as the author of nearly a hundred books for boys that celebrated the rags-to-riches opportunities afforded by the United States, had been accused of molesting boys in the congregation. Alger did not deny it but rather, in the words of church documents from the time, "received it with apparent calmness of an old offender, and hastily left on the very next train for parts unknown."[12]

That same year, on the other hand, the already renowned poet Walt Whitman was fired from his position at the Department of the Interior—not for homosexual acts, but for homosexual poems in his classic work, *Leaves of Grass.* From the time *Leaves of Grass* first appeared in 1855, its segments celebrating homosexual love aroused rage. Critic Rufus Wilmot Griswold, esteemed as the editor of the anthology *The Poets and Poetry of America,* laced his assessment with panic-inducing absolutes when he wrote in the November 10, 1855, issue of *The Criterion,* "In our allusions to this book, we have found it *impossible* to convey *any, even the most faint* idea of its style and contents, and of our disgust and detestation of them, without employing language *that cannot be pleasing* to ears polite." (Italics added.) By so ornamenting his assessment with these absolutes, Griswold occluded the fact that his entire assessment was a blank to be filled in, leaving it to his readers to imagine the poem's disgusting and detestable contents. Entering the realm of panic, Griswold urged that "someone should, under circumstances like these, undertake a most disagreeable, yet stern duty." The governing phrase, "stern duty," was a blank to be filled in that, virtually any way in which readers filled it, resulted in political panic by seeking to strengthen the United States by weakening its First Amendment pillar. Indeed, the city of Boston did just that when it banned *Leaves of Grass.*

A Shift in the Groundwork

The classification "homosexual" did not appear in English until the 1892 translation of Austro-German psychiatrist Richard Kraft-Ebing's 1886 work *Psychopathia Sexualis.* Five years later, British physician Havelock Ellis published *Sexual Inversion,* the first book by an English-speaking author that regarded homosexuality as a mental illness as opposed to a sin or a crime. In the wake of this shift in perspective, state laws regarding homosexuality were changed in Oregon and Idaho during the opening decades of the twentieth century—but not in a way that reflected any shift in panic. Both states enacted statutes enabling medical treatment of convicted homosexuals through sterilization.

The public assertion of gay rights that, among Americans, can be traced to Walt Whitman, grew into a group of men in 1924 when Henry Gerber organized the first officially chartered organization for homosexual men, the Chicago-based Society for Human Rights. Backlash occurred soon after when Gerber was arrested and his organization eliminated by virtue of bankruptcy resulting from his three trials, none of which resulted in a conviction. The presence of panic surfaced at the end of the third trial when the detective who had arrested Gerber asked him, "What was the idea of the Society for Human Rights anyway? Was it to give you birds the legal right to rape every boy on the street?"[13] His question filtered out the fact that the society's stated mission explicitly opposed "seduction of adolescents."[14] What its charter urged was discussion of homosexuality. Political panic was thus demonstrated by arresting Gerber, not for violating a law that any of the three juries could agree he'd done, but by seeking to protect the republic by weakening its First Amendment guarantee of free speech.

Just as Whitman paid a price for his expressions by losing his government job, in the era following Gerber's attempt to organize a public discussion, gay men were increasingly at risk of losing their job. That much of this fear had a political component is revealed by the fact that those careers viewed as vital to the future of the nation were those in which homosexuals were most at risk of being fired. When a University of Texas regent declared in 1944 that "a nest of homosexuals in the faculty" had been discovered, the revelation made national news.[15] So too did the 1948 revelation of what one newspaper termed, "the near fantastic story of mad homosexual parties" involving faculty at the University of Missouri.[16] Education was a career field particularly vulnerable to panic over homosexuals, much as it was in the panics over Catholics and communists, since education entails preparing the nation's future guardians. The fact that parents, too, contribute significantly to preparing their children for the nation's stewardship often contributes to, rather than diminishes, education as a flashpoint for panic. What may seem to be an irony results from parenting being so filled with uncertainties— uncertainties that tend to be exacerbated as a parent's ability to control a child's choices diminishes when the child leaves the home for school. Increased uncertainties regarding one's child can render a person more susceptible to panic-inducing claims about education than to comparable claims regarding other career fields.

Panic, in the form of doing that which one fears, also affected careers in the military or those that involved security clearances, and ultimately any job in the federal government. Fearing the nation was endangered by gays in any aspect of government service, those in panic endangered the nation by shattering its Fourteenth Amendment's guarantee of equal protection under the law. During World War II, a man ejected from the military when his homosexuality was discovered wrote to an advice columnist, "I feel I might as well end it all . . . How can I ever face my family?" When the letter writer noted that, prior to serving in the military, "I was the president of our company and made $10,000 per year," he revealed his fear that this revelation of his homosexuality would also derail his career in private enterprise.[17] Fear of such career consequences was further validated when, also during the war, a father wrote the same columnist, "To think, here I am a prominent business executive and I find my son dismissed from the navy for such degeneracy! . . . I've told him to stay away from home and try to launch his life anew in some other city."[18] Those in the private sector who feared gays weakened their company's economic prospects consequently weakened the nation's economic legacy as the Land of Opportunity.

Peak of the Panic

Panic over homosexuals became most widespread during the years that followed World War II by virtue of being connected to the panic over communism. In addition to congressional investigations into communists in government positions, other federal efforts were specifically focused on gays. "Senator Wherry Says 3750 Government Men, Women Are Sex Perverts," headlined a 1950 wire service report on "a full-scale Senate investigation to rid the government of perverts . . . and new legislation designed to rout out homosexuals."[19] Echoing nineteenth-century warnings of imminent danger from radicals, the report went on to tell readers of "a plan of Communists to sabotage and damage Washington in case of war with Russia . . . using sex degenerates for subversive purposes."

President Dwight D. Eisenhower bestowed credibility on such fears by issuing an executive order declaring, "The appointment of each civilian officer or employee in any department or agency of the Government shall be made subject to investigation . . . [regarding] habitual use of intoxicants to excess, drug addiction, sexual perversion."[20] Further credibility was provided by Secretary of State Dean Acheson when he revealed that ninety-one homosexuals had been recently dismissed from the State Department because "they are easy targets for blackmail or threats to expose them."[21] A variation of doing that which one fears surfaces with this edict, the variant being *effecting* that which one fears. What potentially made gays in government jobs "easy targets for blackmail" was that those in panic caused gays to be fired from their government jobs. Had the government not fired workers for being gay, "threats to expose them" would not have made them "easy targets for blackmail."

Others in panic urged the government to go even further. On February 16, 1950, Washington-based columnist Gene Howe told readers of "gossip going around Washington . . . that many of the intellectuals who are playing with Communistic ideas are funny men," referred to more specifically in the next sentence as "effeminate." Howe entered the portal to panic through the use of unverified claims and absolutes, characterizing *all* homosexuals as thinking alike and feeling alike when he claimed, "They are misfits, they are unhappy . . . and they welcome any opportunity to avenge themselves on society as they know it." Howe then passed into the realm of panic by advocating that which he feared via a blank to be filled in when he advocated, by quoting an unnamed authority, "'Drive the funny men out of Washington and have all of them over the country catalogued and under surveillance and the menace of Communism would be lessened greatly,' says a prominent Washington man who knows the ropes."[22] Panic resided in Howe urging government action against a group of citizens, whether or not they have violated any law, in order to protect the United States, whose pillars include the constitutional guarantee of due process of law.

Imagery used in the panic over communists ("secret cell," "spy ring") closely resembled that applied to homosexuals ("nest of homosexuals," "homosexual ring").[23] Such imagery also closely resembled that which had been applied to convents during the panic over Catholics ("abode of licentiousness and deception," "league with the devil").[24] Such imagery in turn resembled covenants with the devil previously applied to accused witches in Salem.[25] The element of panic that is the common denominator in these recurring images is secrecy. Conveying secrecy adds both a blank of mystery and intention—intention being secrecy's implication that those involved are engaged in acts so abhorrent, or of such danger to the nation if known, they do not want others even to imagine them. Imagining them is precisely what such a blank to be filled in does.

In addition to fueling the panic over homosexuals with panic then raging over communists, the intensity of the panic over homosexuals was further fueled as a backlash to a renewed effort by gay Americans to achieve equal rights. In 1950, Harry Hay formed a gay rights group called the Mattachine Society. "America, On Guard! Homosexuals, Inc.," headlined a feature in the May 1954 issue of *Confidential*. "Don't sell the twisted twerps short!" it told readers. "Once they met in secret. Today, they've organized as the 'Mattachines,' with a goal of a million members and a $6,000,000 bankroll!" Further backlash followed when gay women soon formed an organization, the Daughters of Bilitis. The crescendo of panic now increasingly engulfed them too in employment prohibitions. Previously, gay women often eluded such discrimination under the guise of "spinsters." But they had not eluded derision. As far back as 1784, a reader of Boston's *Independent Chronicle* wrote, "Passing up State Street a few days since, I was met by one of those hermaphrodites who infect our streets, her hat fiercely cock'd, and a cane which she exercised with such agility as far out did out most profes'd beaux." The letter writer employed a blank to be filled in with the word "infect," which left it to readers to determine what weakening of the body politic resulted from such infection. When the letter concluded, "Those of sense and virtue must ever despise such beings," it employed two more blanks to be filled in, leaving it to readers to determine what constituted "sense" and "virtue," and hinged those blanks to side-by-side absolutes in his phrase, "*must ever* despise."[26] That the letter was reprinted in other papers reveals that awareness of, and disdain for, lesbians was widespread.

Even as panic over gay men and women flared nationwide, it was markedly less intense in regard to careers not viewed as vital to the security of the nation, and in regard to gays who did not publicly advocate for their rights. A particularly vivid illustration of this aspect of the panic is the career of Liberace, a flamboyantly effeminate pianist who skyrocketed to fame and fortune during this era. "Women, from five to sixty-five, go for him," California's *Long Beach Independent* told readers on March 23, 1954, though the article did add, "Men generally are not so enthusiastic." For all his flamboyance, Liberace never advocated for gay rights; in fact, he went to great lengths to imply he was not gay.[27] He told one interviewer that "he volunteered for military service in 1941 . . . but a spinal injury, causing a nervous disorder, made him ineligible."[28] He sued the scandal magazine *Confidential* after an article in its July 1957 issue reported that he "minced down the ramp from the plane . . . [and] upon being introduced to the young publicity man . . . was getting ideas." The exposé then asserted that Liberace "wasted no time persuading the press agent to join him in his suite for a drink. The latter went along with the invite, figuring it was his job to keep Dimples happy. He had no idea that in a few short minutes he would be fighting for his honor." Declaring that the statements were "defamatory, vulgar, rude, and completely untrue," Liberace succeeded in obtaining a $40,000 settlement from *Confidential*.[29]

Widespread Panic Begins to Abate

A seed that would contribute to decreasing the panic over gays sprouted shortly before the peak of the panic in the 1950s. In 1947, the results of the first Kinsey Report, a massive study of the sexual histories of over 12,000 Americans, was released. It was conducted by Indiana University professor Alfred C. Kinsey. A wire service article that appeared in newspapers nationwide reported, "Homosexuality has been practiced by . . . nearly forty percent of unmarried men reaching the age of forty." The report sought to avoid generating panic by pointing out that this "does not mean all these men are homosexuals, in the sense of continuing the practice."[30] Prior to what Kinsey verified statistically regarding human sexuality, legislators and judges had already reflected in shifting laws and sentences. In 1938, California passed laws that sought to treat homosexuality as a mental illness rather than a crime. Several other states followed suit.[31]

As in other panics, signs that widespread fear was diminishing intensified the panic among some who remained fearful. In the wake of California's judicial changes, a January 29, 1947, editorial in the *Long Beach Independent* (the same paper that later wrote benignly of Liberace, as discussed previously) warned that "where the courts are lenient, that community becomes dangerous for children to walk the streets." The assertion entered the portal to panic with this unverified claim that fewer children were molested by homosexuals in jurisdictions imposing prison sentences on people convicted of any homosexual act than in jurisdictions where homosexuality was treated as a mental illness and child molestation as a crime. Asserting absolutes, the editorial went on to declare that "*all such tendencies* are criminal tendencies" and that "one *never* knows when such an offender may become a sadistic ravager of some child or adult." (Italics added.) When the editorial then stated, "Women fear being out alone at night," it employed the fallacy that concluded Socrates was a cat by having its readers believe:

> *There are homosexual men who commit sexual assaults.*
> *Women fear sexual assaults, particularly at night.*
> *Women fear homosexuals at night.*

Clearly filtered from this reasoning is that women who fear being out alone at night do not fear being raped by a homosexual. The editorial in the *Long Beach Independent* contained an additional unverified claim that has long been widely believed and is a highly potent element in the panic over homosexuals. It is the assumption that homosexuals have a greater predilection for pedophilia than heterosexuals. Data has repeatedly shown that the percentage of homosexuals who are pedophiles is not measurably different from that of heterosexuals who are pedophiles.[32]

In 1963, with both panic over homosexuals and panic over communists no longer as widespread as they had been a decade earlier, Congressman John Dowdy of Texas introduced legislation to deny the Mattachine Society its tax-exempt status as a nonprofit organization. When objections were raised as to the constitutionality of the bill, Dowdy's reply might be seen as the peak of the panic's intensity, but was more akin to the execution of dogs during the waning of the panic over witchcraft. Seeking to reenergize both panics, Dowdy pointed to laws denying tax-exempt status to communist organizations, then employed an absolute when he asserted, "As far as I know, *all* the security risks that have deserted the United States have been homosexuals."[33] (Italics added.) Dowdy's assertion stopped short of entering the portal to panic since it was governed by the phrase, "as far as I know," thereby allowing for the fact that he knew very little about the very few desertions from the United States to enemy nations. Dowdy's bill was defeated, evidence that his remarks came at a time when panic over gays was beginning to decline.

An increasing number of gays now joined with efforts by the Mattachine Society to combat such intensified rage. Antigay rage detonated on June 28, 1969, in what has come to be known as the Stonewall Riot—a melee that triggered backlash in news coverage that blamed gays for what transpired. "Hundreds of young men went on a rampage in Greenwich Village shortly after three A.M. yesterday after a force of plainclothes men raided a bar that the police said was well known for its homosexual clientele," the *New York Times* reported. "The crowd grew to close to four hundred during the melee."[34] The raid was the third on a Greenwich Village gay bar in a two-week spate of raids on bars catering to gays (the bar in this instance being the Stonewall Inn).

While gays were the victims of the police raid and the *Times* coverage, the episode galvanized many to combat victimization by becoming more assertive. Not long after the raid, a November 1, 1969, *Washington Post* article was headlined, "Protesting Homosexuals Seize City Hall in S.F." A November 17, 1969, *New York Times* feature was entitled, "The Woman Homosexual: More Assertive, Less Willing to Hide." A June 28, 1970, article in Tucson's *Star-Citizen* with the headline "Gay Power Openly Flexes Its Muscles" began with an interview of a once secretly gay marine who was now a school teacher telling of his dream to live openly in a small town such as the one where he grew up. "I wouldn't hide anymore. I'd go to the people and tell them I'm gay and that I don't want to seduce their eight-year-old sons or turn them into flaming faggots."

Once again a backlash of panic reignited throughout the country. Homosexuality was now accorded the absolute of being "the greatest moral evil of our time" by a minister addressing the annual meeting of the Seventh-day Adventist church.[35] Singer and former Miss America finalist Anita Bryant became a leading figure in a movement called Save Our Children. "As a mother, I know that homosexuals cannot biologically reproduce children; therefore, they must recruit our children," she warned in her 1978 book *At Any Cost*. In seventeen words, Bryant was able to employ two fallacies, a filtered fact, an unverified claim, two false claims, and a blank to be filled in. The entire statement was predicated upon an unverified claim that homosexuals seek to reproduce homosexuals. Its opening phrase, "as a mother," served solely to induce panic among parents with a false claim, since motherhood is not required to know that homosexual sex cannot result in pregnancy. When Bryant stated "homosexuals cannot biologically reproduce children," she employed a claim that, as a mother, she ought to have known to be false. Homosexuals can, indeed, biologically reproduce children. In addition to filtering the fact that many people who have engaged in homosexual acts have also been the biological parents of children, Bryant also filtered the fact that the preponderance of research indicates the percentage of homosexual offspring (biological or adopted) of homosexual parents is no different than the percentage of homosexual offspring of heterosexual parents.[36] Governing the statement is a blank to be filled in, "recruit," which left it to readers to determine what constituted such recruitment and led the reader to the fallacy that whatever elements a reader *correlated* with homosexual recruitment *caused* homosexuality.

As seen most vividly in the panics over communists and capitalists, alarm breeds alarm. Alarmed by Anita Bryant's influential voice, the now nationally organized gay community mounted a campaign against her, spearheaded by a boycott of Florida oranges and orange products until such time as she was fired from her position as spokesperson in television commercials for Florida's orange growers. As had happened to gays and communists, Bryant lost her job and an opportunity that was in the works to star in a network television show. Bryant in turn, reacted with increased panic-inducing vehemence. "When the homosexuals burn the Holy Bible in public, how can I stand by silently?" she declared in a fund-raising letter sent out for Save Our Children.[37] Absent from her unverified claim are any examples of incidents in which homosexuals burned the Bible.

Backlash, as an aspect of the panics over gays and women (whose feminism Bryant also opposed despite her own longtime career), surfaced anew, as many Americans now voiced reinvigorated opposition to homosexuals. Syndicated columnist Max Rafferty wrote on July 9, 1977, that he was "lining up in the Bryant Brigade" because "Anita doesn't want her children taught in tax-supported public schools by sex perverts." Rafferty's political panic over gays surfaced when he employed two blanks to be filled in by asserting, "We cannot have it because the actual survival of our country in the years ahead depends upon a generation which will be *straight,* not *distorted.*"[38] (Italics added.) In a November 30, 1977, letter to the editor of California's *Freemont Argus,* a reader wrote, "Just as the queers seek to silence Anita Bryant, now you want to silence people like me." Not silenced at all by virtue of the paper publishing his letter, he warned that homosexuality "precedes degeneration and death for the nation's state." Fully entering the realm of panic, the reader advocated "degeneration and death" of the nation's founding pillars when he wrote, "The Declaration of Independence says that certain inalienable rights come from the creator. But God says perversion is an abomination." While the spirit of the Declaration of Independence became embodied in the Constitution, this letter writer sought to replace the Constitution's prohibition of a state religion with the Bible as the state religion. Moreover, the letter writer filtered out from the Bible its decree of the death sentence for homosexuals, unless he indeed believed it to be a capital crime—in which case he also either believed or filtered from the Bible its decrees of death for adulterers and, in Numbers 15:32–36, a person who picks up a stick on Sabbath.

As repeatedly seen, verbally expressed panic is often followed by violently expressed panic. On November 27, 1978, less than a year after becoming the first openly gay person elected to the San Francisco Board of Supervisors, Harvey Milk was assassinated. Also as repeatedly seen, his assailant was a deeply troubled person who found a place for his pathology in the panic over gays. Milk was murdered by fellow board member Dan White, who had recently resigned for what he had said were personal reasons but then sought reinstatement. Milk's assassination was but one of a spate of violent assaults on homosexuals during this era of backlash in response to the gay rights movement. Two years after Tennessee Williams wrote of being gay in his 1977 memoirs, the sixty-seven-year-old Pulitzer Prize–winning playwright was beaten by five teenage boys in a ritual that has come to be known as "gay bashing." Gay women, too, soon became the victims of violent assaults. In 1988, Rebecca Wight was shot to death and her companion, Claudia Brenner, wounded by Stephen Ray Carter when he realized the two Appalachian Trail hikers were gay. In 1995, Roxanne Ellis and Michelle Abdill were murdered in Medford, Oregon, after voicing opposition in local news interviews to a proposed state law allowing restrictions on homosexuals.

The intensity of these episodes was further fueled as backlash in response to the fact that gay men and women were not only proclaiming their sexuality in these years, but increasingly rallying around a cornerstone of the fear that homosexuals endangered the strength of the nation: the ban on gays in the military. As early as 1966, the Mattachine Society began organizing parades in a campaign to end the ban. Seeking the support of those who supported the war in Vietnam more than they opposed gay rights, the Mattachines announced that "there are seventeen million homosexuals in the nation, most of whom would be eager to fight for their country."[39] Soon, however, the Mattachine Society set this issue aside, not wanting to be associated with what was becoming an unpopular war. It resurfaced, however in 1990 and 1991 with the far more popular Persian Gulf War. In this instance, the American military was widely perceived as liberators freeing Kuwait from an invasion by Iraqi dictator Saddam Hussein's troops.

No sooner had gays resumed their effort to serve in the armed forces than the fear that homosexuals threatened the nation's strength resurfaced. Explaining his reasons for opposing gays in the military, Army colonel Michael E. McAleer declared of himself and fellow service members, "We all take an oath to obey and fight and defend the Constitution and defend the beliefs of Americans."[40] Filtered from the statement was the fact that gays who had entered the military took the same oath McAleer took. Moreover, unverified (because untrue) was that any military oath included a vow to defend "the beliefs of Americans." It was a significant false claim as it formed the basis for McAleer's conclusion that Americans believed homosexuality is "against Christian ideals." Out of his fear for the nation's foundations, McAleer revealed his panic by hurling a political grenade at the First Amendment in order to inscribe Christianity as the national religion.

That political panic is neither the province of conservatives or liberals surfaced when the *Washington Post* reported on August 19, 1991, that Secretary of Defense Dick Cheney, a man frequently labeled as a conservative, "rejected as 'a bit of an old chestnut' the idea that homosexuals present a security risk to the country." Quite possibly Cheney's view emanated from his having a gay daughter whom he knew was not a security risk to the country. Whatever its source, Cheney's view was quickly becoming widespread. In 1993, Congress enacted a military regulation popularly known as, "Don't Ask, Don't Tell," which prohibited the rejection or dismissal from military service based on homosexuality, unless that person openly demonstrated "a propensity to engage in homosexual acts." Backlash, a key element in the panic over homosexuals, was built into this new policy even as it promoted greater acceptance of gays. Such backlash resided in its acceptance of gays in the military—unless a gay soldier asserted his or her homosexuality in any way.

Ten years later, government punishment of homosexuals receded when the Supreme Court ruled in 2003 that the Texas sodomy law was unconstitutional. Its decision in *Lawrence v. Texas* ended all such laws throughout the nation. In so doing, it reversed the court's 1986 decision in *Bowers v. Hardwick,* which had upheld Georgia's sodomy law. That the Supreme Court voted 5-to-4 in 1986 to uphold such laws and 6-to-3 to strike them down in 2003 provides a measure of the rate at which panic over homosexuals was diminishing.

In his dissenting opinion, Justice Antonin Scalia revealed that Supreme Court justices are as susceptible to panic as anyone else. "Today's opinion is the product of a Court . . . that has largely signed on to the so-called homosexual agenda," he wrote, employing a blank to be filled in with his use of the term, "homosexual agenda."[41] Though Scalia did not invent the term, stamping it with the imprimatur of a Supreme Court justice bestowed credibility on a panic-inducing phrase that gained sufficient traction as to title many of this era's spate of antigay books, such as, *The Homosexual Agenda: Exposing the Principal Threat to Religious Freedom Today* (2003); *The Lavender Tidal Wave: Exposing the "Gay" Agenda in America* (2004); and *The Agenda: The Homosexual Plan to Change America* (2005). The credibility bestowed by Justice Scalia's use of the term was further extended to the panic-inducing elements alarmists often used to fill in this blank. When Connaught Marshner, director of the Child and Family Protection Institute, wrote in a June 9, 1984, *Washington Post* column, "Our nation must resist pressure to carry out the homosexual agenda," she filled the blank with another blank when she asserted the agenda included seeking "converts among children." The word "converts" required readers to determine what acts or statements constitute such conversion. Tucked inside this blank within a blank was yet another element of panic, the correlation = causation fallacy. As with Anita Bryant's use of the word "recruits," this use of the word "converts" implied that whatever elements the reader correlated with homosexual conversion caused homosexuality.

Justice Scalia's dissent in *Lawrence v. Texas* also strung together panic-inducing filtered facts when it stated, "Many Americans do not want persons who openly engage in homosexual conduct as partners in their business, as scoutmasters for their children, as teachers in their children's schools, or as boarders in their home." Filtered was the fact that the ruling did not prohibit Americans from refusing to form a business partnership with a gay person or refusing to have a gay person as a boarder in their home. It did not forbid scout organizations from refusing to allow gays to be scoutmasters, as evidenced by the fact that the Boy Scouts of America continued—legally, albeit controversially—to do just that. It also had nothing to do with the separate legal issue of refusing employment in a public school on the basis of sexuality. It simply said Americans could not be arrested for consensual homosexual acts. Such irrational conclusions from a Supreme Court justice demonstrate that, even among highly educated individuals, their panic often intensifies when they perceive widespread panic to be receding. Indeed, as Justice Scalia could perceive in lower court rulings, widespread panic over gays was continuing to recede. In 2010, a federal court ruled that the ban on openly gay members of the military was unconstitutional. The decision was not appealed to the Supreme Court because Congress, three months later, repealed "Don't Ask, Don't Tell," thereby equalizing military restrictions on sexual behavior.

Panic Over Love

A bill to legalize gay marriage was introduced in Massachusetts in 1972 by a newly elected state legislator named Barney Frank. The effort failed, but the fact that it was proposed in a state legislature revealed a building momentum. As far back as 1967, when the December 3 *New York Times* reported on an Episcopal theologian who saw no sin in "homosexual acts between persons who intend a permanent union," Americans were aware of the notion of gay marriage. As with other assertions by gays for equal treatment, backlash followed. "I don't want homosexual marriages legalized any more than any other things like lying, cheating, stealing, drunkenness, killing," declared a reader of the Sarasota *Herald-Tribune* in an August 3, 1996, letter to the editor. His statement not only filtered out the fact that lying, cheating, stealing, and killing are not acts between consenting parties, but also filtered that the acts listed are viewed by homosexuals in the same variety of ways as they are among heterosexuals. Fully entering the realm of panic, the letter went on to declare, "What we need to do in America is get back to practicing right from wrong with a moral conscience of what our creator desires and commanded." By employing the blank to be filled in, "what our creator desires and commanded," to govern the sentence, the statement sought to strengthen the nation by weakening the First Amendment pillar that prohibits laws solely on the basis of "what our creator desires and commanded."

Following in the footsteps of Justice Scalia's irrational conclusions, the attorney general of Georgia demonstrated panic in 1991 when he revoked a job offer to a young woman upon learning she and her female lover had recently been joined in a Jewish marriage ceremony performed by a rabbi. "She came along and said, 'I'm going to engage in conduct which is not recognized, sanctioned, or condoned by Georgia law,'" the attorney general,

Michael Bowers, explained to justify his withdrawal of the job offer as "strictly a legal question."[42] Bowers entered the portal to panic by filtering out the fact that the young woman had never purported to have a civil marriage, nor had she ever sought tax, insurance, or any other financial benefits for spouses. Thus the state attorney general entered the realm of panic when, seeking to protect the state by adhering to strictly legal behavior, he weakened the state by not sticking to strictly legal behavior. As the young woman herself said, "There is nothing in Georgia law that says two women cannot have a marriage ceremony."[43]

Far more panic-inducing than even Justice Scalia's dissent from that Supreme Court decision were the warnings of author Michael Savage, who foresaw in the ruling "a loaded gun pointed at the heart of traditional marriage." Savage sought to induce panic when he wrote, "I feel as if we're living in the last days of the ancient Roman Empire, which fell when this kind of degenerate behavior was allowed to take over the public and then the military."[44] The statement not only filtered out homosexuality in the Roman Empire during its most powerful era, but also any other factors that contributed to the decline and fall of Rome. By this filtering, the statement became an absolute: Homosexuality destroyed the Roman Empire. Savage additionally employed the panic-inducing element of secrecy in his explanation of why the court had reversed its previous *Bowers* decision, which had upheld laws prohibiting homosexual acts, when he spoke of seeing "the invisible hand of Ruth Ginsberg at work behind the scenes. She's doing her best to bring an end to American democracy." As verification of this claim, he wrote, "Look how the high court in Israel has snatched power and authority from other branches of government."

Michael Savage is yet another example of how alarmists cannot be stereotyped. Though his views on the fall of the Roman Empire suggest he is not very well educated, he holds two masters degrees and a PhD from Berkeley. And though his statements regarding Justice Ginsberg and Israel give every appearance of being (and may well be) anti-Semitic, Michael Savage was born Michael Alan Weiner, the son of Jewish parents. The reasons for Michael Weiner Savage's panic are psychological, rather than logical. For

this reason one cannot reason with people in panic. Barney Frank understood this when confronted at a town hall meeting by a constituent holding a
placard showing President Obama with a Hitler mustache. When she asked
Frank "Why are you supporting this Nazi policy?" he replied, "Ma'am, trying to have a conversation with you would be like trying to argue with a
dining room table."[45]

The backlash over the notion of gay marriage was so widespread that in
1996 Congress passed and President Bill Clinton signed into law the Defense
of Marriage Act (DOMA). The law denied federal spousal benefits to gay
men and women who were married in any state that had legalized same-
sex marriage. At the time, no state had legalized gay marriage, though in
2004 Massachusetts became the first state to do so. In 2013, the Supreme
Court struck down key provisions in DOMA. Other states subsequently
commenced legalizing gay marriage.

Remaining Wildfires of Panic

Between 1990 and 2010, forty-five gay men and women were murdered in
the United States for no other reason than that they were gay. Most of these
victims attracted little or no attention. One who did was Matthew Shepard,
a college student in Laramie, Wyoming. The brutality with which he was
beaten senseless on October 12, 1998, then lashed to a fence and left there to
die attracted national attention. That attention, in turn, triggered a backlash
by members of a small Kansas church under the leadership of its minister,
Fred Phelps. Intruding on the Shepard family's funeral with placards declaring "God Hates Fags," the group made network news. With this springboard
to the national spotlight, Phelps and his followers went on to intrude on
other newsworthy funerals, not only of men and women who were gay but
also funerals for soldiers killed in combat, asserting that God was punishing
the United States for allowing gays in the military.[46]

Throughout the episodes of American panic over homosexuals, the underlying political element, as opposed to personal, has remained the fear
of national weakness, envisioned as effeminacy. When columnist Charley

Reese warned in 1997, "The reason nations fall when they become effeminate is that they cannot cope," he echoed the 1787 warning previously cited from the *Vermont Gazette:* "Shall effeminate fops undermine a fabric raised by wise politicians and brave warriors?" When Reese elaborated by claiming, "Effeminate men can be cruel, but they are not brave," he filtered out the bravery of those gay men who dared to combat the police raiding the Stonewall Inn. When he added, "Warrior qualities such as courage, boldness, unselfishness, and an ability to organize are needed in peace as well as in war," he filtered out precisely those qualities having been demonstrated by the gay men and women who organized and marched for equal rights, not to mention the unknown numbers of gay men and women who served in the armed forces, faithfully but silently, often while facing danger to life and limb. Based on this filtered foundation, Reese entered the realm of panic by asserting that this strong nation, founded as a quest for liberty and political equality, was in danger of becoming weak because gay Americans were becoming more liberated and politically equal.

Eleven

"America is under siege, facing a hostile invasion on its own soil.... The invaders are ILLEGAL IMMIGRANTS, their battleground is the U.S.-Mexico border, what's at stake is the money, security, and freedom of all Americans."

—Jon E. Dougherty, ILLEGALS: THE IMMINENT THREAT POSED BY OUR UNSECURED U.S.-MEXICO BORDER (2004)

Periods of widespread alarm over Latinos entering the United States first surfaced in the opening years of the twentieth century and have continued to the present. This alarm, which at times has entered the realm of panic, echoes past panics over Eastern European immigrants in the late nineteenth and early twentieth centuries, Chinese immigrants in the mid-nineteenth century, and Irish immigrants in the 1840s.

In the early years of the United States, few Latin Americans immigrated into what was then a nation that extended only to the Mississippi River and did not yet extend to the Gulf of Mexico. (The boundaries of the United States first touched the Gulf of Mexico with the 1803 Louisiana Purchase.

The frontage also expanded with acquisitions from Spanish West Florida in 1810 and 1813, with Florida becoming part of the United States in 1819, and Texas in 1845.) To the extent that immigration was taking place, far more United States citizens were emigrating to Latin America (most to a region of Mexico called Texas). When Latin American lands began gaining independence from Spain in the 1820s, many Americans aspired to spread the democratic traditions—if not the borders of the United States—into these newly emerging nations. Latinos were typically viewed at this time as having "a great facility of acquiring knowledge . . . [and] much attached to the great cause of independence and liberty." So wrote John M. Niles in his 1825 book *A View of South America and Mexico*. Even darker-hued Latinos, Niles told readers, "are orderly and industrious and make good citizens . . . and many of them have been much devoted to the cause of liberty."

These attitudes changed with the Mexican War, from which the United States acquired both a lot of new land and a lot of new citizens. That these citizens were darker hued led Vermont congressman George P. Marsh to say, in opposing the war, "What evidence is there that the possession of New Mexico, or California . . . can be attended with any solid advantage to the people of this country? They are inhabited by a mixed population . . . incapable of sympathy or assimilation with our own . . . unfitted for self-government, and unprepared to appreciate, sustain, or enjoy, free institutions." Marsh's absolute, "incapable of assimilation," echoed alarms regarding Native Americans and would echo anew in the panics over Chinese and Jews. Another absolute, "unfitted for self-government," likewise echoed claims regarding Catholics and would recur in the panics over African Americans and women.

First Widespread Panic

The first influx of Latinos into the United States occurred at the same time and for the same reason as the first influx of Chinese: the California Gold Rush. The panic over these Latinos was further fueled by the fact that the United States shared a long and open border with Spanish-speaking Mexico. Competition for the gold soon resulted in similar violence. Americans destroyed a gold mining settlement of Chileans in September 1849.[1] In 1850, another group of American miners passed a resolution requiring "all foreigners, except persons engaged in permanent business, to leave Tuolumne County within fifteen days." Some 1,200 Mexicans packed up and moved on rather than face the consequences.[2]

But an additional fear fueled more widespread fear of these Latino encampments. "The number of Mexicans has been doubled within a short time in that region," South Carolina's *Charleston Courier* told readers on June 22, 1849, going on to warn of the possibility "this jewel is wrested from the hands of the North *Americanos* to form a great and powerful nation, the mistress of the Pacific." Widespread panic over these Latino immigrants was held in check, however, by a far more immediate concern regarding a jewel being wrested from the United States—the American South. That jewel did indeed come loose during the Civil War, in which Confederate colonel John Baylor declared of the New Mexico Territory: "The Mexican population are decidedly Northern in sentiment, and will avail themselves of the first opportunity to rob us or join the enemy."[3] Indeed, both New Mexico and California, where the majority of Latino Americans lived, had opted to remain loyal to the Union—the state of California by rejecting secession and the Latinos in what was still the New Mexico Territory by opposing the brief creation during the war of a Confederate state of Arizona (whose boundaries traversed from Texas to California). But the loyalty demonstrated by Latinos had little effect on northern attitudes. Union General Henry Halleck said his New Mexican soldiers were "worse than worthless."[4]

Two events in the closing decades of the nineteenth century altered the nation's social landscape in ways that resulted in far more Latinos entering the United States. The first of these events was the end of Reconstruction in the South in 1877. No sooner had occupation by Union troops ended than persecution of African Americans intensified. By the turn of the century, so many African Americans were leaving the South that, to fill the void, impoverished Mexicans began to arrive as farm workers.

The second event was the nation's 1898 victory in the Spanish-American War, one of the results of which was the acquisition of Puerto

Rico. Like their Mexican counterparts, many impoverished Puerto Ricans migrated to become farm laborers—but not in the southern states. "The Porto [*sic*] Rican immigrants who are announced as on their way to New Orleans under contract to work on the plantations of Hawaii may not, and probably will not, be allowed to land," Boston's *Daily Advertiser* wrote in November 30, 1900, adding that federal authorities had been sent to New Orleans to prevent any of the Puerto Ricans from stepping off the ship. The reason these Puerto Ricans were forced to remain on board was that, quite possibly, they could not be deported if they chose to remain after coming ashore; since they were from an American territory, they could make the claim they were United States citizens.[5] An element of panic resided in the fear that all Puerto Ricans, being Latino, were widely viewed as a toxic element in the nation's body politic. By not permitting them to leave the ship in New Orleans, the authorities did that which they feared. Seeking to protect the United States they lifted the gangplank on the Fourteenth Amendment's guarantee of "equal protection under the law."

At the time, however, whether or not Puerto Ricans were citizens was a hotly contested question. In 1903, the city of Chicago prohibited its Puerto Rican residents from voting in the city's mayoral election, based on its claim that being a United States territory did not confer citizenship upon its people.[6] One year later, the Supreme Court sidestepped the citizenship issue but did rule that Puerto Ricans could not be denied unrestricted entry into the United States.[7] Congress officially bestowed citizenship on Puerto Ricans in 1917. In so doing, it conveniently rendered their young men eligible for the draft in World War I.[8]

Simultaneously, alarm was increasing over the number of Mexican immigrants, whose numbers had increased with the expansion of American agriculture. Despite the fact that Mexican farm workers had taken it upon themselves to venture from the South to as far as the Northwest, the *New Orleans Times-Picayune* told readers on January 7, 1909, that Mexicans were "unambitious, listless, physically weak, irregular and indolent." By 1914, the federal government dispatched railroad trains to Los Angeles, San Francisco, and Portland to round up Mexican immigrants and deport them.[9]

During this era, what would become the most murderous episode in the panic over Latinos suddenly detonated. "Officials in Brownsville, Texas, claim that they have unearthed a widespread plot to kill every white American from Brownsville to Arizona along the border, take towns and set up governments, free what is termed enslaved Mexicans and negroes, and commit other depredations," Oklahoma's *Hobart Republican* reported on February 6, 1915. Newspapers across the country reported this warning under headlines, such as in Georgia's February 21, 1915, *Columbus Enquirer-Sun,* "Negroes and Mexicans Want Republic in Tex." Elements of panic that contributed to this alarm surfaced when the *Hobart Republican* article told readers, "It is said that papers giving the details of the alleged proposed organization were found upon a man recently arrested for sedition." But the authorities released none of the details, meaning they did that which these Mexicans were accused of having done: They cloaked the plot in secrecy, but with a significant difference. Maintaining the secrecy in announcing the secrecy had the effect of inducing panic by generating blanks to be filled in. The public was left to imagine which Mexicans and how many Mexicans were planning to attack unknown targets.

Still, as with allegations of secret organizations of women, the alarm was not spun from thin air. A militant Mexican named Basilio Ramos, Jr., had recently entered the United States with a manifesto that sought to incite rebellion among Mexican Americans and African Americans. Ramos was soon discovered when other Mexicans revealed his plans to the authorities. His arrest, however, did not end the alarm. Two other Mexican Americans were soon charged in the conspiracy. The *Columbus Enquirer-Sun*'s February 21 coverage connected the two men to "circulars printed in Spanish [that] were distributed throughout South Texas," an assertion unsupported by any evidence and not included in the government's charges. Several days later, all the charges against the two men were dropped.

Ramos's plot, though aborted, continued to fuel panic in otherwise nonpolitical incidents. Headlines such as "Mexican Bandits Raid Ranches Across Border," in California's July 9, 1915, *San Jose Mercury,* aroused fears of invasion that led to headlines such as "Hope to Conquer Texas," in the

August 10, 1915, *Kansas City Times*. So widespread was the fear that President Wilson dispatched troops to the region. Their commander, General Frederick Funston, bestowed credibility on the fears when he declared he had information indicating "more than 3,000 Mexicans [meaning Mexican Americans] are pledged to a revolutionary organization already."[10] As with the earlier release of information on "a widespread plot to kill every white American from Brownsville to Arizona," Funston named neither the Mexicans nor the source of his information, thereby not only preserving their alleged secrecy, but in doing so adding fuel to the panic by generating a blank to be filled in.

In response to General Funston's remarks, the citizens of Laredo, Texas, issued a statement declaring, "We represent all shades of political belief and all local political factions, and we absolutely know that . . . all factions here are cooperating as American citizens to restore order and obtain adequate protection for our families and property."[11] Their words were soon supported by news reports such as that in the August 9, 1915, *Grand Rapids Press*, which told readers of Jesus Garcia, "a well-known Brownsville Mexican who gave information to the authorities concerning the raiders' movements [and] died today from wounds in last night's battle." Nevertheless, the response of those in panic effected that which one feared via the same circular process seen in the panic over gay government workers during the Cold War. On August 10, the *Kansas City Times* told readers, "It is claimed that for the last ten years Mexicans have held weekly meetings at [Jesus] Garcia's home. American neighbors assert that many members of the present bandit gangs were among those attending the weekly meetings." Not just Jesus Garcia, but all Mexican Americans were now viewed with suspicion due to the ability of secrecy—or the accusation of secrecy—to effect that which it fears. In this instance, some number of loyal Mexican Americans began carrying firearms out of fear that they might come under attack by those who feared them to be secretly disloyal. This effecting of that which one fears surfaced when the *Star* article continued: "The habit of peaceful Mexicans in this section of going armed constantly has made it difficult for the authorities to distinguish between the bandits and inoffensive citizens."

In Mexican American communities, white vigilantes went house to house searching for and taking any firearms they found. Two Mexican Americans were fatally shot in July, ostensibly for resisting arrest. In August 1915, Texas Rangers summarily shot and killed three Mexican Americans suspected of disloyalty. That same month, Montana's *Anaconda Standard* reported an incident in the border town of Nogales, Arizona: "Several hundred American soldiers engaged in a riot on the streets tonight as the result of a rumor that the Mexicans had threatened to take their guns away." Two hundred Mexicans fled across the border to escape pursuit from the soldiers. The following month the *Washington Post* reported on September 28, "Thirty dead Mexicans have been found within the past twenty-four hours [in Texas] near San Benito, Mission, Progreso, Chapin, and Mercedes. The bodies are lying along the roads and in the brush. Whether they were killed in a fight or were shot down on sight cannot be learned." On October 2, the *Albuquerque Morning Journal* reported, "The bodies of eleven Mexicans were found today on the American side of the Rio Grande near Donna. . . . Several of the bodies were identified as members of a family residing near Donna, Texas."

As seen in the panic over communist subversion (and as soon will be seen in the panic over Arab and Muslim-Americans), foreign policy conflicts can fuel domestic panic, and did in the case of Latinos. In May, 1916, Mexican revolutionary leader Pancho Villa, angered by President Wilson's support for the government of Mexico, invaded the town of Columbus, New Mexico, reportedly killing nineteen Americans and burning the town.[12] The following year, in the midst of World War I (though prior to the entry of the United States in that war) German Foreign Secretary Arthur Zimmermann sent a telegram to his nation's ambassador in Mexico, intercepted en route, that proposed urging Mexico to join Germany and its allies by promising to give back to Mexico regions of Texas, New Mexico, and Arizona. Both incidents sparked far more distrust of Mexico than of Mexican-American, but neither incident diminished the fears of those who distrusted the loyalty of Mexican Americans.

From the Gold Rush to the Great Depression, violence against Mexican immigrants and American citizens of Mexican descent was rife but statistically difficult to assess since such data was not always recorded. Some indication is provided, however, by scholars who have focused on lynching in the United States. Their estimates indicate that mobs lynched approximately 600 Latinos during those years.[13]

Fuel from Other Panics

As the crisis along the Mexican border subsided, those who remained in panic over Mexican immigrants fueled their warnings by connecting them to other concurrent panics. "The importance of the question of immigration from Mexico can hardly be overestimated. . . . It is tied up with the greatest of all our problems, that of race mingling," former Texas congressman James Slayden declared in 1921, studding his certitude with the absolutes "*can hardly* be overestimated" and "*greatest* of all our problems." (Italics added.) Slayden then asserted an unverified (to say the least) claim in declaring that "the average Mexican is as prodigal as the Negro."[14]

Another Texas congressman, John Box, urged legislation in 1919 and again in 1927 that would declare Mexicans "are not and cannot become Americans."[15] Box based his proposed prohibition of citizenship on his assertion that "the Mexican peon is a mixture of Mediterranean-blooded Spanish peasant with low-grade Indians. . . . Into that was fused much Negro slave blood." In urging Congress to protect "American racial stock from further degradation," Box revealed that the foundation of his assertions were unverified claims hiding inside a blank to be filled in.[16] The blank was the word governing his warning, "degradation," which left it to others to determine what constituted the gradations of race. Hiding inside that blank were unverified claims that, whatever one thought constituted such degradation, supposedly endangered the nation.

Yet again demonstrating that political panic is not confined to poorly educated people and the politicians who exploit them, University of California zoology professor Samuel J. Holmes applauded the Box Bill in "Perils of the Mexican Invasion," an article he authored in the May 1929 issue of the prestigious *North American Review*. Holmes based his use of the word "invasion" on population data derived not from census records but from a California State Fair contest for the largest family of which first prize went to a Mexican family with sixteen children. "This excessive fecundity is of course exceptional," Holmes conceded, but it was good enough for the professor to consider it "indicative of the breeding habits of this class of our population." Fueled by this poorly verified claim of immigration being tantamount to invasion, Holmes went on to claim that Mexicans "have little understanding of our government or institutions, and are usually indifferent to political questions." Having thus asserted an absolute that claimed all Mexicans think alike, Holmes went on to echo voting-bloc alarms heard years earlier during the panic over Catholics: "When they vote at all they commonly do so at the dictation of some boss." Echoing prior alarms, Holmes stated, "Of all the foreign stocks represented in any considerable numbers in our population, the Mexicans appear to be the least assimilable."

The Great Depression through World War II: More Immigration, Deportation, and Panic

Following close on the heels of Holmes's 1929 article, the Great Depression hit overpopulated and underemployed Puerto Rico particularly hard. But its people also had a particular avenue of escape as American citizens. "Free entry of Puerto Ricans into this country is causing a slum condition here," the *New York Times* reported on May 20, 1937. The article cited a federal official describing Puerto Ricans as "unable to perform ordinary labor because of climatic conditions, his physique, and his susceptibility to ailments."

Massive immigration of Puerto Ricans was countered by massive deportation of Mexicans. Deportation of illegal immigrants is not necessarily an act of panic, particularly when, as during the Depression, so many citizens were out of work. That panic fueled these mass deportations, however, is suggested by the fact that they commenced *prior* to the economic collapse in 1929. The 2,087 Mexicans deported in 1928 represented an increase of 37 percent over the 1,519 deported in 1927. More vivid evidence of panic surfaced during the Depression. Of the nearly 350,000 Latinos who were deported or fled, historians have estimated that approximately 60 percent were American citizens.[17]

As in the Civil War, the nation's entry into World War II did not sidetrack the panic over Latinos, despite the fact that more than 200,000 Puerto Ricans and Mexican Americans served in the armed forces. In this respect the panic was similar to the panic over African Americans, whose service in the nation's military—which, like that of Latinos, also commenced with the Civil War—did little to alter attitudes. Wartime service of Catholics, Jews, Chinese, and Japanese, on the other hand, did contribute to reducing widespread panic. Since war truly does threaten the security of the nation, the inconsistency of attitude change toward those who have put their lives on the line to defend the nation illustrates how deeply rooted in irrational beliefs political panic can be.

During World War II, the panics over the two groups not affected by wartime service, Latinos and African Americans, dovetailed further via a fashion in clothing: the zoot suit. This particular style in menswear originated in California among young Mexican and Mexican Americans and soon spread to African Americans. For some white Americans, the zoot suit was less a garment filled with a man than a fashion blank to be filled in. *Los Angeles Times* columnist Lee Shipley quipped on April 2, 1942, that it took a good deal of courage for a young man to wear a zoot suit in places like Los Angeles where "he is sure to encounter men in uniform. The latter have taken to stepping up to zoot suit wearers and politely asking, 'May I have this dance, Miss?'" The same paper filled in the garment with a very different fear in an October 6, 1942, headline: "Zoot Gangsters Knife and Rob More Victims."

Zoot suiters as effeminate and zoot suiters as gangsters formed a peculiar but explosive mix that detonated into riots in 1943 between whites in the military and Latinos in zoot suits. Initially, the *Los Angeles Times* reported the city's violence with bemusement. "Zoot Suiters Learn Lesson in Fights with Servicemen," headlined its June 7, 1943, coverage, which began, "Those gamin dandies, the zoot suiters, having learned a great moral lesson from servicemen, mostly sailors, who took over their instruction three days ago, are staying home nights." Not staying home were sixty-one "wearers of the garish costume"—a blank this article filled when it continued, "that has become a hallmark of juvenile delinquency." The news article stated that sixty-one Latinos wearing zoot suits had been arrested and jailed after conflict "arose as a result of beatings of individual sailors by juvenile street bands." Filtered from the report was any explanation as to why Latino youth might gang up and beat members of the military in a time of war.

Inadvertently, the same newspaper had accurately reported the cause of the riots some days earlier. On June 8, columnist Ed Ainsworth wrote in a light-hearted piece, "A zoot suiter starts down the street and by the time he gets a half block he is a walking advertisement for the Garden of Eden." As later investigations revealed, the violence was perpetrated not by bands of Latinos attacking servicemen but by bands of servicemen stripping Latinos in zoot suits for sport. But as Ainsworth's column also revealed, the sport went further. "Anybody discovered wearing one is liable to wear, very shortly, a face whose resemblance to a human one is purely coincidental," he quipped. "Many young men of the haut monde—or zoot suit type—after interviews with sailors, are taking up a new style described as the Receiving Hospital Mode." Camouflaged in Ainsworth's patter was panic. Fearing that zoot suit wearing Latinos represented a danger to the nation, he applauded violence that endangered the United States when its law enforcement authorities denied equal protection under the law to those who wore zoot suits.

This denial of equal protection soon bloomed into full panic when governmental bodies actively participated in the panic. The city council of Los Angeles considered a proposal that, as described in the June 10, 1943, *Los Angeles Times,* would make it "a jail offense to wear zoot suits with reat pleats within the city limits of Los Angeles." The following day, the paper reported that a municipal judge in the city offered probation to a nineteen-year-old Latino "if he would consent to have his flowing duck-tail haircut, pride of the zoot suiter, shorn from his head." More ridiculous, were it not so ominous, was a report in the *Times* the following day that California state legislator Jack Tenney was launching an investigation of "evidence indicating that the zoot suit demonstrations are Axis sponsored."

That such panic was widespread surfaced when nationally syndicated columnist Westbrook Pegler wrote of the violence in Los Angeles. "There is nothing to be gained by pretending that the American soldiers and sailors started this trouble," he told his readers on June 14, 1943, then employed absolutes in asserting that "when they are moved to mob action against *any* element of the community . . . *it is plain* that they are acting under great provocation."[18] (Italics added.) Pegler further revealed this panic was now widespread when he explained how Tucson, Arizona, had averted such violence when a local judge declared that "anyone brought before him wearing a zoot suit would be found guilty"—thereby vividly demonstrating the denial of the Constitution's equal protection under the law.

Pegler's column also provided clearer insight to the cause of the zoot suit violence. "Nobody seems to understand the zoot suiters," he admitted before speculating, "It may be bravado." Filtered from this speculation was why bravado did not cause teenage boys of European descent to attack American servicemen. Pegler's idealization of men in the military filtered out the possibility that some may have harbored harsh feelings about putting their lives on the line for this "degenerate exhibition of youthful mass hysteria"— Pegler's words when connecting, with the use of an absolute, Latinos and African Americans: "Indirectly but *unmistakably* this cult got its inspiration . . . on Broadway with hundreds of them [African Americans] writhing, twitching, and howling gibberish to the horrible squeals and squawks of the jive bands." (Italics added.)

Panic over African Americans both fueled and acquired fuel from the zoot suit riots. Days after the riots started in Los Angeles, rioting erupted in African American communities in Detroit; Philadelphia; Baltimore; Evansville, Indiana; and Beaumont, Texas. That the zoot suit served as the conduit of rage is evidenced by news coverage such as a report from Detroit that described "a clash between high school youths and servicemen and negro zoot suiters"; a headline on the Baltimore riots that announced, "Zoot Suit Negroes Cause Disturbance"; and an article headlined "Zoot Suit Riot in Philadelphia," which commenced, "Four Negro boys wearing zoot trousers and 'pancake' hats were attacked and badly beaten today by twenty-five white boys."[19]

Postwar Panic

"I have been down Mekiko way myself. . . . I have gone into the market places to bandy imprecations with those swarthy merchants," Ralf Charles Kircher wrote in his April 25, 1946, column, *Fagin Fogg's Fiddlesticks*. Appearing in Chicago's *Garfieldian*, Kircher went on to compare the political sensibilities of Mexicans to those of Texans by quipping about the Rio Grande: "I tried to buy it as a souvenir, and while any Mexican will claim to own it and offer it cheap, the state of Texas would not do business." Though cloaked in humor, Kircher's remarks suggest that the service and sacrifice of Latino Americans in World War II had little, if any, impact on attitudes toward Latinos.

Not cloaked in humor, and more detailed in its revelations, were the attitudes expressed in a 1954 letter to the editor of a college newspaper. Responding to student Ruben Salazar's article on discrimination against Mexican Americans by the school's fraternities and sororities, a fellow student replied, "Is your social life a failure? Have you been spurned? Perhaps the answers to these questions will shed light upon your feeling of inferiority and consequent attack upon all that is, at least striving for, properness and correctness." Tucked inside the letter writer's use of the blanks to be filled in, "properness" and "correctness," were unverified claims that Ruben Salazar lacked whatever readers of the letter determined as proper and correct behavior. The letter continued, "I belong to a church and a family, Salazar; I am also an American citizen"; it thus proceeded further into the portal to panic by implying the unverified claim that Ruben Salazar did not belong to a church and false claims that Salazar was not a citizen or a member of a family. The letter writer entered the realm of panic when he concluded, "Organizations to secure and retain *moral,* religious, and political freedom are not wrong, Salazar, and opposition to them stems either from *ignorance* or *ill-breeding.*"[20] (Italics added.) Panic was demonstrated by the letter writer justifying the rejection of Ruben Salazar for reasons promoting that which he feared. His reasons were *immoral* by virtue of false claims, *ill-bred* by virtue of blanks to be filled in that rudely withheld the reasons for Salazar's rejection, and *ignorant* in 1954 if based on a belief that skin color is the cause of one's character. Notably, Ruben Salazar went on to a distinguished career at the *Los Angeles Times* and as news director of a Spanish-language television station. His career was cut short when he was killed by police during the August 29, 1970, National Chicano Moratorium March against the war in Vietnam.

After World War II, emigration from Puerto Rico surged as a result of renewed political upheaval on the island and from many of its young men returning from war and seeking to create families in the more prosperous mainland of the United States. This renewed influx of Puerto Ricans renewed that aspect of the panic over Latinos. Also renewed were alarms that added fuel to the fear of Latinos by renewing its connection to the panic over African Americans. "The racial problem as between whites and Negroes, as between whites and Mexicans, as between whites and Puerto Ricans intensifies each year," syndicated columnist George Sokolsky wrote in 1957 in regard to a New York grand jury investigating unofficial segregation in the city's schools. "A grand jury investigation . . . would have to be truthful to be worthwhile," he stated, using this maxim to lend credence to his subsequently telling readers that such segregation reflects the "racial difference in maturity of children in certain environments." More specifically, Sokolsky's column asserted that "the sex compulsions in mixed groups, particularly among children from . . . homes in which sex played an unorthodox role . . . such factors cannot be dealt with politically."[21]

Sokolsky's claims barged far into the portal to panic. After being left on their own to determine what constituted "maturity," readers were lured further into the portal by unverified claims that racial differences caused whatever they used to fill in the blank of "maturity." His phrase "sex compulsions in mixed groups" employed a second unverified claim inside a blank to be filled in. Readers were first left to determine what constituted the effect of mixed groups on sex compulsions, which then triggered an unverified claim that whatever a reader determined to be the effect of mixed groups on sex compulsion differed from sex compulsions in "nonmixed groups." Seen here is a different way of employing an absolute.

While we have seen absolutes conveyed in idealizations, such as idealized references to the Founding Fathers, Sokolsky conveyed such idealization through its opposite when he referred to "homes in which sex played an unorthodox role." The phrase created the notion of homes in which sex played an *orthodox* role, such homes being ideal. From this duality, yet another unverified claim emerged via the implication that "racial difference" caused unorthodox sex.

Squarely in the realm of political panic had been those New Yorkers who amended the state constitution in 1921 to require that voters must be able to pass a literacy test in English. More commonly used in southern states to deny voting rights to African Americans, such tests represented panic in that their use to keep the nation from becoming politically weak weakened the nation's constitutional guarantee of equal protection under the law. By 1958, some 150,000 to 200,000 citizens in New York who had been born in Puerto Rico were denied the right to vote on this basis. Still, the denial of voting rights to Puerto Ricans not fluent in English failed to mitigate the panic, just as barring the entry of Chinese into the country did not mitigate that panic. In this era, columnist Jack Lait accused New York Congressman Vito Marcantonio of "importing Puerto Ricans by the planeload to build his vote."[22] Lait told his readers, "They vote as they are ordered," thereby echoing past panics in which alarmists invoked the absolute that all members of a particular group think alike. Tapping into another panic in that era, he warned, "By 1960, the city will have 1,000,000 of these migrants, and if they vote as overwhelmingly for extreme left-wing leaders as they do now, they could prove a powerful, and in certain circumstances, sinister political force." Readers were left to fill in the blank as to what constituted a sinister, extreme left-wing political force—communism being the most obvious choice. Filling that blank in just that way, New York City mayor William O'Dwyer accused Marcantonio of tricking "Puerto Ricans in this city into unwittingly supporting communism."[23]

New York was not alone in its panic over Puerto Ricans, as it was not the only place to which they migrated. Puerto Ricans who responded to calls from Walla Walla, Washington, for fruit and vegetable pickers had to agree to return to Puerto Rico after the harvest in order to be hired. But, as the *Olean Times Herald* lamented on June 8, 1950, "Since they have the same rights as other Americans, nobody can prevent them from staying." So many residents of Youngstown, Ohio, where Puerto Ricans worked in the steel mills, viewed them as a bad influence that in 1952 one city councilman proposed that they "be removed from the area."[24]

A common denominator in the alarms sounded over Puerto Ricans and those sounded over Mexican migrant workers was, in fact, a verifiable claim: both groups spoke Spanish. In 1997, Phyllis Schlafly, who had advanced her career via the panics over communism and, later, women, availed herself of this panic, too. Now a syndicated columnist, Schlafly employed a metaphor that was not a blank to be filled in, by virtue of the clarity of its meaning, then followed it with an absolute when she declared, "Once inside our union, Puerto Rico would be a modern *Trojan horse* . . . and do *irreparable* damage to our nation."[25] (Italics added.)

Connecting her alarm to fears of domestic terrorism that were con-tributing to panic over Muslim Americans, Schlafly then asserted an un-verified claim: "Many Puerto Rican extremists are known to have received terrorist training in Cuba." But her alarm extended to all Latinos when she wrote, "The most important issue about Puerto Rico is whether Americans are willing to admit a fifty-first state whose people don't speak English . . . the language of our Declaration of Independence and our Constitution." Her warning filtered out the fact that neither document loses its meaning in Spanish. The overall statement entered the realm of panic through double doors. It did that which it feared in its seeking to keep the nation strong by denying voting rights to the American citizens of Puerto Rico who do not speak English (just as literacy tests, by then illegal, had done in New York), thereby weakening the nation's constitutional guarantee of equal protection. And it did that which it feared by seeking to keep the nation strong by op-posing citizenship for people who do not speak the language in which the Declaration of Independence was written, thereby weakening the nation by altering its founding principle in that document, rendering it, "all *English speaking people* are created equal."

Phyllis Schlafly was not the first to sound such alarms. Indeed, they had been put into action in 1981 when Virginia made English its official language. The bill's sponsor in the legislature, Raymond Guest, told the press his concerns regarded proposals being discussed that would require bilingual education. Unstated was that official documents, such as election and referendum ballots, now need only be issued in English. One month later in Congress, California senator S. I. Hayakawa announced he would propose a constitutional amendment making English the nation's official language. "Unless such an amendment is adopted," wire services reported Hayakawa warning, "Hispanics in California, Texas, Florida, and Arizona will demand by the year 2000 that Spanish be made a second official language."[26] Credence was bestowed on Hayakawa's warning by virtue of his having been a professor of semantics and a college president. Yet filtered from this scholar's list of states was New Mexico, which had required all its laws to be published in Spanish and English until 1935, when the mandate was allowed to expire since it was no longer needed. Yet bilingual New Mexico never, since its acquisition in the Mexican War, had done (to borrow the words of Phyllis Schlafly) "irreparable damage to the nation."

Congress did not pass Senator Hayakawa's amendment, but in 1984 Kentucky senator Walter Huddleston introduced it again. Congress still opted not to enact it. By 2007, however, twenty-seven states had joined Virginia in making English their sole official language. In so doing, they echoed a past episode of panic. In 1919, Pennsylvania's *Harrisburg Patriot* reported on April 21, "Nebraska has taken a step which shows that, while the war ended six months ago, some of the lessons taught by it have not been forgotten or ignored." The step Nebraska had taken was to prohibit grade school teachers from using any language other than English. In 1919, German was the language striking fear in the hearts of many Nebraskans. So many German immigrant families lived in the state that teachers who could speak German often used it with grade school pupils not yet fluent in English. When, in reference to World War I, the *Harrisburg Patriot* employed the phrase "the lessons taught by it," it functioned much like a land mine of unverified claims planted beneath a blank to be filled in. Readers were first left to decide the lessons learned from the war, then whatever they determined those lessons to be detonated into unverified claims that speaking German caused those factors. This earlier panic over language and loyalty was not limited to Germans or Nebraska. Legislators in Illinois were so fearful that language had a greater impact on loyalty than the Constitution that they enacted a law in 1923 making the "American language" the state's official language.

That something more than language contributed to alarms regarding Spanish surfaced when alarms were also sounded regarding the possibility of Puerto Rico becoming a state. In 1990, syndicated columnist and television commentator James J. Kilpatrick declared, "Bluntly and without qualification, statehood for Puerto Rico is an intolerable proposition."[27] Kilpatrick based his view on unverified claims hidden in a blank to be filled in when he asserted that Puerto Rican "culture is essentially an Hispanic culture." The phrase left it to readers of his column to determine what constituted Hispanic culture, which in turn led them to unverified claims that, whatever they determined those elements to be, that culture was a danger to the United States. The following year, columnist Jeffrey Hart echoed alarms sounded in the panics over Catholics and Chinese when he voiced opposition to Puerto Rican statehood with blanks to be filled in the form of his questions, "Do they have our constitutional tradition in their bones? Do they share our historical traditions?"[28] Fearing that the voting power Puerto Ricans would acquire should their territory become a state would endanger the nation, Kilpatrick and Jones advocated weakening the nation's founding principle that "all men are created equal."

On the other hand, echoes of John M. Niles's 1825 view of Latinos as orderly, industrious, and devoted to the cause of liberty could be heard on December 5, 1960, when Arizona's *Phoenix Republic* wrote, "They didn't sail past the Statue of Liberty, but in common with all immigrants, these people have . . . hope, children, few possessions." The statement captioned a photo of Cuban immigrants deplaning at Miami's airport. Arriving at the height of foreign tensions between the United States and recently communist Cuba providing the Soviet Union a platform for its military, these anti-communist

Cuban refugees served as a counterweight to the fear that all Latinos were susceptible to communism.

Nevertheless, instances of panic flickered following the influx of these Cubans into the United States. An April 1, 1961, editorial in Virginia's *Danville Bee* referred to the "horde of Spanish-blood Cubans, some of them up to no good," leaving it to readers to fill in the blank as to what "Spanish-blood" contributes to the character of Cubans. Leaving no blanks to be filled in, a November 23, 1965, letter to the editor of the *San Antonio Express* vehemently declared, "I am dumbfounded by . . . our State Department allowing Cubans by the tens of thousands to immigrate to this country . . . [given] the possibility of trained and planted saboteurs, insurrectionists and spies, besides the communistic leanings resulting from years of living under communist rule." Vehemence, however, is not necessarily panic. For all his or her vehemence, this alarmist spoke only of the "possibility" of Cuban saboteurs and insurrectionists sneaking into the country, as opposed to making an unverified claim that they had. The letter did, however, assert an unverified claim that living under communist rule, even for the six years that Cuba had been so ruled, results in communist leanings.

Being refugees from communism, the Cubans who arrived over the next two decades by planeloads, boatloads, and, on occasion, loaded onto makeshift rafts, were granted legal status as immigrants. Far larger numbers of other Latinos who flowed into the United States were unable to obtain such status. "They say anyone who wants to curb illegal entry is a racist, and by using that dramatic word they hope to stop all debate on the serious subject of illegal aliens," Helen Graham, a leader in an organization seeking tighter restrictions on immigration, wrote in a June 3, 1992, column for California's *Ukiah Journal*. Graham's statement entered the portal to panic via its use of the two absolutes ("anyone," "all") and reached the threshold to the realm of panic when it asserted the unverified claim, "The truth is that black and Hispanic Americans are the most adversely affected by all immigration, particularly by illegal immigration."

It is one thing to employ an absolute by saying, "All Latinos are lazy"; or a blank to be filled in such as, "Latinos are a degraded race"; or employ

the correlation = causation fallacy, for instance, "Latinos are a danger because they commit more crimes than whites." But unverified claims differ
insofar as they often present a roadmap for action that can lure those in the
portal into the realm of panicked actions. Claims such as Helen Graham's
contributed to others doing exactly that. In 2011, Alabama passed a law
penalizing businesses that, knowingly or unknowingly, hire illegal immigrants. The state added muscle to the law by requiring, as opposed to simply
enabling, police to demand documentation from any worker they suspect
to be an illegal immigrant. Thousands of jobs went vacant and remained
vacant, despite the fact that 7.2 percent of Alabama's workforce had been
and remained unemployed in the months following the law's enactment
and its immediate enforcement.[29] Panic resided in Alabama's causing that
which it sought to cure. Seeking to improve the state's economy by lowering
unemployment, its crackdown on illegal immigrants damaged its economy
by rendering the state's farms, factories, and service industries in need of
workers.

Facts that emerged from the impact of Alabama's law had little impact
on those in panic. At center stage in the conflict was Arizona, since it had
been the first state to enact such a law. Those opposed to Arizona's and other
such laws often claimed they were not opposed to implementation of immigration regulations but to what they claimed these new laws cloaked: panic
over Latinos. In turn, television and radio commentator Glenn Beck accused
many of those opposed to Arizona's law of being the ones inducing panic.
"Are you comparing the systematic cold-blooded extermination of millions
of Jews to America making sure people are here legally?" he asked on his
April 27, 2010, Fox News network broadcast. Beck was commenting on several such references, including a political cartoon that had appeared that day
drawn by syndicated cartoonist Jimmy Margulies. It depicted Hitler with a
mustache in the shape of, and labeled, Arizona. Political cartoons are often
blanks to be filled in; that is the essence of the art form. Still, Beck was not
wrong. Tucked inside this cartoon was a panic-inducing fallacy along the
lines of that which concluded Socrates was a cat. After viewers of Margulies's depiction of Hitler with an Arizona-shaped mustache determined what

Arizona had in common with Hitler, whatever association they made triggered the fallacy:

> Arizona has done X.
> Hitler did X and went on to commit genocide.
> Therefore, Arizona is on a path to committing genocide.

Comparisons to Nazi Germany have also been used by Glenn Beck, himself no stranger to panic-inducing alarm.[30] Regarding illegal aliens, however, Beck represents yet another example that alarmists cannot be stereotyped. "Businesses don't hire illegal aliens because they can't find American workers; they hire illegal aliens because they don't want American workers," he declared in an April 27, 2008, appearance on the television network CNN. Elaborating on "how capitalism does not work," Beck continued, "Illegal aliens mean no workers' comp claims, no age, race or sex discrimination lawsuits . . ." He followed his continuing list with a panic-inducing statement from the panic over capitalist corporations: "They're not employees at all; they're corporate slaves."[31]

In addition to cartoonist Jimmy Margulies, Colorado congressman Jared Polis also compared Arizona's crackdown on illegal immigrants to Nazi Germany—but not in a panic-inducing way. "It is absolutely reminiscent of the second-class status of Jews in Germany prior to World War II, when they had to have their papers with them at all times and were subject to routine inspections at the suspicion of being Jewish," Polis declared in a *Politico* article that appeared the day before Glenn Beck challenged such comparisons. Even Polis's use of the absolute, "absolutely," did not function as a panic-inducing element since it described the verifiable claim that Arizona's law was "reminiscent" of the specified Nazi laws. Polis did go further, however, in expressing his alarm when he went on to declare, "I fear that Arizona is headed for a police state." While this statement is vehement, it is yet another example that vehemence is not necessarily panic. Had Polis said, "Arizona is headed for a police state," he would have entered the portal to panic via an unverified claim.

As it turned out, Arizona was headed toward becoming a police state in which all Latinos, not just illegal immigrants, were in danger of becoming second-class citizens. "The stand-off between the federal government and a high-profile Arizona sheriff accused of discrimination against Hispanics escalated Tuesday," the *Washington Post* reported on April 3, 2012. "Justice [Department] officials have accused Maricopa County Sheriff Joe Arpaio's department of illegally detaining Hispanic residents . . . saying in a report that the officers have engaged in a 'pattern or practice of unconstitutional policing' by unlawfully stopping, detaining and arresting Hispanics."

Arpaio himself revealed his panic in the title of his 2008 book *Joe's Law: America's Toughest Sheriff Takes on Illegal Immigration, Drugs, and Everything Else that Threatens America.* While it is not automatically panic when his subtitle claims illegal immigrants to be a threat to the nation, it became panic when his title advocated "Joe's Law," as opposed to American law.

Arpaio's warning, in the subtitle of his book, that illegal immigrants were a threat to the nation echoed the title of Congressman Tom Tancredo's 2006 book *In Mortal Danger: The Battle for America's Border and Security.* The panic in Arpaio's title, *Joe's Law,* also surfaced in the title of a 2005 book by Congressman J. D. Hayworth and Joe Eule, *Whatever It Takes*—a title that filtered out constitutionality in regard to the book's subtitle: *Illegal Immigration, Border Security, and the War on Terror.* The references in these titles to "illegal immigration, drugs, and everything else that threatens America" and "illegal immigration, border security, and the war on terror" fueled their warnings by tapping fears from other current panics—most notably, the panic over Muslims.

Twelve

"Some of the most influential Islamic spokesmen and leaders in the United States … envision not only a Muslim president, but that the United States Constitution be replaced or amended so as to comply in all particulars with ISLAMIC SHARIA LAW."

—Robert Spencer, STEALTH JIHAD:
HOW RADICAL ISLAM IS SUBVERTING
AMERICA WITHOUT GUNS OR BOMBS (2008)

In the tidal wave of immigration to the United States between 1880 and World War I, some 100,000 Arabs, mostly from Syria and present-day Lebanon, joined the 25 million immigrants who arrived in that era. That 90 percent of this initial wave of Arabs was Christian is not nearly as significant to political panic as the fact that very few non-Muslim Americans have ever been aware of this fact. Americans of Middle Eastern or Islamic descent remain widely viewed as the same, thereby grouping Muslim and Christian Arab Americans with Americans who are Muslims but not Arabs—the latter including Americans with backgrounds from Turkey, Albania, Bosnia, Indonesia, regions bordering the Caspian Sea, regions of Africa, and African Americans who belong to the Nation of Islam. In some instances, Hindus and Sikhs have also been mistaken for Arabs.

While panic over American Muslims is a relatively recent phenomenon, negative attitudes toward people in Islamic nations are not. Planted in the American social landscape by European colonists, negative attitudes grew from three seeds. Two were seeds that also grew into panics over African Americans, women, and gays: beliefs ascribed to the Bible and beliefs ascribed to Nature. The third was a seed that grew to entangle itself in the panics over Catholics and communists: foreign conflicts perceived as character conflicts, whereby groups in the United States were viewed as willing tools of foreign leaders.

This third seed was in full flower in England when it began to colonize the future United States. At that time, the Ottoman Empire had expanded from its Islamic base in present-day Turkey in all directions, including westward to the outskirts of Vienna. Europeans understandably feared that Ottoman expansion threatened their nationhood and religion. The Hagia Sophia, that magnificent Christian basilica in present-day Istanbul, had been turned into a mosque and served as a towering symbol of religious intolerance often inflicted by Ottoman authorities. Political conflict being perceived as a conflict of character surfaced in Thomas Herbert's 1638 book *Some Yeares Travel into Divers Parts of Asia and Afrique,* in which he related incidents alleging barbaric cruelty by Muslims. Herbert told readers of "a needy souldier [who] drawes up a catalogue of his good service and clothes it in want, humbly intreating favour and some stipend. . . . For his saucinesss he is almost drub'd with many terrible bastinadoes to death." In Herbert's telling, the sultan then turned to the scribe who penned the request for the illiterate soldier and "that hee should never write worse, makes his hand to bee cut off." Spicing his book with sexual barbarity, Herbert told of a woman who "in a lustfull bravado" petitioned her region's potentate "for help, her good man proving too weak to conquer her." The book then related that the potentate "promises her a present satisfaction. . . . They give an Assinego [a simpleton] an ophiate lustfull potion, which inrages the beast, who by a forced connexion basely glutted her; but in the end banisht her life also." Herbert concluded, "If I should summe up his variety of tortures . . . his men-eating hags of hell; his cannibal hounds . . . his ripping men's guts and the like . . . such is the hard-heartednesse of Mahemitans, a wicked people for cruell inventions."

Such attitudes were planted in the social landscape of the first colony of the future United States, Virginia, by one of its founding leaders, Captain John Smith. Just prior to the 1607 settlement at Jamestown, Smith had joined European forces seeking to repel the Ottoman Empire from present-day Romania. Suggestive of beasts, Smith wrote in a highly popular 1630 book that the "noise of the miserable slaughtered Turks was most wonderful to hear."[1] Suggestive of slaughtering livestock, he described numerous Turks he had beheaded. The element of panic surfaced when Smith went on to describe his soon becoming a prisoner of war. He and his fellow prisoners were, he wrote, "sold for slaves, like beasts in a marketplace." Referring to himself in the third person, Smith wrote that his new Turkish master had his foreman "strip him naked, and shave his head and beard so bare as his hand; a great ring of iron . . . riveted about his neck." He and his fellow slaves were worked in ways "a dog could hardly have lived to endure, and yet for all their pains and labors, no more regarded than a beast." By regarding his beheadings and massive slaughter of Turks as if they were beasts because he believed Turks treated others as beasts, Smith did that which he feared—a hallmark of panic.

In the new United States, political conflict perceived as a conflict of character was the first anti-Muslim seed to sprout. Prior to the American Revolution, American ships had been protected by the British Navy but afterward they were on their own. Indeed, they were even more unprotected since the new nation—states loosely united under the Articles of Confederation—maintained only a minimal navy to protect its ports. Consequently, American ships could be commandeered with little risk. Muslim privateers, operating from bases in North Africa, so often captured American ships that George Washington expressed his rage when he characterized these Muslims as "banditti who might, for half the sum that is that paid to them, be exterminated from the earth."[2]

Alarm swirling toward panic can be detected in a widely published news account from 1785. "Americans beware!" warned three fellow citizens in an open letter telling of their capture, followed by being marched through the port of Algiers "stripped of all our wearing apparel, and brought to a state of bondage and misery." Tucking an unverified claim in a blank to be filled in, their letter declared, "The severities which we endure are beyond your imagination." Leaving it to readers to imagine what severities they endured, this blank then triggered an unverified claim that, whatever one imagined, the reality was worse. Curiously, the letter also stated that the British consul had "taken us into his house."[3]

Despite the fact that the number of Muslims in the United States at this time was miniscule, composed almost entirely of those slaves who had belonged to Islamic tribes in Africa, fear of domestic subversion by Muslims already existed. In 1790, Peter Markoe published a novel entitled *The Algerine Spy in Philadelphia*. "I am arrived," the title character ominously announced, going on to marvel that he, an Arab, "is lodged under the roof of a Pennsylvanian" yet Americans remain "unconscious of danger." Subversion in the novel, however, was on the part of the author, not its Muslim spy. Markoe depicted the Muslim spy as a crafty but intelligent character whose views, like our own views, reflected his past experiences in life. He is, in effect, a man created equal. From this basis, the fate of the spy in Markoe's all but forgotten novel resonates more profoundly today, amid panic over Muslims that is far more extensive than when it was written. In the course of acquiring and sending information on the United States to his superiors, the spy falls in love with the United States and decides to defect. Still, Markoe revealed his own potential for panic over American Muslims. In the novel's closing line, the spy reveals his decision by declaring, "Open thy arms to receive Mehemet the Algerine, who, formerly a Mahometan, and thy foe, has renounced his enmity, his country, and his religion, and hopes, protected by thy laws, to enjoy, in the evening of his days, the united blessing of freedom and Christianity."

Markoe's novel appeared amid continuing depredations on American shipping that ultimately led to the nation's first overseas military conflict, the Barbary War. In August 1805, the United States won a major victory with the capture of Tripoli, an achievement that remains embedded in the opening line of the *Marines' Hymn:* "From the Halls of Montezuma to the shores of Tripoli." Francis Scott Key, in a poem he later revised that became the national anthem, likewise celebrated this victory when he wrote that "the turban'd head bowed to the terrible glare. / Now, mixed with the olive, the laurel shall wave, / And form a bright wreath for the brows of the brave."[4]

The deletion and continued obscurity of this verse reflects the dissipation of American fears of Muslims—until those fears were revived in the latter half of the twentieth century.

The Arrival of Muslims

During the Civil War, one of the nation's few Muslim citizens, Nicholas Said, served in the 55th Massachusetts Regiment. The unit's memorial book stated that he "wrote and spoke fluently the English, French, German, and Italian languages; while there is no doubt he was master of Kanouri, his vernacular, Mandra, Arabic, Turkish, and Russian."[5] Alarm is absent in these words, but all three seeds of the panic to come can be found sprouting in what was not recorded, such as Nicholas Said having sought to avoid the widespread stereotype of Muslims by changing his name from Muhammad Ali ibn Said.[6] Racial attitudes attributed to Nature were revealed by Said's presence in the memorial book, since the 55th Massachusetts Regiment was one of the units created for African Americans. The religious seed too sprouted in the life of Nicholas Said. His very presence in the country was so unusual, the *Atlantic Monthly* published parts of his memoirs in its October 1867 issue. In these memoirs, Said assured his fellow Americans, "Reader, do not misunderstand me, I was a Mohammedan; I am now, in belief, a Christian." But Said pointed out (revealing the flip side to Peter Markoe's fictional Algerine), "I cannot help thinking that the way I was baptized was

not right, for I think that I ought to have known perfectly well the nature of
the thing beforehand."

The ways in which white Americans accepted and did not accept Nicholas Said turned out to be the ways in which they accepted and did not accept
the scores of Arabs who arrived with other immigrants during the decades
connecting the nineteenth and twentieth centuries. "Not a single exception
has been encountered to the testimony of Americans who have business dealing with them that they are perfectly honest and reliable," Louise Seymour
Houghton wrote in a 1911 assessment for charitable organizations, though
she added, "If it be true that only a care for reputation keeps them honest,
it is certainly striking that . . . totally ignored by the communities in which
they live, [they] have not suffered morally by isolation."[7]

During this era, American perceptions of Muslims and Arabs were put
on display at the 1893 World's Columbian Exposition in Chicago. Over 27
million people saw its exhibits of "Arabs [who] prostrated themselves on the
ground and cried aloud to Allah," in the words of one reporter, who was further awed as "eunuchs stood in line with beauties of the harem."[8] Paralleling
the conversion to Christianity of Nicholas Said and the fictional Algerine
spy, Istanbul was rechristened Constantinople (its Greek name prior to its
conquest by Muslims in 1453) in the exposition's recreation of its streets.
Hundreds of Middle Easterners also came to Chicago for the Exposition, not
as exhibits but as immigrants seeking a start by selling rugs and other Middle
Eastern goods to fairgoers. None was accompanied by a harem or eunuchs.

While many homegrown Americans were alarmed by the nation's growing number of immigrants, that portion of immigrants who were Arabs did
not arouse particularly greater panic. In a May 18, 1894, report on one of
the era's many labor demonstrations, the New York Herald blandly listed,
"The majority of the mob seem to be Hungarians, Arabs, and tramps." Likewise little noticed were the creation of mosques in places such as the Detroit
suburb of Highland Park in 1920; Michigan City, Indiana, in 1924; Ross,
North Dakota, in 1929; and Cedar Rapids, Iowa, in 1935.[9]

Though this first wave of Arab immigrants did not trigger widespread
alarm, pockets of panic did exist. Some Americans sufficiently feared Middle

Easterners as a threat to the nation that efforts were made to prevent them from becoming citizens. "A strong fight has been made against the granting of naturalization papers to [George] Najour, on the grounds that he is a Mongolian," Alabama's *Montgomery Advertiser* reported on December 4, 1909—"Mongolian" being an umbrella term at the time, along with "Oriental," for anyone from anywhere in Asia. U.S. District Court judge W. T. Newman, however, declared Najour eligible for citizenship. But not every federal judge agreed. Another federal judge declared that Syrian immigrant Farris Shahid was not entitled to citizenship. "What is the race or color of the inhabitants of Syria?" Judge Henry A. M. Smith was quoted as asking in the June 25, 1913, *Macon Telegraph,* and then answering, "It is impossible to say. . . . One Syrian may be of pure, or almost pure, Jewish, Turkish, or Greek blood, and another the pure blooded descendant of an Egyptian, an Abyssinian, or a Sudanese." Nature, in the form of unverified claims about race, was now flowering in this early episode of panic over Arab Americans. In this instance, the judge's admission of confusion brought into focus two recurring and contradictory elements in this panic, both emanating from the nation's founding. The first is the proclamation in the Declaration of Independence that all men are created equal. The second, to which this judge referred in his ruling, was the Naturalization Act of 1790. It declared "any alien, being a free white person . . . may be admitted to become a citizen." While freed slaves becoming citizens was the predominant fear, it was not the only fear accounting for the use of the word "white" in the 1790 law. In that year, the *Philadelphia Packet* had declared on March 23, "Spain affords a melancholy example for us to be warned from: I allude to the mixing [of] the Moors . . . with the ancient inhabitants."

Religion, too, contributed to these early pockets of panic regarding Arabs as a threat to the nation. "The god of Islam is an absolute, autocratic ruler," Henry Suksdorf wrote in his 1911 book *Our Race Problems.* His statement filtered out that God is also the absolute ruler to Christians and Jews. Suksdorf went on to assert, "Islam is no monotheistic religion. A host of angels, archangels, devils and saints, all endowed with divine powers, aid Allah in the government of the world." Filtered from these statements were any examples demonstrating how Islamic angels, archangels, devils, and saints differed from Old Testament angels and Christian saints, not to mention the devil. Based on these filtered foundations, Suksdorf warned, "A tiny but swelling streamlet of these denizens of Semitic Asia has found its way to our shores; and if we do not close our gates in time, this undesirable and impro-gressive element may become a factor for evil in the formation of our nation."

As in the early years of the republic, political conflicts with Muslim nations again came to be viewed as conflicts with the character of Muslims and Arabs. This time the foreign conflict was World War I, during which Armenian Christians were slaughtered by Muslim Turks and the Ottoman Empire was allied with Germany. Shortly after the United States entered the war, the *Boston Globe* reported an incident in nearby Quincy in which a man "with a loaded rifle [was] shooting at all the Syrians he could find and smashing the windows in the homes of Syrian residents."[10] No one was killed, but one Arab American, Elias Haggar, was wounded by a shot in the head that narrowly missed his brain. More ominous was an all-out battle in Hawkinsville, Georgia, in which two Arab Americans were killed and a native-born American seriously wounded in September 1917. "The trouble is said to have started," the local newspaper reported, "over the drafting of a Syrian enemy alien, Thomas Simon, who is said to have relatives in the Turkish army." The accusation led to a fist fight that led to the Arab Ameri-can's family taking refuge in their dry goods store where, with "loaded Win-chester rifles and revolvers" they engaged in "a pitched battle."[11] Still, such incidents remained isolated. Far more frequent were reports such as that in Maine's *Kennebec Journal* in the days following the nation's declaration of war: "Mitri Gabour of Fall River visited Brig. Gen. Clarence R. Rogers, commanding the department of the Northeast, today, and offered to raise a regiment of Syrian-Americans. Gabour, a veteran of the Spanish-American war, said he already had organized a company of 106 Syrians in Fall River."[12]

The upheaval of World War I demolished the already weakened founda-tions of the Ottoman Empire. The resulting political turmoil in the empire's former domains sent more Middle Easterners fleeing to other countries, in-cluding the United States. Panic, however, continued to manifest itself only in relatively isolated incidents in the years leading to and through World War II. Ahmed Hassan's application for citizenship was rejected in 1942 when Judge Arthur Tuttle invoked both race and religion in his ruling: "Apart from the dark skin of the Arabs, it is well known that they are part of the Mohammedan world and that a wide gulf separates their culture from that of the predominantly Christian peoples of Europe." Tuttle echoed fears from previous panics when he added, "It cannot be expected that as a class they would readily intermarry with our population and be assimilated into our civilization."[13] As before, however, not all judges agreed. In an identical legal challenge in a different federal court, Judge Charles Wyzansky overturned the 1944 denial of Mohamed Mohiriez's citizenship application. His ruling cited commonality, in the form of contributions by Arabs to mathematics and science that "remind us, as they would have reminded the Founding Fathers, of the action and interaction of Arabic and non-Arabic elements of our culture."[14]

It was into this social landscape—fissured but so far relatively stable—that a second wave of Arab immigrants commenced, following a major aftershock in the political landscape of the Middle East that followed the political earthquake of the demise of the Ottoman Empire. The major aftershock, which occurred on May 14, 1948, was the creation of the State of Israel.

Rise of Widespread Panic

In 1949, a Senate committee urged amending the Displaced Persons Act that followed World War II to include 10,000 Arab refugees who had been displaced by the warfare that erupted on the heels of the creation of Israel. Between then and 1967 (the year of the Six Day War in which Israel captured the West Bank, the Golan Heights, and the Sinai Peninsula), tens of thousands of Arabs migrated to the United States. In one respect they differed from comparable numbers of Arabs who migrated to European countries. Those who chose the United States came to the nation most politically and economically supportive of Israel. Despite what for them was a profound disagreement with the prevailing American view of Israel, more profound political and economic dreams drew them here.

During these years, violent acts by Arabs plagued Israel but no Arab had yet committed a violent political act in the United States. That changed on June 5, 1968, when Jordanian immigrant Sirhan Bishara Sirhan assassinated presidential aspirant Robert F. Kennedy. The Associated Press described Sirhan as having "a swarthy complexion and wiry hair" and being "violently pro-Jordan and anti-Israel."[15] It didn't take long for fears of Arab Americans to spread and to surface. One week after Robert Kennedy's assassination, a June 30 letter to the editor of the *New York Times* declared, "We have enough blind, home-grown hatred in this country without importing more each month. I refer to immigrants from Arab countries . . . where hatred is tantamount to a national policy, indeed, almost a religion." This letter writer thus revealed political conflicts with Arab nations becoming conflicts of character, based on unverified Nature-based and religion-based claims about the Arab mind. Absent from most of these news reports and personal assertions was the fact that Sirhan Sirhan was a Christian. And a troubled one at that, having reportedly left the Orthodox Church into which he was born to become a Baptist, then leaving that faith to become a Seventh-Day Adventist.[16] Whatever his personal pathology, it ultimately found a place to nest in rage over supporters of Israel, such as Robert F. Kennedy.

A 1969 editorial in one New York newspaper told readers that Jerusalem's Jewish mayor "and others really tried to understand the Arab mind, admittedly a terribly difficult thing to do."[17] An Associated Press report that year referred to the "enigmatic Arab mind of Sirhan Bishara Sirhan."[18] A 1972 article in a Florida newspaper referred to "the inscrutable Arab mind."[19] As the news media repeatedly asserted a sense of mystery regarding "the Arab mind," they created an overarching blank to be filled in. Increasingly, Americans filled it with fears resulting from acts of terrorism by Arabs against Israelis. Those fears soon turned into actions.

"Plans to build the first Los Angeles mosque are being opposed," the *Van Nuys News* reported on May 10, 1973. The protest was based, ostensibly, on concern that the mosque would add to traffic congestion. After all the legal avenues were exhausted, this objection remained overruled, but by then the funds of Muslims used to defend the mosque's construction left insufficient funds to construct it. The protest was a harbinger of the panic American Muslims would face—panic that seeped far further into the nation's political landscape on November 4, 1979, when Iranian militants stormed the American embassy in Tehran and commenced holding fifty-two Americans hostage for more than a year. Islamic forces in Iran had recently overthrown its U.S.-backed monarch, replacing him with a cadre of religious leaders headed by Ayatollah Ruhollah Khomeini, who pronounced the United States the "Great Satan." Not long after the Iranian hostage crisis began, it came to be depicted as a conflict of character. Syndicated columnist Charley Reese, urging a military response, told his April 23, 1980, readers, "Dealing with the Moslem mind is like working with mules. The first thing you have to do is get their attention."[20]

Still, alarm was not yet widespread. Under the headline "Islamic Religion Spreading Throughout America," the *Santa Fe New Mexican* told readers on August 23, 1981, that there are now "about four million Americans who practice the faith," and went on to explain its basic precepts. On April 28, 1982, no alarm was included in Texas's *Seguin Gazette* when it ran an article on an Islamic-oriented condominium and retail center in San Antonio. Southwestern Virginia's *Radford News* similarly voiced no alarm on June 17, 1984, when informing readers that a mosque being built in Blacksburg will be "the only Islamic center for hundreds of miles [to which] worshippers are expected to come on Fridays from across Virginia, North Carolina, South Carolina, Tennessee, and West Virginia." Not so, however, when Chicago's *Daily Herald* reported on June 10, 1992, "Peggy Stiegemeir said she did a double take as she was driving down Tyrrell Road on her way home . . . when she spotted more than a dozen people wearing turbans gathered around their leader, praying." The group turned out to be local Muslims who, having obtained the needed permits to construct a mosque on the site, were praying for Allah's blessing of the project. Residents in the Chicago suburb of Gilberts commenced an organized campaign, much as had happened in Los Angeles, to halt the mosque's construction.

During the years leading up to this 1992 conflict in suburban Chicago, terrorists in Beirut, Lebanon, had begun taking foreigners hostage.

By 1992, twenty-five Americans had been abducted there, three of whom died. In addition, Arab terrorists had hijacked an American airplane bound for Rome in 1985, resulting in the murder of passenger Robert Dean Stethem, a U.S. Navy diver. His body was then dumped on the tarmac at Beirut's airport. Three months later, a wheelchair-bound American Jew, Leon Klinghofer, was murdered by Arab terrorists who had hijacked the cruise ship *Achille Lauro*. Klinghofer's corpse and wheelchair were then dumped overboard. In 1988, a bomb planted by Arab terrorists destroyed a Pan Am flight as it flew over Lockerbie, Scotland, en route to New York, killing all 259 aboard, including the flight's 189 Americans. The accumulation of such acts contributed to the protest over the Gilberts, Illinois, mosque. This protest acquired further fuel when, in February 1993, a car bomb planted by Arab terrorists exploded in the garage of New York's World Trade Center. Six people were killed and more than a thousand injured. Back in Gilberts soon after this attack, the town council annexed the property where the mosque and adjoining school were to be located. The *Daily Herald* reported on April 13, 1993, "No one approached the board during the public hearing on the annexation and there was no discussion among the trustees prior to the vote."

Throughout the nation, alarm over Arab terrorism—as opposed to panic, since the terrorism was a verified fact—was now spreading. Alarm intensified, less by unverified claims of planned attacks than by actual incidents in which planned attacks were averted by discovery and arrests. But panic, too, was beginning to swirl from this alarm, as evidenced in the wake of a bombing on February 20, 1995, that destroyed the Alfred P. Murrah Federal Building in Oklahoma City, killing 168 people, including 19 children. Under the headline "The Threat From Islamic Fundamentalists," a column the following day in Maryland's *Frederick News-Post* told readers, "Those who bomb in the name of religion have a longer reach than the terrorists of old." The assumption that Muslims were responsible for the Oklahoma City bombing filtered out information made public hours after the attack that the FBI had issued warrants seeking two white men. The two men turned out to Timothy McVeigh and Terry Nichols.

Though Muslims were not responsible for the Oklahoma bombing, the same assumption resurfaced a year later when a bomb exploded at the 1996 Olympic Games in Atlanta. Buttressing the assumption was the fact that, ten days earlier, a TWA flight had exploded minutes after takeoff from New York. "Terrorism struck the Olympics for the first time since Munich in 1972," an Associated Press report declared, referencing the murder of Israeli athletes by Arab terrorists at the 1972 Olympics. The report told of a warning called in to the 911 emergency line moments before the blast, but filtered out from its initial reports that the 911 operator had said the caller sounded like a white man.[21] Even after the operator's report appeared in the news media, some Americans continued to filter it out. One state representative in Pennsylvania acclaimed the effectiveness of the Mossad, Israel's version of the CIA, thereby continuing to focus suspicion on Arab terrorists, of whom he declared, "I don't care how you get them; I don't care if there's an accident that's not investigated."[22] Panic resided in his seeking to protect the United States by not caring about the Constitution. Ultimately, investigations revealed that the airplane exploded as a result of a mechanical defect and that the person responsible for the Olympics bomb was American-born Eric Robert Rudolph, who was neither Arab nor Muslim.

Neither finding, however, was sufficient to stanch the growing number of Americans who assumed Muslims to be predisposed to terrorism, particularly since this assumption was being further fueled by a new foreign conflict. Increasingly, the United States was finding itself at odds with the leadership emerging in Afghanistan. Known as the Taliban, it implemented Shariah law, a 1,400-year-old legal code that emanated from the Koran and rulings by the prophet Mohammad. Shariah law resulted in the Taliban decreeing punishments such as that reported by the *Syracuse Post-Standard* on March 8, 1995: "With a crowd of thousands watching, the Islamic judge announced that three young men had been convicted of robbing travelers. The convicts were brought forth. Two doctors promptly severed the right hand and left foot of each man, sending blood spurting in all directions." Such incidents overseas caused more Americans to attribute U.S. political conflicts with Muslim governments to conflicts with the character of Muslims.

Correspondingly, more Americans did not want more Muslim Americans. Four months after the 1996 Atlanta bombing, Adil Awadh, a Muslim immigrant arriving from Iraq, was placed in jail upon arrival and held there as a "security risk."[23] Awadh, a physician, and seven other detained Iraqis had fled to the United States after a failed effort by their CIA-backed resistance group to topple their nation's anti-American dictator, Saddam Hussein. Government-created blanks to be filled in were conveyed in wire service reports that stated, "Although U.S. officials won't disclose their evidence, the Iraqi refugees and their attorneys believe the United Sates thinks the men are Saddam's spies."[24] Not until June 1999 was Awadh cleared of any suspicions and released. Ten years later, and amid virtually no fanfare, Adil Awadh became the Arabic media advisor for the Israel Project, an Israeli-American group seeking to bridge differences in perceptions between the Arab and Israeli presses.

Awadh was among the first of a growing number of Muslim immigrants held in detention on the basis of suspicion that they were secretly planning to commit terrorist acts. While these claims of secret terrorist conspiracies remained unverified, verifiably secret was the government's bases for its suspicions, which it repeatedly refused to disclose. Intentionally or not, this government secrecy served as a panic-inducing blank to be filled in, just as it did when Palestinian immigrant Hany Mahmoud Kiareldeen was jailed for nineteen months in 1998–1999 without trial or access to the evidence against him, before being released and cleared of suspicion. At the time of his release, twenty-four immigrants, nearly all of them Muslim, were being held without charge or access to the evidence against them.[25] Despite the government's refusal to reveal the evidence against these men, the fact that federal officials detained these immigrants bestowed credibility on the fears of those who assumed Muslims were predisposed to acts of terror. In 1998, the number of panicked residents in Leesburg, Virginia, forty miles outside Washington, D.C., was now large enough to block a planned Islamic school in their town. This time, fears were not cloaked in parking and traffic issues, as they had been in Los Angeles and Gilberts, Illinois. An anonymous handbill warned neighbors in Leesburg that "thousands of Middle Eastern strangers would be roaming our streets while we work."[26] Across the

Potomac River in Frederick, Maryland, opposition two years later stopped a mosque from being built. Ostensibly the issue was environmental, having to do with tapping into city sewer lines. But the Monocacy Valley Church was granted permission to use the sewer lines while the proposed mosque, on adjacent property, was not.

Not everyone in the nation or in Frederick, Maryland, was panicked. "Nothing has disgusted me more than the vicious politics that has frustrated the Frederick Islamic Society's latest attempt to build a mosque," Roy Meachum wrote in his September 1, 2000, *Frederick News* column. As in Leesburg, the mosque was not built. And voices such as Roy Meachum's were soon to be muffled beneath bodies and rubble when, twelve months later, Muslim terrorists leveled both towers of the World Trade Center and demolished a section of the Pentagon.

September 11, 2001: Widespread Panic

No American Muslims were implicated in the September 11, 2001, attacks. The attacks, however, triggered such fear of Islamic terrorists that American Muslims were, more than ever before, victims of those whose fear crossed into the realm of panic. "People have called saying they are going to split my head open and kill my children," James Zogby, director of the Arab American Institute, told reporters.[27] Nearly half the e-mails and phone calls Zogby received told him to go home. For Zogby, going home meant going to Utica, New York, where he was born into an Arab American family that was Catholic. A letter to the editor in the September 16, 2001 *Syracuse Herald American* declared, "How did these people get into our country? We let them in. . . . This is not a racial letter. It is a fact-based letter. Not only keep them out, get them out. . . . Every foreigner let in to America in the last five years: Sorry, gotta go home now. . . . We are taking our country back and we are keeping it." This letter writer's clearly panicked words were echoed in panicked actions nationwide. A Muslim gas station attendant was attacked by a man wielding a machete. An assault rifle poured bullets into another service station where an Arab American was working. A firebomb was thrown into an

Islamic community center. A rug company owned by Arab Americans was set ablaze. A Muslim woman was nearly run over by a driver who then followed her into the store where she fled, threatening to kill her for "destroying my country." Two Muslim girls were beaten on the campus of their college. Public schools in New Orleans were closed after multiple attacks on Muslim students. Outside Chicago, a mob of 300 people sought to descend on an area mosque. Police held them back.[28] Each of these incidents occurred in the first three days following the September 11 attack—days so filled with emotion for all Americans that many reacted with panic. Other panicked acts followed. Balbir Singh Sodhi, neither Muslim nor Middle Eastern, was murdered in Arizona. An immigrant from India, Sodhi was a follower of the Sikh religion, whose men wear turbans. His murderer bragged of his hope to "kill the ragheads responsible for September 11."[29] Another immigrant from India, Vasudev Patel, was murdered days later under similar circumstances. Muslim Waqar Hasan was shot to death in the convenience store he owned on the same day Arab American Adel Karas, a Christian, was killed in his grocery store. Both murders were motivated solely by panicked rage.[30]

Acts of panic were not limited to the hotheaded or less educated. Airline pilots are well educated and among the nation's most emotionally even-keeled. But the hijacking of airplanes to carry out the September 11 attacks raised fears, no doubt, for all pilots—and for a few, panic. In three separate incidents during the two weeks following September 11, two Arab Americans were asked to leave the airplane before takeoff and a third prevented from boarding because the pilots were uncomfortable with them as passengers.[31]

Even during these emotionally charged days, not all Americans shared these views. Thousands of airline pilots did not refuse to fly with Muslims on board. The previously cited letter to the editor that urged mass deportation of all recent immigrants was among several others from readers in the September 16, 2001, *Syracuse Herald-American* that urged the nation *not* to panic. Also appearing in that day's edition, syndicated columnist Cynthia Tucker undertook the difficult question "Wouldn't less freedom be a fair price to pay for more security?" Tucker went on, however, to remind her readers of the panic that followed the attack on Pearl Harbor in 1941. "But we ought to be able to learn from the mistakes of the 'Greatest Generation' as well as from their accomplishments," she wrote. "They made the shameful decision to intern Japanese-Americans for no reason other than ancestry. So we ought to know better than to blame all Muslim-Americans."

It is difficult to assess the impact of these voices urging reason, as there is no way to measure incidents that did not take place as a result of such pleas. What can be assessed is the extent to which such pleas lacked success. As in previous panics, a spate of books appeared with titles such as Robert Spencer's *The Truth about Muhammed: Founder of the World's Most Intolerant Religion* (2006) and Geer Wilders's *Marked for Death: Islam's War against the West and Me* (2012). Such books joined other influential voices that attacked Islam in reaction to the September 11 attacks. Reverend Pat Robertson told viewers of his February 22, 2002, broadcast of *The 700 Club* that Islam "is not a peaceful religion that wants to coexist. They want to coexist until they can control, dominate, and then, if need be, destroy."[32] His assertion filtered from Christian history events, justified by allusions to biblical tenets, that sought to control, dominate, and if need be destroy, such as the Salem witch hunt, the Inquisition, or the Crusades.

Assumptions regarding the character of Muslims were also purveyed in a secretly created 2003 FBI PowerPoint—the title of which the government continued to keep secret when it was obliged to make the text of the Power-Point public in 2011 under the Freedom of Information Act. The presentation, used to provide field agents with "a basic understanding of the origins and history of the Islamic faith," informed these federal agents that "the Arab mind is a Cluster Thinker, while the Western mind tends to be a Linear Thinker." In addition to being an unverified claim, the statement is further notable for characterizing the Arab mind in absolute terms ("is") while characterizing the Western mind in nonabsolute terms ("tends to be").[33]

Sentiments such as those expressed in FBI training or by Pat Robertson have persisted because terrorist acts targeting Americans have persisted. Shortly after the September 11 attacks, Richard Reid attempted to ignite explosives concealed in his shoe while aboard an American Airlines flight. The facts—that Reid was British, a convert to Islam, and not in the United States

but en route there from France—did not lessen the increasing fear of terrorism. "How many breaks does this guy get?" asked one reader of Allentown,
Pennsylvania's *Morning Call* in regard to Reid, objecting to the fact that that,
despite being caught red-handed, the press still referred to Reid as the "alleged
bomber."[34] Fearing unjust government by radical Muslims, this reader's statement advocated weakening that pillar of American justice which deems one
innocent until proven guilty in a court of law. After Reid's use of his shoe to
hide a bomb resulted in more thorough passenger screening at airports, an *Orlando Sentinel* reader urged that these time-consuming screenings be limited to
Arabs. "[W]hile most Arabs are not terrorists," he wrote, "all recent terrorists
were Arabs."[35] His panic resides in his having filtered out the fact that Richard
Reid was not an Arab and that numerous recent terrorist acts in the United
States were perpetrated by non-Arabs—most notably the 1995 destruction of
Tulsa Oklahoma's Federal Building by Timothy McVeigh and Terry Nichols.

Following Reid's arrest, the public learned that this would-be terrorist was the son of a Jamaican-born drug addict and that, like his father,
Reid had been a petty criminal with numerous convictions and prison stints.
Richard Reid appears to have acted out of profound personal needs that
he justified by connecting them to political views. In this respect, his actions were akin to those of Harry Orchard, Leon Czolgosz, and Alexander
Berkman, as discussed in their respective political panics. In understanding
political panic, their significance resides in the fact that the result of their
violent acts are, as scholar Omar Khraishah points out, "insignificant when
compared to the reactions and perceptions they forged."[36]

While individual acts of terror are often committed by personal rage
emanating from causes other than the cause in whose name the act was perpetrated, not all acts of terror fit this pattern, nor does this pattern necessarily
lessen concern. Months after Richard Reid's attempt in December 2001, six
American Muslims of Yemeni descent were arrested near Buffalo, New York,
when it was discovered they had attended the same terrorist training camp
in Afghanistan as the September 11 terrorists. In 2003, U.S. army sergeant
Hasan Karim Akbar, a convert to Islam born Mark Kools, hurled grenades
into the tents of fellow soldiers, killing two officers and wounding fourteen

other soldiers. Six Muslims, four of whom were Americans, were arrested in 2007 when federal agents learned of their preparations for a terrorist attack on Fort Dix, New Jersey. In 2009, American Abdulhakim Mujahid Muhammad, who had changed his named from Carlos Bledsoe when he converted to Islam, murdered an army recruiter and wounded another in Little Rock, Arkansas. Later that year, an American-born army major and psychiatrist of Palestinian descent, Nidal Malik Hasan, killed thirteen people at Fort Hood, Texas, and wounded twenty-nine others in a shooting spree. Two months after that, Nigerian Umar Farouk Abdulmutallab attempted to detonate a bomb hidden in his underwear while aboard a Northwest Airlines flight from Amsterdam to Detroit. Faisal Shahzad, an American citizen born in Pakistan, was arrested in 2010 for attempting to detonate a car bomb in Times Square. In 2011, Naser Jason Abdo, an American-born soldier whose mother was a native Texan and father a U.S. citizen of Palestinian descent, was convicted for assembling a bomb to attack a restaurant frequented by troops from nearby Fort Hood.

These incidents are indeed evidence of a threat posed to the nation by people who are Muslim or Arab Americans. Still, the presence of widespread panic over American Muslims and non-Muslim Arab Americans is evidenced by the comparative lack of intense panic regarding comparable incidents perpetrated during the same years by Americans of European descent. In addition to the murders and assaults previously cited, police arrested Robert Goldstein in 2002 when they discovered explosives he was assembling in preparation for attacks on mosques in Florida. In 2003, Earl Krugel, a member of the violence-prone Jewish Defense League, pleaded guilty to charges of plotting to bomb a Los Angeles mosque and the office of a Lebanese American congressman. John M. Russell, a non-Muslim army sergeant, murdered five fellow soldiers in a 2009 rampage at the military base to which he was assigned. A map of Fort Drum, New York, along with night vision equipment and a cache of weapons were discovered in the motel room of non-Muslim Lloyd R. Woodson in 2010. In 2011, Michael Enright was arrested after he slashed the throat of cab driver Ahmed Sharif while shouting, "As-salaam alaikum"—meaning, ironically, "Peace be unto you."

Police found a journal kept by Enright that characterized Muslims as "murderers without a conscience."[37] In 2012, a mosque in Joplin, Missouri, was
destroyed when torched for the second time in two years by an arsonist.[38]

Despite these acts of terror by American of European descent, panic over
Muslims and Arab Americans continued to spread. A December 7, 2002 letter to the editor of Georgia's *Savannah Morning News* began, "The attack
was a complete surprise on Sunday morning, December 7, 1941," and went
on to link Japan's attack on Pearl Harbor to Muslims in the United States in
ways that resonated with prior alarms over Catholics, Chinese, and Latinos,
by declaring, "Our country is again engaged in a conflict, perhaps the most
perilous in our nation's history. . . . This time it is not against a conventional
enemy . . . but against a confrontation of cultural values. Our very way of life
is at stake." The letter went on to propose "rounding up all those of Muslim
ancestry and deporting or placing them in internment camps. Naturally,
constitutional scholars would cry foul, but it is difficult to understand why
giving illegal aliens the boot could be considered unconstitutional." Panic
permeates these remarks, most notably in equating "all those of Muslim
ancestry" with "illegal aliens" and, on that basis, advocating actions that are
unconstitutional out of fear that our constitutional way of life is threatened.

Reminiscent of the loyalty oaths demanded amid widespread panic over
Communists and, in an earlier era, freemasons, a November 19, 2002 letter
to the editor of Florida's *St. Petersburg Times* declared, "It is outrageous for
any Muslim American to criticize the President without first condemning
the murders by Muslims on Sept. 11, without condemning the fundraising
by American Muslims to support the families of suicide bombers, without
condemning Arab Muslim states for incarcerating American Christians,
without condemning Arab Muslim states whose government are not democ-
racies . . ." The list continued. Panic resided in filtering out comparable pre-
requisites for criticism by any other group in which members of that group
had supported or perpetrated violence or tyranny. Also filtered from these
declarations were anti-terrorist acts of loyalty on the part of Muslim and
Arab Americans. Filtered, for example, was the fact that the arrest of the six
Muslim Americans of Yemeni descent who had attended a terror training

camp in Afghanistan resulted from, as *USA Today* had reported on September 16, 2002, "a tip from within a large Yemeni community." Among many other newspapers reporting this fact, the *Los Angeles Times* further reported on a recent recruitment ad for the CIA on the inside cover of the financial magazine, *Arab-American Business*.

By now, the intensity of the panic caused repercussions to events even after certain incidents turned out to be misunderstandings. On September 14, 2002, a *St. Petersburg Times* article told of a concerned citizen who informed police that she thought she overheard three men "who looked to be of Middle-Eastern descent" talking in a Georgia coffee shop about going to Miami and "bringing it down." Providing police with a license plate number, the men were pulled over after "one of the two cars they were in ran a toll booth without paying." These initial news reports also included that the incident was a misunderstanding. The young men, two of whom were American citizens, were medical students en route to begin residencies at a Florida hospital. None had any connection with terrorist activity. The *St. Petersburg Times* did note, however—possibly tongue-in-cheek—that it remained unanswered "whether any of the three was cited for running a toll booth." Nevertheless, a September 18, 2002 letter to the editor of Allentown's *Morning Call* revealed the intensity of its writer's panic when it stated, "The headline on the Sept. 14 story of the three Arabic medical students allegedly overheard discussing terrorist plans in a Georgia restaurant was 'Muslims Detained in Terror Scare: It Was All a Mistake.' . . . [I]t would be more accurate for the headline to have read: 'Muslims Detained in Terror Scare: Was It All a Mistake?'" Panic resided in the reader urging the use of a blank-to be-filled in. This individual was not the only one panicked in spite of the incident having been a misunderstanding. So too were the administrators of the hospital to which the medical students were traveling, who expelled them from their residency program upon their arrival. The hospital later altered its decision. As for running the toll booth, videotape revealed that charge, too, was unfounded.[39]

At present, the aftershocks of fear from the September 11 attacks continue to reverberate, periodically triggering acts of panic. Closest, both physically and emotionally, to the World Trade Center was controversy in 2010 over plans to build a mosque two blocks away. "This is not about religion; it's about this particular mosque," New York gubernatorial candidate Rick Lazio stated, filtering out the fact that prior to September 11, Muslims prayed at the World Trade Center itself in Islamic prayer rooms destroyed in the attack. Demonstrating the high need for certitude that filters facts such as these prayer rooms was an August 29, 2010, letter to the editor of the *Colorado Springs Gazette* that asserted via the use of an absolute, "I am *certain* that the efforts to build a mosque near ground zero is *only* the Muslims thumbing their noses at America by rubbing salt into the wounds of this great country." (Italics added.) Another letter in that day's edition asserted an unverified claim in the form of a blank to be filled in created by its question: "How many mosques in the U.S. have already been found to be recruiting and training areas for these same extremists?" Readers were left to determine the number of mosques engaged in this unverified claim. Though the World Trade Towers had fallen, it turned out the nation's pillars were still standing. The mosque was built. It and the multifaith facilities and programs included in its original design opened in 2011.

Similar protests sought to prevent mosques from being built in Murfreesboro, Tennessee; Temecula, California; and Sheboygan, Wisconsin. Murfreesboro's Muslim community faced not only demonstrations and legal challenges in its efforts to build a mosque, but also vandalism, bomb threats, and arson. "Residents at a public hearing maintained that Islam was not a religion," the *New York Times* reported on August 19, 2012, "and that the mosque was an outpost in a plot to undermine the Constitution with Shariah law."

The fear of a plot by American Muslims to replace American laws with Shariah laws spun off of the antimosque protests. Syndicated columnist Diana West wrote a November 19, 2010, piece headlined, "We Need to Stand Up and Say, 'No to Shariah.'"[40] Oklahoma enacted a law prohibiting the state from enacting or enforcing Shariah laws. Similar proposals were made in some two dozen other states. These efforts were endorsed by former Speaker of the House and presidential aspirant Newt Gingrich when he asserted, "Shariah is a mortal threat to the survival of freedom in the United States."[41] Gingrich's warning filtered out the fact that Article VI, Section 2 of the Constitution explicitly prohibits any foreign law from taking precedence over the laws of the United States. Since Gingrich and state legislators knew, or should have known, of this clause in the Constitution—a section so prominent it has been termed the "supremacy clause"—their statements and actions give an indication of the degree to which these politicians were seeking to avail themselves of political panic.

In 2012, Congresswoman Michele Bachmann, at the time a presidential aspirant, echoed the panic over communists when she called for an investigation "into potential Muslim Brotherhood infiltration into the United States government."[42] In particular, Bachmann questioned the loyalty of Huma Abedin, a Muslim American born in Kalamazoo, Michigan, who was a high-level aide to Secretary of State Hillary Clinton. Also as in the panic over communism, Bachmann's suspicions were not based on any actions or statements by Abedin but on people with whom Abedin had been associated. "The mother, brother, and deceased father of Huma Abedin . . . are connected to the Muslim Brotherhood," Bachmann asserted, expressing concern that "she, too, by extension, may be working on the organization's behalf." Similarly echoing the panic over communists, Congressman Peter King initiated an investigation in 2011 by the House Homeland Security Committee into the "radicalization of the American Muslim community and homegrown terrorism." Employing an absolute, King declared in an interview on Fox News, "The fact is that *nobody* had a closer relationship with the Muslim community than I did before September 11," thereby seeking to lead viewers further into the portal to panic via two blanks to be filled in when he went on to say, "Since then, I've been disappointed that *a number of* their *leaders* did not cooperate with law enforcement." (Italics added.) At no point did King say who those leaders were, let alone how many. In 2012, King took such official congressional inquiries to a new level when he announced his committee's next investigation: "American Muslim Response to Hearings on Radicalization within their Community"—a hearing investigating responses to a hearing.

At present, panic over American Muslims continues. But it also contin-ues to replicate the patterns of American panics dating back over 200 years. In all probability, it will continue to replicate those patterns by fading away as Muslim Americans continue to do what they have so far done: replicate the patterns of every other immigrant group in the history of the United States.

Conclusion

"We have met the ENEMY, and he is US."

—Pogo

When Walt Kelly refashioned Commander Oliver Perry's famous dispatch from the War of 1812—"We have met the enemy and they are ours"—for his comic strip, the character Pogo was referring to litter and pollution. His irony, however, equally applied to political panic. Still, while none of us is immune from such panic, the question remains as to why some panic when others do not. To a large extent, the answer resides in John Douglas and Mark Olshaker's observation, cited at the outset of this book, regarding everyone being attracted in varying degrees to conspiracy theories because they offer comprehensibility and certitude. All of us require some degree of certitude. Without it, we would walk down a sidewalk the same way we cross a creek on wet rocks. But the extent to which we each need certitude varies. A readily recognizable instance is jealousy. Virtually everyone, at some point, feels jealousy—the sense of threat to the certitude of a relationship. In the same way that some people are more prone to jealousy than others, some are more prone to feeling the nation is in danger than others.

The way we acquire certitude is by assembling perceptions into a pattern. The more reliable a pattern proves to be over time, the greater our sense of certainty. The process is the same whether it concerns walking down a sidewalk or seeing a person wearing a pointed white hood and robe that, for many Americans, fit a pattern of a violent racist. The process is also the same at more abstract levels, such as deciding whether or not to adopt patterns presented by others. We may dismiss a warning of disaster from a street corner orator if the claims of such people have poorly correlated with later events, yet not dismiss the same warning if it appeared in the *Washington Post*—the patterns composed of its reports being, for many, more reliable than those of street orators.

Here, then, is the critical juncture at which the correlation = causation fallacy so frequently contributes to political panic. While correlation does not imply causation, *it does cause assumption.* And assumption often plays a role in pattern recognition, the process so essential it enables us to walk down a sidewalk with more certitude than we would cross a creek. That correlation *causes* assumption can be seen in the example:

IF YOU CAN READ THIS
YR ИIAЯB IS MKNG ASMⴖTIONS
AND cREATNG Ɐ PTTRN.

Having correlated certain shapes with letters that have certain pronunciations, readers of the above example will assume that shapes similar to certain letters will be pronounced like those letters if that assumption contributes to forming a pattern. At more complex levels, however, not all of our minds generate the same pattern. These differences often result in different assumptions, accounting for differences in the way people walk down snowy sidewalks, or walk through a group of gays, or walk or don't walk by a group of young black men on a quiet street at night. How we assemble patterns is not just some cognitive technicality—and the differences in how individuals assemble them are not unemotional.

Alarm versus Panic

The episodes explored have revealed that political panic is most clearly evident when it entails doing that which is feared. Recognizing the way such actions emanate within an individual provides insight into groups and conflicts that are highly volatile at the present time. Foremost perhaps, as of this writing, is the Tea Party movement. Many of those who identify themselves as supporters of the Tea Party are panicked, but those who have demonstrated panic have done so in regard to certain issues while others have done so in regard to other issues. To regard the Tea Party as a group in panic would be to regard its members as a bloc, a view that is itself panic-inducing.

One concern of many associated with the Tea Party is, as the movement's name implies, taxes. The 1773 Boston Tea Party was a protest against a tax on tea—or, as previously mentioned, a protest against taxation without representation. Few, if any, Tea Party adherents have protested federal taxation of 618,000 citizens living in the District of Columbia who have no voting representation in Congress, since the Tea Party's alarm regards taxes that have enabled the federal government to, in their view, overexpand. In many instances this alarm has been vehemently expressed. But vehemence itself is not panic and this underlying alarm is not, in and of itself, panic since it is based on a verifiable claim: taxes have enabled the federal government to expand. When, however, such alarms filter out which government programs represent overexpansion, they do then enter the portal to panic.

Other groups that are often currently viewed as panicked are those opposed to abortion and those opposed to gun control. Both issues have sparked vehemence and incidents of panic. Between 1993 and 2012, eight physicians and staff at clinics providing abortions have been murdered by individuals advocating the sacredness of life. Some believe these killings to be justified revenge against people whose actions endanger the moral foundations of the nation. But those who murder to protect the nation's moral foundations weaken those foundations by dispensing with the Constitution's moral guarantee of due process of law.

Many gun rights advocates have also displayed vehemence but not necessarily panic. Some however have revealed panic, such as those who identify with an organization called Save Our Guns. Its 2012 website declared that the "first American Revolution" was fought in response to wrongs that included "tyrannical government and gun confiscation." The statement entered the portal to panic with the unverified (indeed, false) claim that gun confiscation was a cause of the American Revolution. The Declaration of Independence listed the reasons for the Revolution; none had to do with gun confiscation. By describing the American Revolution as the *first* American Revolution, the statement created a panic-inducing blank to be filled in: What will be the *second* American Revolution? Those who fill it in by advocating a second revolution based on the government failing to abide by reasons for which it was not established in the American Revolution have entered the realm of panic.

Still, the underlying alarms over abortion and over gun control are based on verifiable claims—though others have challenged the verification. In the case of those who oppose abortion, that fundamental challenge has centered on a debatable but vital question: When does life begin? In the case of those who oppose gun control, the challenge has centered on the debatable question: What significances does the Second Amendment's opening phrase—"A well regulated militia being necessary to the security of a free state"—have on the sentence it modifies—"the right of the people to keep and bear arms shall not be infringed"? To the degree that a person opposes any instance of abortion or gun regulation due to certainty that his or her underlying claim is valid, that person is susceptible to panic to the same extent. Likewise, to the degree that a person opposes those opposed to abortion or gun control because of certainty regarding the invalidity of the underlying claims, that person too is susceptible to panic. Regarding abortion, author Cristina Page attached an absolute to an unverified claim—through which she entered the portal to panic in her opposition to the prolife (anti-abortion) movement—when she wrote, "Women should stay home to raise children. This is a *bedrock* pro-life idea."[1] (Italics added.) Similarly, author Barry Howard Minkin entered the portal to panic when he made the unverified claim that the National Rifle Association is a "racist" organization whose members "distort our Constitution to support their right-wing agenda."[2] That Page viewed the anti-abortion movement and Minkin viewed the National Rifle Association as dangers to the nation surfaced in the titles of their respective books: *How the Pro-Choice Movement Saved America* and *Ten Great Lies that Threaten Western Civilization.*

Nonpatterns of Panic

One might expect that political panic is more intense or frequent during times of war or national economic hardship. Neither, however, is consistently the case. Warfare has triggered episodes of political panic. Those instances include the panics over Japanese Americans during World War II, over Arab Americans following the 9/11 attack, the brief but notable panic over Jews during the Civil War, and the intensified panic over communists during the period of national peril known as the Cold War. But the panics over Catholics and Chinese were sidetracked during the Civil War, as was the panic over women during both world wars. On the other hand, during both world wars panic over African Americans continued, as did panic over Latinos during World War II.

Economic fears have triggered incidents of political panic. The influx of Chinese immigrants that followed the discovery of gold in California resulted in violence as native-born Americans competed with Chinese immigrants in the gold mine regions and for other opportunities spawned by the bonanza. After the Civil War, job competition played a key role in triggering violence in northern cities against African Americans migrating there and vying for the same occupations. Anti-Semitism rose to its greatest heights as established businessmen and professionals faced competition from Jews seeking to enter their fields of work. Nationwide economic difficulties have also contributed to panic over Latinos.

But political panics have also erupted in the wake of national *success*. The panic over Catholics became widespread following the acquisition of the Louisiana Purchase, due in large part to fear that control of this vast new region was in danger of being hijacked by priestly agents of the pope. Following the nation's acquisitions from the Mexican War, the value of which was further bolstered by discoveries of vast deposits of gold, panic erupted over Chinese and Latinos immigrants. The reason national success can contribute to political panic is that the more one acquires, the more one may fear its loss.

This aspect of success applies to power as well as wealth. After World War II, the United States emerged for the first time in history as the preeminent power in the world. Among the fears generated by the nation's new status was one that was also new: alarm over education being inadequate to maintain this supremacy. This alarm may indeed have validity, but an aspect that is noteworthy in terms of political panic is that the alarm has been expressed in terms of superior education in whatever nation the United States most economically feared at the time. Initially, American education was reported to be inferior to that of the Soviet Union. Later reports showed it lagging behind education in Japan. More recently, American education is reported as inferior to that in an array of industrializing Asian nations.[3] Noteworthy as well is that these fears have filtered out the United States having maintained economic preeminence throughout those past decades.

Whether the underpinnings of a political panic have to do with power, wealth, culture, or religion, all involve the fear of a loss of autonomy. Autonomy is not control of others; it is control of oneself. The fears that form political panic regard the possibility that others will take or reduce our ability to control our own lives or our nation. To some extent, others do limit what we can do as individuals, just as other nations limit what the United States can do. It is the boundary of that extent that can generate conflict—and it is those conflicts that occasionally give rise to political panic.

Is America Different?

Never has political panic in the United States risen to the level of Nazi Germany. Along with the murder of 6 million Jews, Adolph Hitler's panic-inducing hysteria also resulted in that government sending to concentration camps proportionately massive numbers of Romani (Gypsies), homosexuals, and communists. While such massive and horrific government-sponsored barbarity has not happened here, the question remains: Could it happen here? Indeed, the question is not new; it has recurred just as often as political panic. In 1934—a year in which Hitler became chancellor of Germany, fascist leader Benito Mussolini was firmly in control of Italy, and the Communist Party in the United States had drawn more than 100,000 votes in the last presidential election—Nobel Prize–winning novelist Sinclair Lewis published *It Can't Happen Here,* speculating as to how it could happen here. Twenty years earlier, Populist Party leader Thomas E. Watson took the opposite view in regard to the fear of Catholics when he wrote, "What happened in Europe can't happen here."[4] Conversely, in 1915, Walter H. Stowe wrote in *The Importance of American Church History,* "We are daily witnesses to the growing claim of the state to an all-embracing power over the life of its citizen. . . . To those who say 'it can't happen here,' we reply: 'It has already happened here.'"

Are Americans a politically different breed? As in other countries, the United States has had episodes of ethnic cleansing, as seen in incidents involving the mass deportations of Latinos in the 1930s, the relocation and confinement of Japanese Americans in World War II, the expulsion and murder of Chinese Americans and African Americans, and the widespread advocacy of genocide that accompanied even more widespread and murderous ethnic cleansing of Native Americans. Yet even these horrendous acts have never attained the scale of tyranny described in the warnings of the nation's alarmists. While many factors have prevented persecution in the United States from yet reaching such scale, most of those factors emanate from seeds planted after the witchcraft panic in colonial Massachusetts. Slow though they have been to sprout, those seeds were the proclamation of equality in the Declaration of Independence and the democratic processes and rights embedded in the Constitution.

Many citizens of the United States have wrestled mightily, often violently, with the nation's unprecedented proclamation of equality and with due process of law. Each time, though rarely easily, the nation's foundational documents ultimately won. With each victory, the United States did indeed generate a new political breed of Americans, many of whom nevertheless continued to wrestle with the nation's self-proclaimed ideals. They, like those who preceded them in this struggle, feared the American way of life was being challenged. In one respect, their fears were valid: The American way of life *was* challenged and, in many instances, did end up changing. Those changes can be seen in the ways the nation has veered closer to the ideals of its founding documents, in spite of resistance from those who feared the nation was veering away from them.

Still, there is very little likelihood that political panic will ever vanish from the United States. Fear, like pattern recognition, is necessary for survival. As such, fear will always be available to alarmists, for whom the United States provides particularly fertile soil. Here their speech is unfettered, and the path to power is open to anyone who is sufficiently convincing. Fears such as those discussed in this book will recur among those who lack faith in freedom and democracy. Such fears, as we have seen, can trample freedom, but they have yet to conquer it. Truly, the price of liberty is eternal vigilance—keeping guard not only at our windows but also at our mirrors.

Notes

Introduction: To Light a Candle

1. William Gribbin, "Antimasonry, Religious Radicalism, and the Paranoid Style of the 1820's," *The History Teacher,* 7, no. 2 (February 1974): 240.
2. Curtis Gallenbeck and Karl U. Smith, "Systematic Formulation and Experimental Analysis of the Phenomena of Thinking and Belief," *Journal of Experimental Psychology,* 40, no. 1 (February 1950): 74–80; Harvey Sussman and Karl U. Smith, "Sensory-Feedback Persistence in Determining Memory," *Journal of Applied Psychology,* 54, no. 6 (1970): 503–8.
3. *Records of Salem Witchcraft Copied from the Original Documents,* vol. 1. (Roxbury, MA: W. Elliot Woodward, 1864), 44-7.
4. Robert Calef, *More Wonders of the Invisible World* (London: Nathaniel Hillar, 1700, reprinted in George Lincoln Burr, *Narratives of the Witchcraft Cases, 1648-1706,* New York: Charles Scribner's Sons, 1914), 343.
5. Calef, *More Wonders,* reprinted in Burr, 372.
6. Burr, *Narratives of the Witchcraft Cases,* 196-8.
7. John Winthrop, "A Modell of Christian Charity" (1630) in *Collections of the Massachusetts Historical Society,* series 3, vol. 7 (Boston: Charles C. Little and James Brown, 1838), 47. The pilgrims who, prior to the founding of the Massachusetts Bay Colony, had established the Plymouth Colony also put forth a founding proclamation, the *Mayflower Compact.* That document, however, was a statement of governance, not of goals. That this distinction was a factor in the 1692 witchcraft panic is borne out by the fact that no one in Plymouth was accused of witchcraft during that year and by the fact that, since its founding, only two people had been tried for witchcraft in Plymouth, both of whom were acquitted and their accusers punished. See Eugene Stratton, *Plymouth Colony, Its History and People, 1620-1691* (Salt Lake City: Ancestry Pub., 1986), 159.
8. Cotton Mather, *A Faithful Account of the Discipline Professed and Practiced in the Churches of New England* (Boston: S. Gerrish, 1726), 195-6.

Chapter 1: Indians

1. John Mason, *A Brief History of the Pequot War* (Boston: S. Kneeland and T. Green, 1736), 30. The Massachusetts colonists made efforts to round up those Pequots who survived. Pequot culture was all but obliterated. Nevertheless, the tribe managed to survive to the present day. In so doing, the Pequots demonstrated that their culture can peacefully coexist with that of whites.
2. Karl Davis, "'Remember Fort Mims:' Reinterpreting the Origins of the Creek War," *Journal of the Early Republic,* 22, no. 4 (Winter 2002): 611-636.

3.   H. A. Fay, ed., *Collection of the Official Accounts, in Detail, of All the Battles Fought by Sea and Land Between the Navy and Army of the United States and the Navy and Army of Great Britain During the Years 1812, 13, 14, and 15* (New York: E. Conrad, 1817), 179–81.

4.   *Annual Messages, Veto Messages, Protest &c. of Andrew Jackson, President of the United States,* 2nd edition (Baltimore: Edward J. Coale and Company, 1835), 59-61; F. P. Prucha, "Andrew Jackson's Indian Policy: A Reassessment," *Journal of American History,* 56, no. 3 (December 1969): 527-539.

5.   Russell Thornton, "Cherokee Population Losses During the Trail of Tears," *Ethnohistory,* 31, no. 4 (1984): 289-300.

6.   Francis Parkman, *Conspiracy of Pontiac and the Indian War,* vol. 2 (Boston: Little, Brown, and Co., 1913), 39; George Bancroft, *History of the United States,* 17th edition, vol. 5 (Boston: Little Brown, 1866), 132.

7.   *William Trent's Journal,* in "Notes and Documents," *Mississippi Valley Historical Review,* 11, no. 3 (March 1924): 390–413; Thomas Brown, *Did the U.S. Army Distribute Blankets to Indians?: Fabrication and Falsification in Ward Churchill's Genocide Rhetoric* (Ann Arbor: MPublishing, University of Michigan Library, 2006).

8.   *St. Paul Pioneer Press* and *Omaha World Journal* quoted in "Lessons of Wounded Knee," *Daily Inter Ocean* (Chicago), January 2, 1891.

9.   Theodore D. Sargent, *The Life of Elaine Goodale Eastman* (Lincoln: University of Nebraska Press, 2005), 39.

10.   *Testimony Relating to the Removal of the Ponca Indians,* 46th Congress, 2nd session, Senate Report No. 670, p. 99; *Federal Cases Comprising Cases Argued and Determined in the Circuit and District Courts of the United States,* book 25 (St. Paul: West Publishing, 1896), 697, 700.

11.   *Report of the Secretary of the Interior for the Fiscal Year Ending June 30, 1885,* vol. 1 (Washington, D.C.: Government Printing Office, 1885), 25.

12.   Rodger Bucholz, William Fields, Ursula P. Roach, *20th Century Warriors: Native American Participation in the United States Military* (Washington, D.C.: Department of Defense, 1996), 1, 2, 5, 10.

Chapter 2: Savagery and Criminality in the Negro

1.   Insult to John Lewis in "Spitting-Mad Protest Takes a Hateful Turn," *New York Post,* March 21, 2010; Obama as witch doctor in Eugene Robinson, "The Favor Jimmy Carter Did Us All," *Washington Post,* September 18, 2009; William L. Ziglar, "The Decline of Lynching in America," *International Social Science Review,* 63, no. 1 (Winter 1988): 14–25; Sherrilyn Ifill, *On the Courthouse Lawn: Confronting the Legacy of Lynching in the Twenty-First Century* (Boston: Beacon Press, 2007), 75-6.

2.   *The Works of Aurelius Augustine, Bishop of Hippo,* ed. Marcus Dods, vol. 2 (Edinburgh: T. & T. Clark, 1881), 324.

3.   Richard Jobson, *The Golden Trade: Or a Discovery of the River Gambra, and the Golden Trade of the Aetheiopians* (London: Nicholas Okes, 1623; reprint, Devonshire: Speight & Walpole, 1907), 65.

4.   Josiah Priest, *Bible Defence of Slavery and Origin Fortunes, and History of the Negro Race,* 5th ed. (Glasgow, KY: W. S. Brown, 1852), 33.

5.   "Speech by Senator John Vardamen," *Readings in Social Problems,* Albert Benedict Wolfe, ed. (New York: Ginn & Co., 1916), 709; "Meet Lester Maddox of Georgia," *New York Times,* November 6, 1966.

6.   Thomas Herbert, *Some Yeares Travels into Africa & Asia* (London, 1638), 18.

7.   James Hunt, *Negro's Place in Nature* (New York: Van Evrie, Horton & Co., 1864), 10.

8.   Thomas Jefferson, *Notes on the State of Virginia* (London: John Stockdale, 1787), 239.

9.   *Political Debates between Hon. Abraham Lincoln and Hon. Stephen A. Douglas* (Columbus, Ohio: Follett, Foster and Co., 1860), 136.

10.   Arthur Jensen, "How Much Can We Boost IQ and Scholastic Achievement?" *Harvard Educational Review,* 39, no.1 (Spring 1969): 82.

11.   "New York, April 7th," *Boston News Letter,* April 14, 1712.

12.   "Report of General Eppes," *Richmond Enquirer,* September 6, 1831.

13. Sarah M. Grimké, *Letters on the Equality of the Sexes and the Condition of Woman* (Boston: Isaac Knapp, 1838), 33.

14. William Gribbin, "Antimasonry, Religious Radicalism, and the Paranoid Style of the 1820's," *The History Teacher,* 7, no. 2 (February 1974), 240.

15. Hinton Helper, *Nojoque: A Question for a Continent* (New York: George W. Carleton, 1867), 15.

16. "From Tennessee," *Milwaukee Sentinel,* August 22, 1867.

17. Frank U. Quillin, *The Color Line in Ohio* (Ann Arbor, MI: Ann Arbor Press, 1913); *Transactions of the Illinois States Historical Society* (Springfield: Illinois State Journal Co., State Printers, 1906); Edward J. Price Jr., "School Segregation in Nineteenth-Century Pennsylvania," *Pennsylvania History,* 43, no. 2 (April 1976): 120–37; Arthur O. White, "The Black Movement against Jim Crow Education in Buffalo, New York," *Phylon,* 30, no. 4 (Fall 1993): 23–48; Albon P. Man, Jr., "Labor Competition and the New York Draft Riots of 1863," *Journal of Negro History,* 36, no. 4 (October 1951): 375-405; Toby Joyce, "The New York Draft Riots of 1863: An Irish Civil War?" *History Ireland,* 11, no. 2 (Summer 2003): 22-7.

18. Alabama incident reported in "Four Negroes Lynched," *San Jose Evening News* (CA), August 8, 1891; Arkansas incidents reported in "Nine Negroes Lynched," *Arkansas Gazette* (Little Rock), October 2, 1891; "Two Negroes Strung by a Mob," *Morning Olympian* (WA), July 15, 1895; Georgia incidents reported in "Seven Lynched," *Worcester Daily Spy* (MA), December 24, 1894; "Lynched," *Grand Rapids Press* (MI), March 16, 1899; "Eight Negroes Lynched," *St. Albans Daily Messenger* (VT), June 29, 1905; Kentucky incident reported in "Nine Negroes Are Reported Lynched," *Belleville News Democrat* (IL), March 15, 1911; Louisiana incident reported in "Eight Negroes Lynched," *San Jose Mercury* (CA), December 13, 1914; Mississippi incident reported in "Five Negroes Lynched," *New York Herald,* July 7, 1892; South Carolina incident reported in "Ten Lynched in the South," *Wilkes-Barre Times* (PA), November 10, 1898; Texas incidents reported in "Paid the Penalty," *Wheeling Register* (WV), June 29, 1892; "Seven Negroes Lynched," *Charlotte Observer* (NC), May 1, 1897; "Nine Negroes Done to Death by White Mob," *Albuquerque Journal* (NM), June 23, 1908; Virginia incident reported in "Four Negroes Killed," *Trenton Evening Times* (NJ), October 18, 1891.

19. John Hope Franklin, "'Birth of a Nation': Propaganda as History," *The Massachusetts Review,* 20, no. 3 (Autumn 1979): 430.

20. 2005 Florida Statutes, Title XLVI: "Crimes," Chapter 776/Section 031: "Justifiable Use of Force."

21. "Florida Expands Right to Use Deadly Force in Self-Defense," *New York Times,* April 27, 2005.

22. Examples of such incidents reported in "Wife Killed Spouse after Abuse," *Orlando Sentinel,* July 18, 1985; "Tests Support Self-Defense Claim," *St. Petersburg Times,* April 12, 1988; "Bar Owner Won't Be Charged in Shooting," *St. Petersburg Times,* July 20, 1991; "Slaying in Self-Defense," *St. Petersburg Times,* December 5, 1993; "Police Won't File Charges in Death of Orlando Teen," *Orlando Sentinel,* May 17, 1994; "Cabbie Kills Attacker," *St. Petersburg Times,* June 3, 1994; "No Charge Filed Against Dad Who Shot Son," *Sun Sentinel* (Ft. Lauderdale), February 1, 1995; "Once Again Crime Victim Shoots, Kills His Attacker," *Orlando Sentinel,* January 5, 1996; "No Charges in Neighbor's Slaying," *Florida Times-Union* (Jacksonville), June 4, 1999.

23. "Wayne LaPierre, Executive Vice President, National Rifle Association, Delivers Remarks at the American Conservative Union's Conservative Action Conference," (Washington: Congressional Quarterly Transcriptions, March 15, 2013).

24. "Post-Newtown, NRA Membership Surges to 5 Million," *USA Today,* May 4, 2013.

25. Florida Stand Your Ground Task Force, *Final Report* (Tallahassee: State of Florida, April 30, 2012).

Chapter 3: The Institution of Freemasonry

1. Kathleen Smith Kutolowsky, "Freemasonry and Community in the Early Republic: The Case for Antimasonic Anxieties," *American Quarterly,* 34, no. 5 (Winter 1982): 543–61;

Steven C. Bullock, "The Revolutionary Transformation of American Freemasonry, 1752–1792," *William and Mary Quarterly*, 3rd series, 47, no. 3 (July 1990): 347–69.

2. "A New Inquisition," *Maryland Gazette* (Annapolis), January 4, 1821; Thurlow Weed, *Life of Thurlow Weed*, vol. 1 (Boston: Houghton Mifflin, 1884), 93.

3. A. P. Bentley, *History of the Abduction of William Morgan* (Mt. Pleasant, IA: Van Cise & Throop, 1874), 7–9; Rob Morris, *William Morgan, or Political Anti-Masonry* (New York: Robert Macoy, Masonic Publisher, 1883), 59–60.

4. Lionel Vibert, *The Rare Books of Free Masonry* (London: The Bookman's Journal office, 1923), 18–23.

5. Steven C. Bullock, "A Pure and Sublime System: The Appeal of Post-Revolutionary Freemasonry," *Journal of the Early Republic*, 9, no. 3 (Autumn 1989), 359–73; "Diary: George Town," *Loudon's Register* (New York), September 28, 1793. A decade earlier, the Continental Congress incorporated Masonic symbols (the "all-seeing eye" and triangles) into the design of the Great Seal of the United States. The Great Seal is sacred by virtue of being that which authenticates the federal government's most vital documents. Neither the all-seeing eye nor a triangle is a uniquely Masonic symbol. None of the other elements in the Great Seal is Masonic.

6. "Case of William Morgan," *New York Spectator*, February 9, 1827.

7. "Morgan," *U.S. Telegraph* (Washington, DC), October 27, 1827.

8. Aspects of the remains indicated the body may not have been Morgan's. It was later identified, with equal uncertainty, as that of another man. The controversy that ensued was too late to halt the hysteria.

9. *The Addresses and Messages of the Presidents of the United States: Inaugural, Annual and Special, from 1789 to 1846*, vol. 1 (New York: Edward Walker, 1846), 73.

10. Randolph Roth, "The Other Masonic Outrage: The Death and Transfiguration of Joseph Burnham," *Journal of the Early Republic*, 14, no. 1 (Spring 1994): 35–69.

11. Frank Gerrity, "The Masons, the Antimasons, and the Pennsylvania Legislature, 1834–36," *Pennsylvania Magazine of History and Biography*, 99, no. 2 (April 1975): 187, 198; "10 Film Figures Face Trial for Contempt," *Washington Post*, January 10, 1948.

12. Calvin Colton, ed., *The Private Correspondence of Henry Clay* (New York: A. S. Barnes, 1855), 306–9.

13. "National Anti-Masonic Convention," *Niles Register*, October 1, 1831.

14. "Political Knavery, Baseness, and Forgery Detected and Exposed," *Cayuga Patriot* (Auburn, NY), September 19, 1832.

15. "Eighth Ward Temperance Society," *New York Spectator*, November 4, 1833.

16. Jim Marrs, *Rule By Secrecy: The Hidden History that Connects the Trilateral Commission, the Freemasons and the Great Pyramids* (New York: HarperCollins, 2000); Graham Hancock and Robert Bauval, *Talisman: Gnostics, Freemasons, Revolutionaries, and the 2000-Year-Old Conspiracy at Work in the World Today* (New York: Element Books, 2004); Bryon Preiss and J. Madison Davis, *Conspiracy and the Freemasons: How the Secret Society and Their Enemies Shaped the Modern World* (New York: St. Martin's Press, 2006).

Chapter 4: The Spread of Popery in This Country

1. All these laws were later rescinded or deemed unconstitutional—except the law enabling the president to deport immigrants from countries at war with the United States. It later contributed to the legal bases for relocating people of Japanese descent (both immigrants and citizens) to confinement camps during World War II.

2. "The Great American Republican Mass Meeting," *New York Herald*, March 22, 1844.

3. Samuel F. B. Morse (under pseud. Brutus), *Foreign Conspiracy Against the Liberties of the United States* (New York: Leavitt Lord, 1835), 58.

4. J. Edgar Hoover, "Communist Party, USA," Federal Bureau of Investigation brochure (ca. 1960-63), reprinted in *Ave Maria Magazine*, April 30, 1960.

5. Anna Ella Carroll, *The Great American Battle: The Contest Between Christianity and Political Romanism* (New York: Miller, Orton, & Mulligan, 1856), 315.

6. Sarah Ellen Blackwell, *A Military Genius: Life of Anna Ella Carroll* (Washington, D.C.: Judd & Detweiler, 1894), 3-18.

7. Anna Ella Carroll, "Plan of the Tennessee Campaign," *North American Review*, 142, no. 353 (April 1886): 343-4; Kenneth P. Williams, "The Tennessee River Campaign and Anna Ella Carroll," *Indiana Magazine of History*, 46, no. 3 (September 1950): 221-48.

8. Isaac Kelso, *Danger in the Dark: A Tale of Intrigue and Priestcraft* (Cincinnati: H. M. Rulison, 1857), 31.

9. W. C. Brownlee, *Popery, the Enemy of Civil and Religious Liberty* (New York: Bowne & Wisner, 1836), 207.

10. Dispute over royalties in "Maria Monk Is In Trouble," *The Herald* (New York City), November 24, 1836; arrest for theft in "Overtaking the Guilty," *The National Union* (Nashville, TN), October 6, 1847; obituary "Maria Monk," *The North Star* (Rochester, NY), October 13, 1848; sales success of the book in Susan M. Griffin, "Awful Disclosures: Women's Evidence in the Escaped Nun's Tale," *PMLA*, 111, no. 1 (January 1996): 93-107.

11. Lyman Beecher, *A Plea for the West* (Cincinnati: Truman & Smith, 1835), 11, 61.

12. Ibid., 95.

13. "The Great Monster Meeting of the American Republicans in the Ninth Ward," *New York Herald*, November 21, 1843.

14. "The Great American Republican Mass Meeting," *New York Herald*, March 22, 1844.

15. "Riot at St. Louis," *Mississippian and State Gazette* (Jackson), August 23, 1854.

16. "Naturalisation [*sic*] Laws." *Trenton Gazette* (NJ), March 20, 1856.

17. Untitled review of *Political Romanism* in *The Methodist Quarterly*, 24 (July 1872): 515.

18. Charles Chiniquy, *Fifty Years in the Church of Rome* (New York: Fleming Revell Co., 1886), 711-36.

19. "Literature," *The Congregationalist*, 80, no. 12 (March 21, 1895): 449.

20. "American Catholics," *Rocky Mountain News* (Denver), May 13, 1894.

21. "Ascribe to Klan Attack on Smith," *New York Times*, March 1, 1923.

22. "Heflin Tells Klan Smith Cannot Win," *New York Times*, July 2, 1927.

23. Paul Blanshard, *American Freedom and Catholic Power* (Boston: Beacon Press, 1949), 47.

24. "Arkansas Baptists to Oppose Kennedy," *New York Times*, September 7, 1960.

25. "Kennedy Affirms Stand on Religion," *Washington Post*, September 13, 1960.

Chapter 5: Millions of Yellow Men

1. Circular from Tacoma submitted to Attorney General by U.S. Attorney W. H. White, cited in Jules Alexander Karlin, "The Anti-Chinese Outbreak in Tacoma, 1885," *Pacific Historical Review*, 23, no. 5 (August 1954): 276-7.

2. *Supplement to the Revised Statutes of the United States*, vol.1, 2nd ed., 1874-1891 (Washington, D.C.: Government Printing Office, 1891), 342.

3. Najia Aarim-Heriot, *Chinese Immigrants, African Americans, and Racial Anxiety in the United States, 1848-1882* (Urbana: University of Chicago Press, 2003), 8-9. See also, Dan Caldwell, "The Negroization of the Chinese Stereotype in California," *Southern California Quarterly*, 53, no. 2 (June 1971): 123-131.

4. "Population of San Francisco," *Albany Evening Journal* (NY), November 14, 1849.

5. "Letter from California," *Pittsfield Sun* (MA), July 29, 1858.

6. "A Calaveras Crusade against the Chinese," *San Francisco Evening Bulletin*, November 19, 1857; "The Chinese Question in Shasta County," *San Francisco Evening Bulletin*, February 9, 1859; "Crusade in Siskiyou County against the Chinese Miners," *San Francisco Evening Bulletin*, March 24, 1860.

7. Ibid.; "A Calaveras Crusade," November 19, 1857; "Attempt to Get Rid of the Chinese in Mariposa," *San Francisco Bulletin*, March 29, 1858; "Anti-Chinese Resolutions of Shasta County, *San Francisco Bulletin*, February 17, 1859; "The Chinese Expelled from Hornitos," *San Francisco Bulletin*, June 4, 1859; "Crusade in Siskiyou County Against the Chinese Miners," *San Francisco Bulletin*, March 24, 1860; Jean Pfaelzer, *Driven Out: The Forgotten War against Chinese-Americans* (New York: Random House, 2007).

8. "Chinese Immigrants," *Sacramento Weekly Union,* May 1, 1852.

9. *Alta California* article reported in "The Chinese in California," *National Intelligencer* (Washington, D.C.), June 16, 1852.

10. "To the Senate and Assembly of the State of California," *Journal of the Third Session of the Legislature of the State of California* (San Francisco: G. K. Fitch & Co., 1852), 373.

11. Ibid.

12. Ibid., 303.

13. Ibid., 373.

14. *The People, Respondent, v. George W. Hall, Appellant,* [no number in original], Supreme Court of the State of California, 4 Cal. 399; 1854 Cal. Lexis 137 (October, 1854).

15. "More Atrocious Outrages on the Chinese," *San Francisco Bulletin,* May 1, 1857.

16. "More Terrible Outrages on the Chinese," *San Francisco Bulletin,* May 19, 1857.

17. Scott Alan Carson, "Chinese Sojourn Labor and the American Transcontinental Railroad," *Journal of International and Theoretical Economics,* 161, no. 1 (March 2005): 83-4.

18. "Advices from North Adams," *Boston Daily Advertiser,* June 24, 1870.

19. "Pig-Tail vs. Paddy, Hans and Cuffee," *New York Commercial Advertiser* article reprinted in *Weekly Georgia Telegraph* (Macon), May 28, 1869.

20. Bret Harte, "Plain Language from Truthful James," *The Overland Monthly,* 5, no. 3 (September 1870): 287.

21. "A New Transatlantic Genius," *The Transatlantic Magazine,* 4, no. 1 (July 1871): 107.

22. The database America's Historical Newspapers contains (as of this writing) 4,545 news articles, editorials, and advertisements with the phrase "heathen Chinee" in the years spanning 1869 to 1919. During the previous fifty years, the database contains no uses of the phrase.

23. "Of Mr. Francis Bret Harte's 'Heathen Chinese,'" [sic], *Lowell Daily Citizen* (MA), December 11, 1878.

24. J. F. Packard, *Grant's World Tour* (Cincinnati: Forshee & McMakin, 1880), 650; Federal Writers' Project, *New York: A Guide to the Empire State* (NY: Oxford University Press, 1940), 258. Notably, a very different perspective—absent any references to inscrutability—appeared in a separate publication of the Federal Writers' Project: *New York City Guide* (New York: Random House, 1939).

25. "Political," *Cincinnati Daily Enquirer,* July 26, 1870.

26. *San Francisco Chronicle* article reprinted in "The Chinese Driven from the Town and Their Homes Burned," *Milwaukee Daily Sentinel,* May 9, 1876.

27. Winfield J. Davis, ed., *History of Political Conventions in California: 1849-1892* (Sacramento: Publications of California State Library, 1893), 371.

28. Ibid., 370

29. "Incendiary Agitators," *San Francisco Bulletin,* November 1, 1877.

30. "Incendiary Agitators–Arrest of Dennis Kearney," *San Francisco Bulletin,* November 5, 1877.

31. "Riot in Denver," *Macon Weekly Telegraph* (GA), October 5, 1880.

32. Willard B. Farewell, *The Chinese at Home and Abroad,* Part One (San Francisco: A. L. Bancroft and Co., 1885), 14; Alfred P. Schultz, *Race or Mongrel* (Boston: L. C. Page, 1908), 230.

33. *San Francisco Call* article reprinted in "The Japs in California," *New Hampshire Patriot* (Concord), February 2, 1870.

34. "Want Japanese Barred," *Fort Worth Register* (TX), August 19, 1900.

35. "The Japs Must Go Too," *Kansas City Star,* January 19, 1896.

36. "Hayes' Stirring Speech against the Japanese," *San Jose Mercury* (CA), September 18, 1906.

37. "Bitter against the Japanese," *Baltimore American,* January 14, 1909.

38. *A Compilation of Messages and Papers of the Presidents: 1789-1908,* vol. 11 (Washington, D.C.: Bureau of National Literature and Art, 1908), 1212.

39. *The Journal of the Assembly during the Thirty-Seventh Session of the Legislature of the State of California* (Sacramento: State Printing, 1907), 72.

40. "Japanese Seizure Ordered by Biddle," *New York Times,* December 8, 1941.

41. "OCD Offices Mushrooming, First Lady Says," *Washington Post,* December 23, 1941.

42. Walter Lippmann, "Today and Tomorrow: The Fifth Column on the Coast," *Washington Post,* February 12, 1942.

43. "Executive Order 9066–Authorizing the Secretary of War to Prescribe Military Areas," February 1942, reprinted in Dorothy Swaine Thomas and Richard S. Nishimoto, *The Spoilage: Japanese-American Evacuation and Resettlement During World War II* (Berkeley: University of California Press, 1946), 9.

44. In addition to public postings, the text of the fliers appeared in newspapers, including the *San Francisco News,* April 2, 1942, under the heading "Western Defense Command and Fourth Army Wartime Civil Control Administration–Instructions to Persons of Japanese Ancestry."

45. Tetsuden Kashima, *Judgment Without Trial: Japanese American Imprisonment During World War II* (University of Washington Press, 2003), 124; 103rd Congress, "Report of the Commission on Protecting and Reducing Government Secrecy," Senate Document 105-2, (Washington, D.C.: Government Printing Office, 1997), Appendix A.

Chapter 6: Wherever the Jew Is Allowed to Establish Himself

1. Only Virginia and New York, in their initial state constitutions, did not prohibit non-Christians from holding public office. When the Articles of Confederation were later replaced by the Constitution, it prohibited religious tests as a qualification for public office. Questions remained, however, as to whether or not this clause in Article 4 applied to state government positions.

2. Peter Wiernik, *History of the Jews in America* (New York: Jewish Press Publishing Co., 1912), 99-103.

3. Ibid.

4. "Editor's Drawer," *Harper's New Monthly Magazine,* 16, no. 95 (May 1858): 854.

5. "Rev. Dr. Raphall's Discourse," *New York Times,* January 5, 1861.

6. *Congressional Globe,* 36th Congress, second session, 217. Despite his avowed racism and dedication to the Confederacy, some in the South cast anti-Semitic aspersions on Judah Benjamin as the Confederacy faced defeat. *Cf.,* Eli N. Evans, "The War Between Jewish Brothers in America," *From Haven to Home: 350 Years of Jewish Life in America,* edited by Michael W. Grunberger (New York: George Braziller in association with the Library of Congress, 2004), 57-8.

7. Joseph Lebowich, "General Ulysses S. Grant and the Jews," *Publications of the American Jewish Historical Society,* vol. 17 (Baltimore: American Jewish Historical Society, 1909), 71-79.

8. "General Grant's Order against the Jews," *Philadelphia Inquirer,* January 9, 1863.

9. "Substance of the Remarks Made by Gen. Howell Cobb," *Macon Telegraph* (GA), January 28, 1864.

10. "Cook's Lecture," *Cincinnati Gazette,* November 16, 1878.

11. [Henry Ford], *The International Jew: The World's Foremost Problem* (Dearborn, MI: Dearborn Publishing Company, 1920), 163.

12. "Ford Is Willing But Won't Finance Any Third Party," *Chicago Tribune,* April 23, 1916.

13. "Coughlin Raps Atheistic Jews And Attackers," *Pittsburgh Post-Gazette,* November 27, 1938; James Rudin, *Christians & Jews Faith to Faith: Tragic History, Promising Present, Fragile Future* (Woodstock, VT: Jewish Lights Publishing, 2011), 88.

14. "Joseph Pulitzer," *People* (NY), April 19, 1891.

15. "Head of Joint Chiefs Criticizes Jewish Influence in the U.S.," *Washington Post,* November 13, 1974; Kevin McDonald, *A People That Shall Dwell Alone: Judaism as a Group Evolutionary Strategy with Diaspora Peoples* (Lincoln, NE: Writers Press Club, 2002), 197.

16. Ibid., 1.

17. "Trio Pushing For War, Says Lindbergh," *Baltimore Sun,* September 12, 1941.

18. Ford, *The International Jew,* 39.

19. Richard Zweigenhaft and G. William Domhoff, *Jews in the Protestant Establishment* (New York: Praeger, 1982), 22.

20. "State Opens Drive to End 'Restricted Clientele' Ads Used by Resorts," *Capital Times* (Madison, WI), August 16, 1949.

21. "Lowell Tells Jews Limit At Colleges Might Help Them," *New York Times,* June 17, 1922.

22. Arthur T. Abernethy, *The Jew a Negro* (Moravian Falls, NC: Dixie Publishing Co., 1910), 7, 11, 105-110.

23. "Meeting of the Colored Men of Huntsville," *Huntsville Gazette* (AL), January 13, 1894.

24. "War in Atlanta Rages Fiercely," *State* (Columbia, SC), May 27, 1913; "Lanford the 'Lieutenant Becker' of Atlanta's Police System is Charge Hurled by Thos. B. Felder," *Macon Telegraph* (GA), May 25, 1913.

25. "Justice Homes's Opinion," *New York Times,* November 27, 1914.

26. "Woodward Is In Limelight Again," *Columbus Ledger* (GA), August 20, 1915. In 1986, Georgia issued a posthumous pardon to Leo Frank, based on insufficient evidence and failure to follow due process of law.

27. North Carolina bombing attempt in "Police Foil Attempt to Bomb Synagogue," *Atlanta Daily World,* February 19, 1958; Skokie, Illinois, bombing in "Synagogue Damaged By 'Bomb' Explosion," *Washington Post,* November 2, 1956; Peoria, Illinois, bombing in "Open Two Investigations in Peoria Temple Bombing," *Chicago Tribune,* October 15, 1958; Jacksonville, Florida, bombing in "Synagogue, Schoolhouse Dynamited," *Washington Post,* August 29, 1958; Atlanta bombing in "Synagogue Dynamited in Atlanta," *Baltimore Sun,* October 13, 1958; Kansas City, Missouri, bombing in "Synagogue Bomb Breaks 51 Windows," *Appleton Post-Crescent* (WI), January 29, 1960; Gadsden, Alabama, bombing in "2 Shot at Synagogue in Fire-Bomb Attack," *Washington Post,* March 26, 1960; Chicago, bombing in "Bomb Synagogue, Threaten Others," *Waterloo Daily Courier* (IA), January 1, 1962; Jackson, Mississippi, bombing in "Jewish Temple Bombed," *Delta Democrat-Times* (Greenville, MS), September 19, 1967; Meridian, Mississippi, bombing in "Bomb Blast Damages Synagogue," *Holland Evening Sentinel* (MI), May 28, 1868; Temple Hills, Maryland, bombing in "Synagogue in Temple Hills Rocked by Bomb in Kitchen," *Baltimore Sun,* January 13, 1969.

28. "The 1992 Campaign," *New York Times,* June 11, 1992.

29. Charley Reese, "Time for Frank Talk on Israel" (King Features Syndicate) in *Garden City Telegram* (KS), July 23, 2007.

30. "Still UnFit to Print," *Washington Post,* January 7, 2011.

31. "Drunken Tirade Turns Anti-Semitic," *Baltimore Jewish Times,* August 4, 2006.

32. "Evangelical Clergy on Mel Gibson," *Washington Post,* August 14, 2006.

33. Ibid.

34. Charley Reese, "Trivia and Tripe," in *Valley Independent* (Monessan, PA), August 9, 2006.

Chapter 7: The Communist Party, USA

1. "Extract from a letter dated, Paris July 27, 1840" *New York Spectator,* August 22, 1840.

2. Sarah Palin, *The Sean Hannity Show,* Fox News Network, September 2, 2012, cited in *Huffington Post,* http://www.huffingtonpost.com/2012/12/04/sarah-palin-obama-socialist_n_2237163.html.

3. "Warning To The Communists," *Chicago Tribune,* November 23, 1875.

4. This recurring element has been observed by numerous historians. See Thomas Robbins and Dick Anthony, "Cults, Brainwashing, and Counter-Subversion," *Annals of the American Academy of Political and Social Science,* vol. 446, (November 1979): 79; David Brion Davis, "Some Themes of Counter-Subversion: An Analysis of Anti-Masonic, Anti-Catholic, and Anti-Mormon Literature," *The Mississippi Valley Historical Review,* 47, no. 2 (September 1960): 205-24.

5. "Nihilistic Preparations," *San Francisco Bulletin,* January 15, 1886.

6. "Dead and Dying," *Milwaukee Journal,* May 5, 1886.

7. Francis X. Busch, "The Haymarket Riot and the Trial of the Anarchists," *Journal of the Illinois Historical Society,* 48, no.3 (Autumn 1955): 247–70.

8. "Fiendish Murderers," *San Jose Evening News* (CA), July 17, 1886; "The Anarchists–Further Disclosure of the Anarchists Plots," *Wheeling Register* (WV), July 19, 1886; "Fielden

Led the Firing," *New York Herald,* July 20, 1886; "Chicago Anarchists," *San Francisco Bulletin,* July 22, 1886; "The Last Link," *Chicago Tribune,* July 28, 1886; "The Evidence for the Defense," *Chicago Tribune,* August 3, 1886; "Pleading for the Anarchists," *Chicago Tribune,* August 13, 1886. One of the defendants committed suicide hours before the Illinois governor commuted the sentences to life in prison for those who had appealed for clemency. Four refused to concede guilt by asking for clemency and were hanged on November 11, 1887. In 1893, Illinois's new governor pardoned the remaining defendants and criticized the trial.

9.   "Mollick Taken By Force," *New York Herald-Tribune,* July 28, 1892.

10. "South Dakota Wants Arms," *Chicago Tribune,* January 10, 1891.

11. American Conservative Union, "Ratings of Congress, 2010," http://conservative.org/ratings archive/uscongress/2010/; "A Turning Point in the Discourse," *New York Times,* January 9, 2011.

12. "Keep Out The Reds," *Chicago Tribune,* August 22, 1894; "Synopsis On Anti-Anarchist Bill," *Chicago Tribune,* August 7, 1894.

13. *Free Society,* September 1, 1901, cited in Marshall Everett, *Complete Life of William McKinley* (NP, 1901), 87.

14. *Proceedings of the First Annual Convention of the Industrial Workers of the World* (New York: IWW booklet, 1905), 1.

15. "Troops At Wardner—Martial Law Will Be Declared In The Camp Today," *Oregonian* (Portland), May 3, 1899.

16. Vladimir Lenin [as N. Lenin] and Leon Trotsky, *The Proletarian Revolution in Russia* (New York: The Communist Press, [c. 1918]), 309.

17. All Haywood statements quoted in, "Sayings of Bill," *Chicago Tribune,* August 13, 1918.

18. *Pittsburgh Leader* publisher Alexander Pollock Moore quoted in "'Is First Blow in Revolt,'" *Kansas City Star,* September 26, 1919.

19. "Agitators Fight Leader of Strike," *Oregonian,* September 26, 1919; "Strike at Bethlehem," *Philadelphia Inquirer,* October 1, 1919.

20. Philip Taft and Philip Ross, "American Labor Violence: Its Causes, Character, and Outcome," *Violence in America: Historical and Comparative Perspectives,* edited by Hugh Davis Graham and Ted Robert Gurr (New York, Bantam Books, 1969), 336.

21. "Seize Books In Cambridge Raid," *Boston Evening Globe,* November 10, 1919.

22. "Communist Test Case is Argued," Associated Press report in *Idaho Statesman,* January 22, 1920.

23. "Dies Body May Be Remembered For Its Attack on Shirley," *Washington Post,* September 4, 1938.

24. Joseph McCarthy, "Speech at Wheeling, West Virginia, 9 February 1950," in Michael P. Johnson, ed., *Reading the American Past,* vol. 2 (Boston: Bedford Books, 1998), 191-95.

25. Even Martin Dies was preceded by congressman Hamilton Fish, Jr. as the nation's preeminent anti-communist. From 1930 to 1934, Fish chaired the House Special Committee to Investigate Communist Activities in the United States.

26. Benjamin Stolberg, "The Red Collapse," *Washington Post,* November 26, 1939; "The Communist Collapse," *Washington Post,* November 28, 1939; "Red Front Organizations," *Washington Post,* November 30, 1939; "Innocent Front," *Washington Post,* December 2, 1939; "The Red Collapse," *Washington Post,* December 3, 1939; "Exit On The Left," *Washington Post,* December 5, 1939.

27. "Un-American Aide 'Purge' Is Urged," *Baltimore Sun,* January 3, 1947.

28. The microfilmed documents, later released under the Freedom of Information Act, proved to be totally innocuous, raising question as to whether they were planted. "U.S. Releases Copies of 'Pumpkin Papers,'" *New York Times,* August 1, 1975.

29. Sam Tanenhaus, *Whittaker Chambers: A Biography* (New York: Random House, 1997), 70.

30. "Mrs. Douglas' View on Reds Challenged," *Los Angeles Times,* August 30, 1950.

31. "The Rosenbergs and Other Spies, Exposed by Russia," *New York Times,* September 27, 1999.

32. "Internal Security Act of 1950" [also known as "McCarran Act]," 64 Stat. 987 (Public Law 81-831), *U.S. Statutes at Large, 81st Congress, 2nd Session* (chapter 1024), 987-1031.

33. Ed Sullivan, "Little Old New York," (syndicated column), in *Oil City Derrick* (PA), June 24, 1950.

34. American Business Consultants, *Red Channels: The Report of Communist Influence in Radio and Television* (New York: Counterattack, 1950), 6-7.

35. Sullivan, June 24, 1950.

36. Bill O'Reilly, *Culture Warrior* (New York: Broadway Books, 2007), 31.

37. Aaron Klein, *The Manchurian President: Barack Obama's Ties to Communists, Socialists, and Other Anti-American Extremists* (Washington, D.C.: WND Books, 2010), ix.

38. "Republican Congressman Claims 78-81 Democrats Are Communists," *Aberdeen American News* (SD), April 11, 2012.

Chapter 8: Corporations Have Been Enthroned

1.   Abraham Lincoln to William F. Elkin, letter dated November 21, 1864, in H. S. Taylor and D. M. Fulwilder, eds., *Lincoln's Words on Living Questions* (Chicago: Trusty Publishing, 1900), 133.

2.   *The Writings of Thomas Jefferson,* Vol. 3, edited by H. A. Washington (Washington, D.C.: Taylor & Maury, 1853), 461.

3.   "The Gadsden Treaty Swindle," *New York Weekly Herald,* May 6, 1854.

4.   H. H. Day, "The Labor Movement," *Pomeroy's Democrat* (Chicago), August 11, 1869.

5.   John Howard Melish, "The Church and the Company Town," *The Survey,* 33, no. 10 (September 5, 1914): 263.

6.   Peter C. Michelson, "Mother Jones," *Machinists' Monthly Journal,* 27, no. 9 (September 1915): 809.

7.   "Urges Workers to Join Their Forces," *Anaconda Standard* (MT), May 4, 1912.

8.   "Unlimited Funds to G.O.P. Campaign," *Charlotte Observer* (NC), August 24, 1912.

9.   "Letters from the People," *Cincinnati Daily Enquirer,* July 16, 1869.

10. "Culberson and Tracy," *Dallas News,* May 31, 1891.

11. "Nashville, Tennessee," *Omaha World-Herald,* October 6, 1896.

12. Kalle Lasn and Micah White, "Why Occupy Will Keep Up the Fight," *Washington Post,* November 20, 2011.

13. *Official Proceedings of the Democratic National Convention Held in Chicago, Illinois, July 7, 8, 9, 10, and 11, 1896* (Logansport, IN: Wilson, Humphreys & Co., 1896), 226–34.

14. "1941 Activity Has Primed Industry for a Record '42," Associated Press report in *Hutchinson News-Herald* (KS), January 1, 1942.

15. Drew Pearson, "The Washington Merry-Go-Round," (syndicated column) in *Coshocton Tribune* (OH), January 25, 1943.

16. John A. Noakes, "Official Frames in a Social Movement Theory: The FBI, HUAC, and the Communist Threat in Hollywood," *Sociological Quarterly,* 41, no. 4 (Autumn 2000): 657–80.

17. John McNulty, "Tom Rath, Commuter," *New York Times,* July 17, 1955.

18. William Whyte, *The Organization Man* (Garden City, NY: Doubleday, 1957).

19. "Farewell Address of President Dwight D. Eisenhower," in *The Oxford Companion to American Military History,* John Whiteclay Chambers II, ed.-in-chief (NY: Oxford University Press, 1999), 439.

20. Paul Bixler, "Editorial: Vietnam—and Beyond," *The Antioch Review,* 27, no. 4 (Winter 1967-68): 418-19.

21. "New Year's Gang" statement in *Madison Kaleidoscope,* August 24, 1970, reprinted in Neil A. Hamilton, *The 1970s* (NY: Facts on File, 2006), 17.

22. John Lewis, "Don't Let Money Rule," *Washington Post,* July 10, 2001.

23. Kevin Phillips, "The New Face of Another Gilded Age," *Washington Post,* May 26, 2002.

24. Sarah Palin Speech at 2010 Tea Party convention, cited in Arianna Huffington, "Tea Party Movement Shouldn't Be Ignored," reprinted from *Huffington Post* in *Sun Sentinel* (Ft. Lauderdale), February 19, 2010.

25. "The Bankers and their Flogging," *Oregonian* (Portland), January 17, 2010.

Chapter 9: Woman Suffrage

1. Senate debate transcript in *History of Woman Suffrage,* vol. 3, edited by Elizabeth Cady Stanton, Susan B. Anthony, Matilda Joslyn Gage (Rochester, NY: Susan B. Anthony, 1886), 203-4.

2. *Familiar Letters of John Adams and His Wife Abigail Adams, During the Revolution,* edited by Charles Francis Adams (New York: Houghton Mifflin, 1875), 149-50.

3. Ibid., 155.

4. James Fordyce, *Sermons to Young Women,* vol. 1 (London: 1778; reprint, London: Cadwell and Davies, 1814), 210, 212.

5. Mary Wollstonecraft, *A Vindication of the Rights of Woman* (London: J. Johnson, 1792; reprint, London: T. Fisher Unwin, 1891), 151-2.

6. Susan Staves, "Elizabeth Griffith," *Dictionary of Literary Biography: Restoration and Eighteenth Century Dramatists,* 3rd series (Detroit: Gale Research 1989); Susan David Bernstein, "Ambivalence and Writing: Elizabeth and Richard Griffith's *A Series of Genuine Letters between Henry and Frances,*" in *Eighteenth Century Women and the Arts,* ed. Frederick M. Keener and Susan E. Lorsch (New York: Greenwood, 1988), 269–76. For specific text amendments by Griffith to idealize her marriage, see Susan Staves, "Traces of a Lost Woman," *Profession* (1995): 36-8.

7. "American A.S. Society—Annual Meeting," *Philadelphia Enquirer,* May 21, 1840.

8. "Declaration of Sentiments Put Forth at Seneca Falls, N.Y., July 19th and 20th, 1848," *Proceedings of the National Woman's Rights Convention* (Cleveland: Gray, Beardsley, Spear & Co., 1854), 70-3.

9. "The Author of 'Mary Lyndon,'" *Sandusky Register,* August 14, 1855; review in *New York Times,* September 8, 1855, reprinted in "Origin, Progress, and Position of the Anti-Marriage Movement," *Boston Advertiser,* September 19, 1855.

10. Wendell Phillips, *Speeches, Lectures, and Letters,* 2nd series (Boston: Lee and Shepard, 1892), 131.

11. *Proceedings and Debates of the Constitutional Convention of the State of New York,* vol. 1 (Albany: Weed, Parsons and Co., 1868), 429, 375.

12. Ibid., 386.

13. John E. Ferling, *The First of Men: A Life of George Washington* (Knoxville: University of Tennessee Press, 1988), 1, 6, 11, 32, 41, 58, 76; A. Ward Burian, *George Washington's Legacy of Leadership* (Garden City, NY: Morgan James, 2007), 16.

14. T. A. Larson, "Petticoats at the Polls: Woman Suffrage in Territorial Wyoming," *Pacific Northwest Quarterly,* 44, no. 2 (April 1853): 74-9; Holly J. McCammon and Karen E. Campbell, "Winning the Vote in the West: The Political Success of the Women's Suffrage Movement, 1866-1919," *Gender and Society,* 15, no.1 (February 2001): 55-82.

15. James Callaway, "Observations & Comment," *Macon Telegraph* (GA), June 6, 1917.

16. "Wilson Hails Women," *Washington Post,* August 18, 1912.

17. Senate Committee on the District of Columbia, *Subcommittee Hearings on Suffrage Parade Under S. Res. 499,* Part I (March 6-17, 1913), 63rd Cong., special session (Washington, D.C.: Government Printing Office, 1913), 27.

18. Ibid., 501.

19. "Picketing Is At End," *Washington Post,* August 18, 1917.

20. *Constitution of the United States of America: Analysis, and Interpretation,* S. Doc. 103-6, 103rd Congress, 1st session (Washington, D.C.: Government Printing Office, 1992), 49.

21. Count Marco, "A Dreadful Book About You Women," syndicated column in *The Victoria Advocate* (TX), August 18, 1963.

22. Betty Friedan, *The Feminine Mystique* (NY: W. W. Norton, 1963; reprint, NY: Norton, 1997), 91.

23. Ralph de Toledano, "New Women's Magazine Completely Inconsistent," syndicated column in *Danville Register* (VA), January 23, 1972.

24. Bob Schmidt, "Women's Liberation Myths," syndicated column in *Pasadena Star-News* (CA), February 2, 1971.

25. *Wall Street Journal* article reprint in "Wall St. Journal–Awareness, Yes, But . . . ," *High Point Enterprise* (NC), October 18, 1969.

26. Alice Widener, "Dear Men: S.O.S.!" syndicated column in *Gazette-Telegraph* (Colorado Springs), December 5, 1977.

27. Eileen M. Gardner, ed., *A New Agenda for Education* (Washington, D.C.: Heritage Foundation, 1985), 45.

28. "Edwardsville Rotarians Hear Mrs. Phyllis Schlafly," *Alton Evening Telegraph* (IL), March 22, 1958.

29. "Primary Election Contests Loom As Filing Is Closed," *Alton Evening Telegraph* (IL), January 23, 1952; "State GOP Keynoter to Speak at Oregon," *Dixon Evening Telegraph* (IL), January 3, 1953; "Mrs. Phyllis Schlafly At Chicago Meeting," *Alton Evening Telegraph,* March 24, 1954; "Conservative GOP Women Plan Meeting," *Independent Press-Telegram* (Long Beach, CA), January 12, 1968; "Final Meeting for Republican Women's Club," *Oak Park Leaves* (IL), May 19, 1960; "27 Women Are Candidates for U.S. Senate and House," *Daily Telegram* (Eau Claire, WI), October 13, 1963.

30. "Assault on America—Falwell: Spiritual Weakness to Blame," *Houston Chronicle* (TX), September 14, 2001.

31. Pelosi called bully in "'Social Justice,' But Not For Americans," *Intelligencer* (Doylestown, PA), April 5, 2013; Clinton accused of having enemies list in "Machiavelli's Disciples," *Idaho State Journal* (Pocatello), December 21, 2013.

Chapter 10: Disgraceful Degradation

1. "The Economics of the Fall of Athens and Rome," *Brownsville Herald* (TX), March 30, 1920.

2. Landon R. Y. Storrs, "Attacking the Washington 'Femmocracy': Antifeminism in the Cold War Campaign against 'Communists in Government,'" *Feminists Studies,* 33, no.1 (Spring 2007): 118-52.

3. *The Writings of George Washington,* edited by John C. Fitzpatrick, vol. 2 (Washington, D.C.: Government Printing Office, 1934), 83-4; cited in Jonathan Katz, *Gay American History: Lesbians and Gay Men—A Documentary* (New York: Crowell, 1976), 24.

4. *Minutes of the Council and General Court of Colonial Virginia,* edited by H. R. McIlwaine (Richmond: Colonial Press, 1924), 42. Citied in Katz, *Gay American History,* 17.

5. William Bradford, *History of the Plymouth Plantation: 1620-1647,* vol. 2 (manuscript journal ca. 1630-51, reprinted Boston: Massachusetts Historical Society, 1912), 315.

6. William Bradford, *History of Plymouth Plantation,* edited by Charles Deane (Boston: privately printed, 1856), 385.

7. Bradford, *History* (Massachusetts Historical Society, 1912), 310.

8. Louis Crompton, "Homosexuals and the Death Penalty in Colonial America," *Journal of Homosexuality,* 1, no. 3 (1976): 287–88. North Carolina retained the death penalty until 1869; South Carolina until 1873.

9. Thomas Jefferson Randolph, ed., *Memoirs, Correspondence, and Private Papers of Thomas Jefferson,* vol. 1 (London: Henry Colburn and Richard Bentley, 1829), 123, 127–28.

10. ("Our city has been in some ferment," *Essex Gazette* (Haverhill, MA), July 7, 1832.

11. "Religious Intelligence," *Boston Advertiser,* March 31, 1866.

12. Gary Scharnhorst and Jack Bales, *The Lost Life of Horatio Alger, Jr.* (Indianapolis: Indiana University Press, 1985), 3, 121-25.

13. Katz, *Gay American History,* 393.

14. Ibid., 389.

15. "Probe Sordid Conditions at Texas College," *The Bee* (Danville, VA), November 18, 1944.

16. "Describes Fantastic Story of Sexual Parties," *Maryville Daily Forum* (MO), May 27, 1948.

17. George W. Crane, "Man Can Remodel His Own Personality," syndicated column in *Wisconsin State Journal* (Madison), February 28, 1944.

18. George W. Crane, "Case Records," syndicated column in *Ogden Standard-Examiner* (UT), March 29, 1945.

19. "Senator Wherry Says 3750 Government Men, Women Are Sex Perverts," *Haywood Daily Review* (CA), May 23, 1950.

20. "Executive Order 10450, Apr. 27, 1953," *Federal Register* 18:2489, in *Code of Federal Regulations, 1949-1953*, vol. 3 (Washington, D.C.: Office of the Federal Register), 936.

21. "Denies Condoning Offenses," *Washington Post*, May 1, 1950; "Perverts Held Dangerous to U.S. Security," *Austin Daily Herald* (TX), December 15, 1950.

22. "Gene Howe Says," syndicated column in *Atchison Daily Globe* (KS), February 16, 1950.

23. Reference to "secret cell" in "Probers Say U.S. Reds Set to Go Underground" *Lima News* (OH), July 3, 1949; reference to "spy ring" in "Ex-Red Reports Federal 'Spy Ring,'" *Washington Post*, July 23, 1948; reference to "nest of homosexuals" in "Probe Sordid Conditions at Texas College," *Danville Bee* (VA), November 18, 1944; reference to "homosexual ring" in "Describes Fantastic Story of Sexual Parties," *Marysville Daily Forum* (MO), May 27, 1948.

24. Reference to "abode of licentiousness" in Andrew B. Cross, *Priests' Prisons for Women* (Baltimore: Sherwood, 1854), 2; reference to "league with the devil" in Rosamond Culbertson, *Rosamond, or a Narrative of the Sufferings of an American Female Under the Popish Priests* (New York: Leavitt, Lord & Co., 1836), 213.

25. Reference to a covenant with the devil in *Records of Salem Witchcraft, Copied from the Original Documents*, vol. 1 (Roxbury, MA: W. Elliot Woodward, 1864), 178.

26. *Independent Chronicle* article reprinted in "Of 'less than Women in the Shapes of Men!'" *Vermont Journal and the Universal Advertiser* (Windsor), May 12, 1784.

27. "Liberace Ends Testimony in London Libel Suit," *Tucson Daily Citizen*, June 9, 1959.

28. "The Liberace Story," *Oakland Tribune* (CA), March 3, 1954.

29. "Liberace Settles Confidential Suit," *Fitchburg Sentinel* (MA), July 16, 1958.

30. "Sex Habits Formed Early," Associated Press report in *Oakland Tribune* (CA), November 19, 1947.

31. State modifications of laws regarding homosexuality in "Prison Probe Report Due on Governor's Desk," *Long Beach Independent*, December 13, 1943; "Delegates Favor State Speed Law," *Manitowoc Herald-Times* (WI), December 6, 1944; "New Penal Program Approved," *Coshocton News* (OH), January 25, 1946; "Mental Exams at Penal Farms," *Hagerstown Daily Mail* (MD), February 17, 1947.

32. Research comparing percentage of homosexual and heterosexual pedophiles in C. Jenny, T. A. Roesler, and K. L. Poyer, "Are Children at Risk for Sexual Abuse by Homosexuals?" *Pediatrics*, 94 (1994): 41–4; Harris Mirkin, "The Pattern of Sexual Politics," *Journal of Homosexuality*, 37, no. 2 (1999): 1–24; Lisa DeMarni Cromer and Rachel E. Goldsmith, "Child Sex Abuse Myths: Attitudes, Beliefs, and Individual Differences," *Journal of Child Sex Abuse*, 19, no. 6 (2010): 618–47.

33. "'Morality' Talk Slows Sex Hearing," *Washington Post*, August 9, 1963. Panic, or its exploitation, came easily to Dowdy. After being convicted in 1972 for bribery and perjury, he was quoted in the April 15, 1972, *Washington Post*, "What happened to me can happen to anybody if they make up their minds to get them." The article went on to note, "Dowdy would identify the 'they' and 'them' who wanted to 'get' him only as the 'Eastern liberal establishment' . . . 'homosexuals' and 'urban renewal interests.'"

34. "Police Again Rout 'Village' Youth," *New York Times*, June 30, 1969.

35. "Speaker Condemns Homosexuality," *Idaho Free Press*, June 12, 1974.

36. Research comparing sexual preferences of grown children raised by homosexual parents to those raised by heterosexual parents in Charlotte J. Patterson, "Children of Lesbian and Gay Parents," *Child Development*, 63, no. 5 (October 1992): 1025–42; Jennifer L. Wainwright, Stephen T. Russell, and Charlotte J. Patterson, "Psychosocial Adjustment, Social Outcomes, and Romantic Relationships of Adolescents with Same-Sex Parents," *Child Development*, 75, no. 6 (November–December 2004): 1886–98; William Meezan and Jonathan Rauch, "Gay Marriage, Same-Sex Parenting, and America's Children," *The Future of Children*, 15, no. 2 (Autumn 2005): 97–115; *Lesbian and Gay Parenting* (Washington, D.C.: American Psychological Association, 2005); Charlotte J. Patterson, "Children of Lesbian and Gay Parents," *Current Directions in Psychological Science*, 15, no. 5 (October 2006): 241–44.

37. "Archive Using Film Fest to Expand Its Collection of KC Gay History," *Kansas City Star* (MO), June 20, 2012.

38. Max Rafferty, "No Gay Teachers," syndicated column in *Syracuse Post-Standard,* July 9, 1977.

39. "Homosexuals Fight Army Ban," *Salt Lake Tribune,* April 17, 1966.

40. "Military's Last Social Taboo," *Washington Post,* August 19, 1991.

41. *Lawrence v. Texas (02-102) 539 U.S. 558 (2003).*

42. "Lesbian Wedding Turns into Test Case," *USA Today,* October 21, 1991.

43. Ibid.

44. Michael Savage, *The Enemy Within: Saving America from the Liberal Assault on Our Churches, Schools, and Military* (Nashville: WND Books, 2003), 29.

45. "Rep. Frank Goes After Health Care Protester," Associated Press report in *Daily Sitka Sentinel* (AK) August 19, 2009.

46. "Westboro Church Plans to Protest DeMarsico's Funeral," *Berkshire Eagle* (Pittsfield, MA) August 30, 2012.

Chapter 11: Illegal Immigrants

1. "Latest from California—Attacks on Chilians [sic]," *Times-Picayune* (New Orleans), September 15, 1849.

2. "Further from California," *Times-Picayune,* September 6, 1850.

3. John Baylor to Henry H. Sibley, October 25, 1861, in *The War of the Rebellion: A Compilation of the Official Records of the Union and Confederate Armies,* series 1, vol. 4 (Washington, D.C.: Government Printing Office, 1882), 135.

4. Ibid., vol. 9, (1883), 634.

5. "Puerto Ricans Barred," *New York Times,* March 25, 1903.

6. Ibid.

7. Gonzales v. Williams, 192 U.S. 1 (1904).

8. Full description of Puerto Rican citizenship controversy in Ray Suarez, *Latino Americans* (NY: Celebra, Penguin Group, 2013), 66-72.

9. "Deportation Car Coming," *Portland Oregonian,* November 30, 1914.

10. "Texans Arm for Threatened Raid," *Anaconda Standard* (MT), August 12, 1915.

11. "Texas Border Is Armed Camp," *Gazette* (Colorado Springs), August 12, 1915.

12. E. Bruce White and Francisco Villa, "The Muddied Waters of Columbus, New Mexico," *The Americas,* 32, no. 1 (July 1975): 72-98.

13. William D. Carrigan and Clive Webb, "The Lynching of Persons of Mexican Origin or Descent in the United States, 1848 to 1928," *Journal of Social History,* 37, no. 2 (Winter 2003): 411–38.

14. James L. Slayden, "Some Observations on Mexican Immigration," *Annals of the American Academy of Political and Social Science,* vol. 93 (January 1921): 121-26.

15. "Box Would Bar Importation of Mexican Labor," *Fort Worth Star Telegram,* October 16, 1919.

16. House Committee on Immigration and Naturalization, *Hearings on Temporary Admission of Illiterate Mexican Laborers,* 66th Cong., 2nd session (1920), 192.

17. Neil Betten and Raymond A. Mohl, "From Discrimination to Repatriation: Mexican Life in Gary, Indiana, during the Great Depression," *Pacific Historical Review,* 42, no. 3 (August 1973): 370–88; Francisco Balderrama and Raymond Rodriguez, *Decade of Betrayal: Mexican Repatriation in the 1930s,* revised edition (Albuquerque: University of New Mexico Press, 2006); *USA Today,* April 5, 2006.

18. Westbrook Pegler, "Fair Enough," syndicated column in *Los Angeles Times,* June 14, 1943.

19. "Police Hold Two Youths in Race Clash," *Huntingdon Daily News* (PA), June 17, 1943; "'Zoot Suit' Negroes Cause Disturbance," *Cumberland Evening Times* (MD), June 22, 1943; "Zoot Suit Riot in Philadelphia," *Reno Evening Gazette* (NV), June 12, 1943.

20. "Letters to the Editor," *The Prospector* (Texas Western College, El Paso), April 3, 1954.

21. George Sokolsky, "New York Scandal Is Over Education," syndicated column in *Lima News* (OH), February 6, 1958.

22. Jack Lait, "Broadway and Elsewhere," syndicated column in *Zanesville Signal* (OH), September 7, 1949.

23. "Marcantonio Plot Charged by Mayor," *New York Times,* November 7, 1949.

24. "Official Denies Puerto Ricans Bad Influence On Youngstown Area," *Coshocton Tribune* (OH), April 1, 1952.

25. Phyllis Schlafly, "Puerto Rico Is Our Modern Trojan Horse," *Alton Telegraph* (IL), October 15, 1997.

26. "Hayakawa to Propose English as Official U.S. Language," *Syracuse Herald-Journal,* April 14, 1981.

27. James J. Kilpatrick, "Puerto Rico: Congress Should Not Make It a State," syndicated column in *Pharos-Tribune* (Logansport, IN), August 29, 1990.

28. Jeffrey Hart, "Puerto Rico: Bush Needs to Explain His Position," syndicated column in *Pharos-Tribune* (Logansport, IN), March 19, 1991.

29. Elizabeth Dwoskin, "Why Americans Won't Do Dirty Jobs," *Business Week,* November 9, 2011.

30. Beck pointed to Nazi Germany in panic-inducing alarms on his May 1, 2007, broadcast on Fox News when he told viewers, "Al Gore's not going to be rounding up Jews and exterminating them. It is the same tactic, however. The goal is different. The goal is globalization. . . . And you must silence all dissenting voices. That's what Hitler did. That's what Al Gore, the UN, and everybody on the global warming bandwagon [are doing]." Panic did not reside in Beck's comparison with Nazi Germany, since he explicitly stated that the Holocaust was not the aspect of Nazi Germany to which he was referring. Where panic resided was in Beck's remarks doing that which he said he was not doing. After stating that Al Gore's campaign to reduce global warming would not lead to genocide, he nevertheless used the reference to loom ominously over his assertion that the *tactic* was the same—a blank to be filled in that Beck then filled with an unverified claim tucked inside an absolute in the phrase, "you must silence all dissenting voices." The absolute, "all," then triggered an unverified claim that Al Gore was silencing all dissenting voices. Beck offered no examples of Gore silencing any dissenting voice; indeed, Beck's dissenting voice contradicted his own claim.

31. Glenn Beck, *CNN Nightly News* (www.cnn.com/2008/US/05/28/beck.immigrantworkers), April 28, 2008.

Chapter 12: Islamic Sharia Law

1. John Smith, *The True Travels, Adventures, and Observations, Of Captain John Smith, into Europe, Asia, Africa, and America, from Ann. Dom. 1593-1629* (London, 1630), 378, 387-8; reprinted online, archive.org/details/truetravelsadven00smit

2. Jared Sparks, ed., *The Writings of George Washington,* vol. 9 (Boston: Russell, Odiorne, and Metcalf, 1835), 243.

3. "The Following Is a Copy of a Letter," *Pennsylvania Evening Herald,* November 19, 1785.

4. Joseph Wheelan, *Jefferson's War: America's First War on Terror, 1801-1805* (New York: Carroll & Graf, 2003), 196. Authorship of these lines in a slightly varied form is attributed to Thomas Green Fessenden in *The Port Folio,* 1, no. 5 (February 8, 1806): 79. Numerous people, including Tom Paine, had penned or adapted lyrics to the melody first sung by London's Anacreontic Society.

5. *Papers of the Military Historical Society of Massachusetts: Civil and Mexican Wars,* vol. 13 (Boston: by the Society, 1913), 290.

6. Nicholas Said, "A Native of Bornoo," *Atlantic Monthly,* 20, no. 120 (October 1867): 485-95.

7. Louise Seymour Houghton, "Syrians in the United States," *The Survey,* 1, no. 27 (October 7, 1911): 957-68.

8. "The Big Fair Opened," *New Haven Register* (CT), May 1, 1893.

9. "Moslem Mosque Will Be Razed," *Benton Harbor News-Palladium* (MI), August 24, 1922; Gregory Orfalea, *Before the Flames: A Quest for the History of Arab Americans* (Austin: University of Texas Press, 1988), 91.

10. "Quincy Syrians Badly Frightened," *Boston Globe,* August 7, 1917.

11. "Syrians Fire on Georgia Citizens," *Daily Times Enterprise* (Thomasville, GA), September 19, 1917.

12. "Syrian Regiment from Bay State," *Daily Kennebec Journal* (ME), May 3, 1917.

13. *In Re Ahmed Hassan,* 48 Federal Supplement (No. 162148), District Court, E.D. Michigan, S.D., 15 December 1942, 844.

14. John Tehranian, "Performing Whiteness: Naturalization Litigation and the Construction of Racial Identity in America," *Yale Law Journal,* 109, no. 4 (January 2000): 838.

15. "Sirhan Wrote of 'the necessity,'" Associated Press report in *Corona Daily Independent* (CA), June 6, 1968.

16. "Sirhans a Family of Little Cohesion," *New York Times,* June 30, 1968.

17. "Another Look at the Middle East," *Daily Messenger* (Canandaigua, NY), February 28, 1969.

18. "Psychiatric Exam Set for Sirhan Sirhan Today," *Oneonta Star* (NY), March 10, 1969.

19. "Strange Sultan's Soggy Story," *Ft. Walton Beach Daily News* (FL), September, 18, 1972.

20. Charley Reese, "Israel Is Our Only Friend in Mideast," syndicated column in *Elyria Chronicle Telegram* (OH), April 23, 1980.

21. "After 911 Call, Operators Spent 10 Minutes Looking for Address," Associated Press report in *Hays Daily News* (KS), July 30, 1996.

22. "Area Residents Want Swift Justice for Bomber," *Altoona Mirror* (PA), July 28, 1996.

23. "CIA Claims Iraqi Refugees Are Security Risk," Associated Press report in *Bedford Gazette* (PA), July 31, 1997.

24. Ibid.

25. Nat Hentoff, "Prosecution in Darkness," *Washington Post,* November 6, 1999.

26. "Opening of VA Muslim Academy Delayed," *Washington Post,* November 6, 1999.

27. "Le Moyne Graduate of Lebanese Descent Told to 'Go home,'" *Syracuse Herald-American* (NY), September 16, 2001.

28. Assault rifle fired in service station, arson at rug company, Muslim woman nearly run over, Muslim girls beaten on campus, and Jefferson Parrish, LA school closure in "Acts of Misplaced Anger," *Gaston Gazette* (Gastonia, NC), September 14, 2001; machete attack on Muslim gas station attendant, firebomb thrown at Islamic community center, and mob outside Chicago mosque, Associated Press report in *Daily News* (Fort Walton Beach, FL), September 14, 2001.

29. "Backlash Murders and the State of 'Hate,'" *Washington Post,* January 20, 2002.

30. Murders of Vasudev Patel, Waqar Hasan, and Adel Karas, Ibid., *Washington Post,* January 20, 2002.

31. "Some Passengers Singled Out for Exclusion by Flight Crew," *New York Times,* September 22, 2001.

32. "Pat Robertson Describes Islam as Violent Religion," *Farmington Daily Times* (NM), February 23, 2002.

33. "From A/AD John Pistole to [NAMES WITHHELD]; Subject [WITHHELD]," (Washington, D.C.: Federal Bureau of Investigation, November 5, 2003; classified by 65179 DMH/MJS, declassified May 20, 2011, accessed January 19, 2014) available from www.aclu.org/files/fbimappingfoia/20111019/ACLURM013039.pdf.

34. "Defendants Can Laugh at Our Justice System," *Morning Call* (Allentown, PA), July 25, 2002.

35. "Rethink Screening," *Orlando Sentinel* (FL), March 5, 2002.

36. Omar Khraishah, e-mail to author, August 29, 2013.

37. "Muslim Cab Driver Ahmed Sharif, Victim in Bloody Attack," *New York Daily News,* August 26, 2010.

38. "Joplin Mosque Razed in Fire," *Salt Lake Tribune* (UT), August 9, 2012.

39. "Be Aggressive but Not Unfair," *Orlando Sentinel* (FL), September 17, 2002.

40. Diana West, "We Need to Stand Up and Say, 'No to Shariah,'" syndicated column in *Tribune-Star* (Terre Haute, IN), November 19, 2010.

41. "In Islamic Law, Gingrich Sees a Mortal Threat to U.S.," *New York Times,* December 21, 2011.

42. "Bachmann Sends Ellison Letter in Response to Muslim Brotherhood Comments," *St. Cloud Times* (MN), July 15, 2012.

Conclusion: The Enemy Is Us

1. Cristina Page, *How the Pro-Choice Movement Saved America: Freedom, Politics and the War on Sex* (New York: Basic Books, 2006), xiii.
2. Barry Howard Minkin, *Ten Great Lies that Threaten America* (San Jose, CA: In-Sight Press, 2007), 142.
3. "More Intensive Training Given In The U.S.S.R. Than Here," *New York Times,* November 7, 1954; "New Study of Soviet Education Contains Warning to U.S.," *New York Times,* January 21, 1962. Relations with the Soviet Union improved with détente in the 1970s, but the same decade saw a severe gasoline crisis in the United States that resulted in a huge increase in the sale of more fuel-efficient Japanese cars. "U.S. badly lags behind Japan," *New York Times,* March 29, 1983. On December 13, 1989, the paper warned, "The typical Japanese student goes to school 240 days a year while the average American youngster goes 180 days, and is exposed to a much less rigorous curriculum." The Japanese economy nearly collapsed in the early 1990s, but China, Korea, and India were emerging as major economic powers. "Most American students are unprepared to meet the high level of performance achieved by Asian students," the *New York Times* reported on May 27, 1994.
4. Thomas E. Watson, *Is Roman Catholicism in America Identical with that of the Popes?* (Thomson, GA: Jeffersonian Publishing, 1914), 74.

Index